The SCIENCE of High-Performance Leadership

# The SCIENCE of HIGH-PERFORMANCE LEADERSHIP

**7 Brain-Based Strategies to Become a Leader Worth Following**

## Sherry Yellin, Ph.D.

*The SCIENCE of High-Performance Leadership*
© 2025 Sherry Yellin, Ph.D.

Published by Thought Leader Academy Publishing
Thought Leader Academy Publishing
3901 N Kildare Ave
Chicago, Il 60641

Cover design by Claudine Mansour Design
Interior design by Liz Schreiter

Hardback ISBN: 978-1-968668-08-2
Paperback ISBN: 978-1-968668-03-7
Ebook ISBN: 978-1-968668-04-4

## In Gratitude

To the Creator of ALL things, who equips us with ALL things, for ALL things. Thank you for the calling and the resilience to carry this message forward.

To Lance—thank you for being my hype man, dreaming with me, listening to my stories on repeat (with interest), turning moments into unforgettable memories, and honoring our vow to get s*&^ done and not f*&^ this up.

To my team—thank you for believing in this project from start to finish. Patty, none of this would be possible without you.

To Callie—thank you for FaceTiming me at wildly inconvenient (and somehow always perfect) moments and for modeling what it looks like to risk failure to be amazing. Sometimes courage skips a generation.

To Nolan—thank you for giving me Beau, the best gift of my life, for miracle stories, and for showing me how to believe bigger, hope deeper, and see clearer.

To my Dad, Mom, and Sister—thank you for being proud of me, though it's hard to explain to others exactly what I do. We get an A+ in family.

To my clients—thank you for sharing your stories, your challenges, your wins, and your learns. It is truly a privilege to watch you shine.

To the organizations that trust us with their vision and their culture—thank you for investing in your people, living your values, and allowing us to be a part of your success.

To the reader—thank you for choosing to be a leader worth following. Our world needs you.

And to my past self—I see you, and you're enough.

Do not be conformed to this world but be transformed by the renewing of your mind.
—Romans 12:2

# Contents

# Are you a leader worth following?

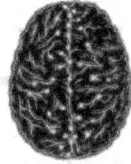

We each get one life. One stretch of time to make it count. For most of us, a staggering 90,000 hours or more of that precious life will be spent at work. And for better or worse, leaders can shape whether those hours feel miserable or meaningful.

He greeted me in the lobby and thanked me for coming. I followed him to his corner office with a breathtaking view of the city. The sun was shining, and the streets were busy on this Tuesday afternoon.

After he closed his door and took his seat behind a large mahogany desk, I asked him, "What makes you think you want to work with a leadership coach?"

He didn't answer immediately.

I gazed at the photos behind his desk of Himalayan hikes, grizzly bear hunts, trout fishing in remote Alaska. He looked like a man who had lived fully.

Finally, he spoke.

"My friend and colleague died last week. One of our vice presidents. Brain cancer."

He swallowed, cleared his throat, and continued.

"At his funeral, person after person talked about how he impacted their lives."

I held the silence.

Then he looked at me like someone seeing himself clearly for the first time.

"I realized no one would ever say those things about me."

Being a leader worth following isn't just about *what* you achieve but *how* you achieve it. It's about multiplying and scaling human potential. It's about impact. Legacy.

And it starts with the brain.

Your brain isn't just part of the story. It *is* the story. It determines every reaction, every decision, every relationship.

In this book, you will learn the CRANIUM methodology, 7 brain-based strategies that connect how people learn best with how leaders lead best. This book removes the guess-work on how to become a leader worth following and create a high-performance culture by leading the way your brain is wired to succeed.

When you lead the CRANIUM way, you do more than get results. You change lives, starting with your own.

Becoming a leader worth following starts here: with the brain, the science, and proven strategies. Your brain is the compass that points the way.

How did I get here?

I wanted to become a college English teacher. That is, until I became a college English teacher. My disillusionment is cap-tured by a meme I once read that said, "Somewhere in hell, peo-ple are grading 5-paragraph essays for all of eternity."

Amid my despair, the brilliant Dr. Sherry Nabors, a dear friend and mentor, asked if I could help her create a workplace education program for a major communications manufacturing company. At the time, providing courses in reading, writing, and math to hourly employees was a new concept. Without hesitation, I said, "Yes!"

I hadn't been in the role for more than a few days when she showed up, a mid-50s, tough, no-nonsense woman. Frankly, she scared me. She walked into my cubicle without knocking, planted herself in the chair across from me, and confidently stated, "Out on that floor, I've got a reputation. I'm known as a bad girl." I heard knuckles cracking and my heart racing. I didn't know whether to smile, to run, or to take notes.

Then she did something I least expected: she started to cry. The armor cracked, revealing not just emotion, but a lifetime of struggle and intense fear of the future. Learning had always been hard for her, leading to feelings of insecurity, shame, and failure. She feared losing her job as the company was implementing self-directed work teams, and her sister, who had always worked beside her, was transferring to a different location. At home, the stress was almost unbearable as she was the sole caregiver for her aging father, trying to make sense of medical bills and doctor reports. She felt unsafe disclosing these challenges to anyone in the company, though she had worked there for over 25 years.

As she shared, I thought of all the students and all the classes I had taught. While teaching college, I felt I had confidence and command of the subject. My students seemed to be engaged and showed improvement. I received positive evaluations, and people frequently requested my class. But as I looked into the tear-filled eyes of this beautiful woman who was terrified of the future and trusting me with her story, I faced something much different, much more sacred and fragile. The stakes were higher. I could not fail her. I could not let her fail herself.

When she concluded, we sat there for some time in silence. I cleared my throat and said,

"I have no idea how to help you. But I promise, I'll try."

We hadn't been working together for very long when I had this overwhelming urge to unscrew the lid, look at her brain, and ask, "What is going on in there?" I knew I could help her if I had the answer to that question. I could also help the other workers who had come forward after they learned she had asked for help. The company had many "left behind" learners who now had renewed hope, hope that, in many ways, was directed towards me.

I was plagued with questions. "Why was learning so hard for them?" "Why weren't the tried-and-true methods of teaching working?" And most importantly, "How does the brain learn?"

I began seeking answers, searching for solutions, changing majors, annoying professors with unrelenting questions, and conducting personal research. Luckily, I was on the cusp of an explosion of information about the brain. Little did I know at the time that U.S. President George H.W. Bush would declare 1990-2000 the "Decade of the Brain."

During this time in history, new technologies allowed scientists to observe the brain while its owner was still alive. We also had new communication pathways via the Internet to get this information to practitioners in almost real time. The findings in neuroscience quickly moved beyond the boundaries of medicine to advance fields such as economics, marketing, and education.

I had a front-row seat to game-changing discoveries and to a rapidly developing field called "brain-based" learning. I learned that the way to optimal performance is by aligning with how the brain learns. We can work with the brain and create extraordinary returns, or we can work against the brain and create extraordinary costs. In many ways, we discovered the Rosetta Stone to human performance.

At first, I applied these findings to improving the workplace education program. But the more I experimented, the more I realized this wasn't just about learning to read or write. This was about unlocking how people think, decide, create, and connect. Leaders needed to know this information. What began in the classroom quickly spilled into the conference room. These same brain-based strategies that guide how the brain learns hold the power to elevate decision-making, spark innovation, strengthen resilience, improve communication, reduce conflict, and build cultures where people and business performance thrive.

So, Sherry and I expanded the vision of the workplace education program to equip others, specifically leaders, with information about brain-based learning and practical ways to apply it. We witnessed improved relationships between the union and management, a safer place to be vulnerable and share concerns, higher trust, improved retention, and a successful move to self-directed work teams.

My focus for the last 30 years has been equipping leaders and teams to lead, learn, and live the way the brain works best using the CRANIUM methodology. Since 2001, my team and I have witnessed unforgettable results with individual leaders, teams, and organizations. We have been extremely blessed to support leaders at every level across multiple industries to celebrate wins such as increased retention, higher engagement, restored relationships, smooth transitions, and lucrative innovations. We've partnered with hospitals as they moved from the lowest-performing in the system to the highest-performing.

We've assisted companies in developing a pipeline of leadership talent, coached struggling leaders who became beloved, high-performing CEOs, and provided ongoing support for teams and individual contributors as they navigated uncertainty, conflict, and pressures in an ever-changing world.

Though we are grateful for every success, the work is just beginning. The stakes are high in a truly complex and uncertain world. Information moves at the speed of a click. Change is constant. Competition is relentless. And despite all of our advances in technology designed to forge connections, we're more disconnected than ever, from ourselves, from each other, and from a shared sense of purpose.

Most workplaces embrace ergonomics to prevent physical injury and reduce strain on the body. But few apply the disciplines of neuroscience and psychology to protect the brain, the very organ that drives every thought, decision, emotion, and action.

We safeguard the body with posture-friendly chairs and anti-fatigue mats, yet we often ignore cultures that cause burnout, low trust, cognitive overload, and disengagement.

For example:

- 85% of workers experienced symptoms of burnout due to work-related stress, with nearly half (47%) taking time off for mental health reasons.[1]
- In 2024, anxiety became the top mental health concern among American workers, surpassing depression and stress.[2]
- In 2024, only 23% of employees globally were engaged in their work,[3] the lowest scores in 10 years.[4]
- Employees' trust in business leaders fell from 80% in 2022 to 69% in 2024.[5]

- Only 26% of employees strongly agree that their workplace is psychologically safe, meaning they feel comfortable sharing concerns and mistakes without fear of embarrassment or retribution.[6]

Most of our workplace cultures are not brain-friendly; they are brain-antagonistic. We can do better.

In 2002, Daniel Goleman, Annie McKee, and Richard Boyatzis stated in *Primal Leadership: Realizing the Power of Emotional Intelligence* that culture or "emotional climate" drives performance. And when surveyed, employees traced culture back to the actions of one person: their leader.[7]

Since then, thousands of studies have reinforced these truths: Culture drives results. Leaders drive culture.

## What kind of leader is truly worth following?

And what kind of culture does a leader create that's truly worth someone investing 90,000 working hours—their talent, their loyalty, and their life?

The answer isn't guesswork.

It's grounded in science and validated by real voices who answered one defining question: "What makes a leader worth following?"

In the pages ahead, you won't just learn theory. You'll learn the CRANIUM methodology, seven proven brain-based strategies.

For each strategy, we'll explore:

- Why it matters to the brain.
- What kind of culture it creates.

- How you can bring it to life through tangible, practical actions.

## How to use this book

This isn't just a book; it's a toolbox for real change. Everything in this book comes straight from the field: insights, actions, and tools we've tested with leaders across industries.

## Make it yours

- Read it solo or with your team to multiply impact and accountability.
- Jump to what you need or read start to finish.
- Play, don't perform. Stay curious, experiment, and notice what works.
- Take action. Each chapter includes practical tools. Try them. Tweak them. Keep what sticks.

## You're in the right place if...

- You want practical tools that work, not just theory that collects dust.
- You're working hard but not getting the results you really want.
- You're new to leadership and want to avoid common traps.
- You feel stuck in "the way it's always been done" and want a smarter way forward.
- You care deeply about building a culture where people feel safe, inspired, and fully alive.
- You know leadership starts with you, and you're ready to grow so others can, too.
- You want your influence to matter and to change lives.

- You see leadership as a sacred responsibility.
- You're ready to accelerate human potential, starting with your own.

Our world needs more leaders worth following. Thank you for being here. Let's get started!

---

## HIGH-PERFORMANCE LEADERSHIP STARTS HERE!

Take the CRANIUM Survey and instantly access your personalized CRANIUM Dashboard, a powerful snapshot of how you're applying the 7 brain-based strategies and where breakthrough is only one insight away.

Scan the QR code or go to yellingroup.com/highperformanceleadership.

---

## ACCESS OVER 30+ FREE BONUS TOOLS

Throughout this book, you'll see "**NAVIGATE TO RESOURCE**" boxes—your gateway to exclusive tools that bring the CRANIUM strategies to life.

To access your free resources, simply scan the QR code or go to yellingroup.com/highperformanceleadership.

Everything you need is just a click away.

# CHAPTER 1

# The Challenge Strategy

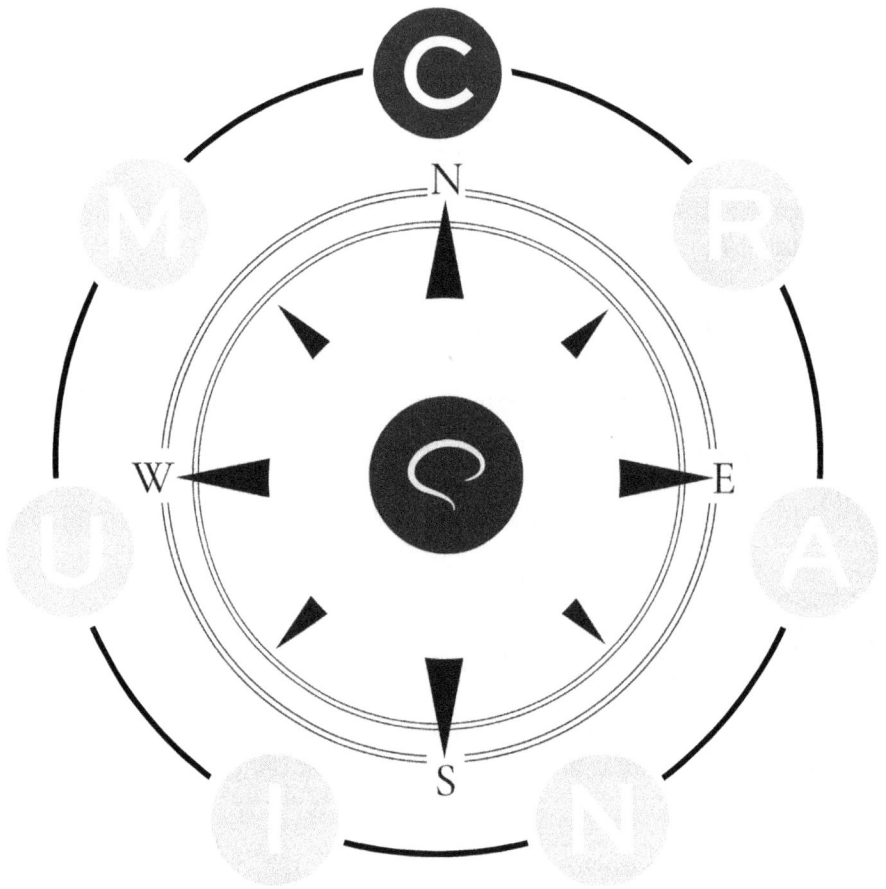

**DECREASE THREAT.**
**INCREASE TRUST.**

**BIG IDEA**

Threat kills, steals, and destroys.

With every decision, we choose to create a culture of threat or a culture of challenge.

## BREAKTHROUGH BELIEFS

Threat to the brain is threat to the brain.

Your current rules are creating your current results.

You can be right, or you can be rich.

# REAL LEADERS. REAL LIFE.

*Unrelenting stress and overwhelm.*

Fatima sits in her office with the door closed, breathing deeply and praying for just 15 minutes of peace with no interruptions, demands, problems, or complaints. She closes her computer and puts her head in her hands. With her heart racing and jaw clenched, she feels the stress crawling up her back and into her shoulders. She questions past decisions, wonders how she got here, and has little hope that things will change. She would rather be under a blanket in a dark room than face another meeting with no clear direction or purpose.

Fatima is a VP in an industry struggling to keep up in a demanding, competitive economy. While her budget and staff have decreased for the last several years, the demands and expectations on her and her team have exponentially increased. She lacks the support she needs to get the job done, but it isn't exactly clear what success would look like even if she had adequate time and resources. She feels like she is drowning in unmet expectations and unrealistic demands.

A workplace once known for innovation, a sense of pride, and community is now a place where people pass each other by in the halls, distracted and disengaged. Departments are suspicious of one another, competing for recognition and a greater slice of the budget. More conversations are spent around "what *could* happen" than "what *is* happening." Meetings are pointless. Promotion seems to be based on favoritism rather than merit.

Then there is Fatima's personal life. While she longs for a home filled with contentment and peace, she lives in one brimming with pressure. She and her husband work long hours to provide for their four children, all in or nearing their teenage years.

The spoken and unspoken demands of their "wannabe" affluent community—private schools, club sports, luxury cars—consume their time and divert their income from essential investments, such as college savings. If she's honest, the last time Fatima and her husband had meaningful time alone was years ago at a weekend getaway. Both are lost in the abyss of "appearance" and "doing."

# YOU'RE WIRED FOR CHALLENGE

*Why your brain thrives on the Challenge Strategy*

A culture of threat is toxic—toxic to ideas, results, performance, personal health, relationships, potential, and possibilities.

The most important message I want to share about the brain is simple: actively minimize threat to achieve the brain's highest performance.

Negative threat impairs the brain and interferes with being our best selves, living our best lives, and achieving all that we can achieve.

We must minimize threat if we seek to create high-performing cultures for ourselves and those we lead and care about, cultures where results come naturally, and cultures where all reach their fullest potential.

What is the most significant "difference that makes the difference" between a threat environment and a challenge environment?

Intentionality.

Challenge environments are created by design. Threat environments happen by default.

A threat environment "just happens," with leaders and influencers giving little thought or resources to building and maintaining the desired culture or course-correcting when there are signs that the culture is sick. A challenge environment happens "on purpose," with leaders and influencers making deliberate decisions to shape the desired culture and investing resources and attention into ensuring the culture stays a priority.

A threat environment results when culture is viewed as a "nice to have." A challenge environment results when culture is embraced as a non-negotiable "must have."

Let's take a closer look at your brain and threat. By understanding how threat impacts the brain, we discover why it is virtually impossible to achieve high performance under threat.

To be clear, the threat we are talking about here is negative threat. Some threat is motivating and essential. For example, in the same way the threat of being eaten by a lion motivates us to run or hide, the threat of failing a class or giving a crappy presentation to the executive team motivates us to prepare and not procrastinate.

Negative threat, the kind that debilitates rather than motivates, typically meets at least three criteria:

- Confusion: We have more confusion than clarity.
- Control: We feel we have little agency, control over or say in the situation.
- Consequences: We anticipate a negative consequence.

Think of a time recently when you perceived an event as a negative threat?

- What created confusion?

- In what way(s) did you feel the event was out of your control? Or that you had little to no choice or say in what was happening?

- What negative consequence were you expecting or dreading?

The pandemic of 2020 presented the perfect conditions for negative threat.

**Confusion**: Almost overnight, we faced immense, unprecedented confusion in almost every area of our lives. Uncertainty surrounded our individual health, our families' health, our economy, our businesses, our children's education, and so forth.

**Control**: We had little choice or voice in how to respond. Masks were mandated, offices, schools, and privately-owned businesses were closed, and major events were cancelled.

**Consequences**: We saw the number of COVID-19 cases escalate, people were suffering, and many of us lost loved ones.

When threat is perceived as negative threat, it has a debilitating impact on our brain to produce the kinds of results we desire for high performance.

Your brain is a treasure. Knowing a few key discoveries about how the brain learns and processes information and events is transformational.

The brain (not technology with a power cord and a data plan) fuels us to be our best selves and live our best lives. Therefore, we need to know a few essential truths about how it works best.

# 3 BIG DEALS

Let's start with what I call the 3 Big Deals. Granted, we have a long way to go in understanding the mysterious equipment we all carry around between our ears, and each person's brain is unique and constantly changing. However, there are a few functional, almost universal, facts that, when applied, can dramatically change the results in every area of our lives.

## Big Deal #1: Your Prefrontal Cortex is Priceless

Big Deal #1 relates to a part of the brain called the prefrontal cortex (or PFC), located at the anterior (front) part of the frontal lobe.

This area of the brain influences functions that are critical to achieving the results we want as high-performing leaders and individuals striving to live our best lives. Some people reference the PFC as the brain's CEO, "the lobe of leadership," or our "Jiminy Cricket." Let's take a closer look.

The PFC has a direct impact on activities essential to high performance, such as:

- Creativity
- Innovation
- Problem solving
- Planning
- Articulating thoughts
- Empathy
- Collaboration
- Adaptability
- Goal setting
- Goal achievement

**NAVIGATE TO RESOURCE**

3 Big Deals:
Video and PDF

The PFC fuels proactive functions such as planning, thinking through consequences, impulse control, and strategic thinking.

Increased activity in the prefrontal cortex also initiates a flood of motivating chemicals in our brain, including dopamine, adrenaline, epinephrine, and norepinephrine. These chemicals facilitate mood stabilization, focus, motivation, the ability to learn and assimilate new information, and the energy to keep doing more of the above.

In recent years, extensive research into the prefrontal cortex has revealed even more astonishing benefits regarding decision-making, impulse control, and self-regulation. When activity in the PFC increases, so too does multiple forms of self-control.

### Motor self-control

Motor self-control is the ability to regulate physical actions, movements, or responses. Think of the childhood game, *Simon Says*. The rules are not complicated; you can move only when someone says, "Simon says." In the same way the PFC assists in winning this game, it also assists when we, under pressure, may need to watch our words, manage our emotions, or resist the urge to throw a punch (yes, it happens).

### Financial self-control

The PFC also heavily influences financial self-control. If you've ever made an impulse buy, you know exactly what I'm talking about. Ever got "new stuff" fever? That urge to acquire a new purse, a new house, or the latest gadget? I have three iPads, none of which are being used. Financial self-control is seeing the new car, smelling the new car, envisioning how sophisticated you will look driving the car, and then remembering you can't *afford* the new car! In the world of leadership results, financial self-control may look like saving to build economic strength for the future or cutting costs even if the decision isn't popular or convenient.

### Emotional self-control

The prefrontal cortex is also involved in the regulation of emotional self-control. It's the ability to manage your emotions, especially in emotionally charged situations. If you've ever attended a child's sporting event, or better yet, been a parent attending your child's sporting event, then you fully understand what emotional self-control does and does not look like. In leadership, it may be refraining from raising your voice, throwing things (yes, that happens, too), or making damaging accusations.

In addition to regulating emotions, the PFC is also involved in self-regulation, which is the ability to stay motivated and disciplined. Several years ago, my sister and I were inspired by our friends running long distances and wearing cool running swag from the races they participated in. The idea to join them sounded great at 9 p.m., but we were much less enthusiastic when the alarm went off at a rainy, cold 5:30 a.m.

Self-regulation in leadership may involve maintaining a positive mindset, staying committed to a project long after the novelty has worn off, or remaining loyal to one's values.

## Cognitive self-control

Cognitive self-control is the ability to control your thoughts. When the PFC is engaged, you can better discern rational and irrational, helpful and unhelpful thoughts. We will dig deeper into the power and deception of thoughts later. For now, remember that your thoughts can (and often) lie, and you don't have to believe and accept every thought you have. Just because it 'feels' real doesn't make it real.

Thoughts are like family members: they are familiar, but when they visit, we don't have to make their room and stay so comfortable that they never want to leave!

## Perspective self-control

As if the previous four types of self-control were not reason enough to protect activity in the PFC, there is also evidence that this magical place in our brains controls our ability to have perspective. *Perspective* derives from Latin roots: *per* (meaning "through") and *spect* (meaning "to see"). Perspective means "to see through," to have the capacity see a situation through someone else's point of view. Let that sink in for a moment.

Think about the critical ability to take another's perspective or shift perspective, especially in reducing threat, building trust, and promoting inclusion and innovation. Imagine how many conflicts could be avoided or resolved if we could genuinely see through the other person's reality. Picture for a moment how communication and innovation could improve if we fully appreciate the perspectives and experiences of others.

Without perspective self-control, there is no collaboration, we limit the possibilities that come from diverse thinking, and no one feels valued and heard.

Here's the problem.

The prefrontal cortex, the part of the brain essential to achieving high-performance results, is fragile. It is highly susceptible to disease and vulnerable to injury. The brain has the consistency of an egg yolk and is housed in a very bony structure, making the slightest head injury a serious injury. The PFC is also particularly sensitive to emotional hijackings, those strong emotional events triggered by negative stress and threat.

This leads to Big Deal #2.

## Big Deal #2: Threat to the Brain is Threat to the Brain

Using the metaphor of a city, the PFC is like the brain's city council, while the brain stem area is more like the city's police department. Like the PFC, the brain stem system is proactive and stimulates important chemicals with one singular focus: to protect us and keep us safe. Sometimes, it helps us achieve our goals, and sometimes, it hinders us. The key is for us to better understand how threat impacts the brain and acquire more tools to manage it mindfully.

Your brain simply responds to threat. Any threat. All threat. Regardless of whether it is physical, like a poisonous snake, or psychological, like a poisonous boss, coworker, or spouse.

Negative threat limits access to those sophisticated PFC functions. It also triggers a surge in protective, stress chemicals such as cortisol that can negatively impact our sleep, immune system, ability to see options, and make informed decisions.

Recall a few moments from your life:

1. When was the last time you were in a large group and were unexpectedly called upon to answer a complicated (or controversial) question or report on a project? How articulate were you?

   Chances are, you scrambled for your thoughts or had the infamous "deer in the headlights" look. Why does that happen? What can we do about it?

2. When was the last time you were reeling in anger because of someone else's actions? How adept were you at truly seeing the situation from the other person's perspective?

   Chances are, you became overly committed to being right and defending your position. Why does this happen? How can we become more aware in the moment?

3. When was the last time you were creative, innovative, energized, and lost in the moment where time and space seemed to disappear?

   Chances are, you were in what Mihaly Csikszentmihalyi named "in flow."[1] This statement often occurs when we engage in something we love in an environment conducive to our best operating style. Why does this happen? How can we create more moments like this?

When threat enters the scene, the priceless functions of the PFC become much harder to access. If we want high-performance results, such as opportunities, inclusion, growth, and self-control, why would we allow threat to take hold and thrive? Even worse, why would we create threat? Threat chokes the part of the brain that fuels high-performance.

The greatest one thing leaders who strive to be high-performing and worth following can do is decrease threat.

## Big Deal #3: Emotions Run the Show

We will explore this further later, but for now, I'd like you to accept that we are not thinking beings who happen to have emotions. Rather, we are emotional beings who happen to think.

We are more emotional than logical. Emotion is involved in everything we do.

Information and experiences are processed first through the emotional center of the brain, commonly referred to as the limbic system. This emotional center decides to consult with the prefrontal cortex and/or the threat part of the brain.

Let's say your team has worked remotely, and you are the lucky messenger who must tell them they are required to return to the office. This information is hitting the team's emotional center first. Their brains are frantically processing the emotions while trying to take in the facts and manage threat (confusion, choice, and control). So, as leaders, we want to be very intentional about how we introduce change. (More on that in later chapters.)

Or, let's say you are a patient who has just received disturbing, unexpected news about your health. An informed physician knows that your brain is not absorbing or remembering anything that follows the sharing of the diagnosis.

We may think we are making logical decisions. In reality, we are making emotional decisions and justifying them with logic.

# THE CHALLENGE STRATEGY IN PRACTICE

*What a Challenge culture looks like*

The Challenge Strategy is about intentionally increasing activity in the PFC by reducing negative threat and engaging emotions that fuel purpose and passion. It is about aligning with how the brain works best, reducing threat, and creating an environment that promotes PFC activity.

Unlike threat, challenge puts the brain in a flow state, creates enthusiasm and engagement, and reduces resistance. It allows us to easily access the sophisticated abilities and results we want for ourselves, those we influence, and those we lead.

Increasing activity in the PFC stimulates motivating chemicals, allowing us to focus, learn, and perform optimally. We "turn on" the priceless functions essential to high-performance leadership, such as speech, willpower, creativity, adaptability, empathy, perspective-taking, and planning.

We must seek ways to reduce the interference of threat and increase challenge in the environment if we want outcomes and results that involve being our best self, bringing out the best in others, expressing creativity and innovation, performing to our fullest potential, intelligently communicating, collaborating, and embracing change. Doesn't that sound like the kind of results we want in our workplaces, teams, schools, homes, relationships, and world?

Challenge gives us an advantage. Let's contrast two cultures—one where threat dominated and one where the Challenge Strategy was actively at work. Notice the differences each presents in terms of measurable results.

## A culture of threat

Early in my career, I experienced firsthand the toxicity of an unhealthy culture, marked by egos, posturing, and division. Me against you. You against me. Us against them.

The union leadership would not, under any conditions, agree with the company leadership. Management lorded over the employees. Employees could not attend professional development classes on "company" time. I once asked for paper clips, and I was given two. One morning, Jim, my supervisor, asked if we needed any supplies in the learning center. I replied that we needed paper clips. That afternoon, he stopped by and placed two on my desk. Sounds like a light-hearted practical joke, right? Not at all. He was completely serious.

Several months later, I experienced a more pronounced example of this threat culture with Jim's boss, Andy. Funny how culture starts at the top. Our team, including Jim, was invited to a national conference in Miami, Florida to receive an award for the training program we had built.

Andy told Jim to take the team out for a celebration dinner on the eve of the awards ceremony. Jim covered the meal with the expectation of reimbursement. We racked up an impressive tab. It was a considerable expense for a middle manager and sole income provider for a large family.

The following evening, our team, Jim, and Andy sat together at the awards ceremony. Before awards were announced, we enjoyed dinner and cheesecake for dessert. The cheesecake looked so delicious that Jim asked for two pieces, which the waiter placed in front of Jim's plate.

Jim was full after he finished his meal and the first piece of cheesecake. He offered his second piece to others at the table. There were no takers.

All was peaceful until Andy firmly stated: "Jim, you WILL eat that second piece of cheesecake."

Our initial genuine laughter died down to silence when we realized Andy was serious.

Andy stood up, stared down at Jim, and said: "You WILL eat every bite of that cheesecake, or I will not approve the reimbursement for last night's dinner."

Our team sat in complete silence as we watched our boss demoralized. He forcibly ate every bite of the second piece of cheesecake. Our heads dropped, and we empathized with our boss, who had been reduced to a 6-year-old not allowed to leave the table until every pea on his plate was eaten. Embarrassed. Belittled. Humiliated.

In that moment, the voice in my head became very loud and clear: "Dysfunctional! Unhealthy! Toxic! Abort!" I was determined to leave that job just as fast as I could.

From office supplies to management styles, this was a culture of threat. Leaders became bigger by making others smaller. The scarcity mentality (there is not a big enough pie for everyone to have a piece—pardon the pun) ruled. People were driven by fear, and the results proved it.

Talented and high performers—including me—left as quickly as we could find another opportunity. All feared attempting anything involving risk or demonstrating initiative for fear of failure or reprimand. Few dared to say what they really felt. Most privately shared their frustrations and resentments for hours on end inside and outside the company. We took that stress and heaviness home with us and passed it on to our families. Meetings were a waste of time, productivity suffered, and the company was not positioned to meet the rapidly changing demands of the communication field in the early 1990s.

Today, the parking lot is empty, and weeds grow through the concrete cracks. If I were to tell you the company's name, most of you would go back in the archives of your mind and say, "Yeah, I remember them."

## A culture with the Challenge Strategy advantage

In contrast, my next career adventure led me to a defense manufacturing organization with assembly lines, safety glasses, hard hats, and 24/7 operations. Here, employees at all levels and on all shifts were encouraged to attend personal and professional development classes all on company time, regardless of whether the topic was directly tied to their current job. Employees who aspired to move into a leadership role were encouraged to take leadership classes.

People were trusted. Novel idea.

The internet as we know it today had only recently became available when I accepted this job. Most companies at the time had restrictive policies concerning internet use. The internet was available on a "need to use only" basis. Most companies during that time were suspicious of internet use, limiting access to senior levels. It was not accessible to the hourly employee for fear of hindering productivity or being used for nefarious purposes.

This company's approach was very different. They trusted their employees and urged them to explore and learn about the internet and how it held information they could use on and off the job. They knew technology was the future. They believed that the skills employees at all levels had with accessing information, the greater the likelihood they would use it to become more efficient, innovative, and productive in their positions and careers.

It was a culture that encouraged collaboration, celebrated accomplishments (large and small), and recognized individuals and teams for outstanding contributions. Managers coached and served rather than bossed. Leaders were promoted based on their teams' results, growth, and performance rather than tenure. Ideas were exchanged, challenging issues were placed front and center to address directly, and every performer had an equal opportunity to grow and develop professionally.

In this culture, leaders became greater by developing (rather than belittling) other leaders. The abundance mentality prevailed over scarcity mentality. The organization operated with the fundamental belief that the pie was big enough for everyone to have a piece. It was collaboration over competition.

People were rewarded and recognized for growing, taking risks, embracing innovation, and demonstrating initiative. They felt safe to express their ideas and opinions. Talent flocked to interviews; high performers stayed and brought their high-performing friends. Productivity was high, and mistakes were truly viewed as learning moments. This company thrives all these years later, surviving mergers, technological advances, and economic ebb and flow.

These two contrasting cultures experienced very different results. Their results demonstrate that there is no positive, meaningful return in allowing or creating a threat environment characterized by fear, stress, and overwhelm.

The greatest one thing leaders can do is identify and recognize threat. As Dr. John Medina powerfully explains in his book, *Brain Rules: 12 Principles for Surviving and Thriving at Work, Home, and School*, threat is as crippling to the brain as arthritis is to the body.[2] If someone has arthritis internally, there are external, visible physical signs. You may see twisted backs, gnarled fingers, or slow movements. Similarly, if a team, organization or individual has internal threat, there are observable, external signs. We just have to pay attention to what they are.

In cultures where leaders ignore the Challenge Strategy, a few observable signs are:

- Honest feedback is rare. Team members may play "nice," but there is no genuine, transparent sharing of thoughts, concerns, and ideas.
- Negative behavior patterns persist, continue to grow, and spread to others. They are often ignored and never directly addressed or reprimanded, at least not with the person engaging in the negative behavior.
- More discussion occurs *after* the meeting than *during* it.
- Promotions are based on outcomes, regardless of how those outcomes are achieved.
- An "us" against "them" mentality prevails.
- High-potential talent treats the role as a stepping stone.
- Goals and objectives are time-consuming, obligatory exercises with little meaning or impact.
- Turnover is high and engagement is low.
- Recruiting is costly because the brand fails to attract top talent.
- Morale is low due to defeat, helplessness, and apathy.
- A deafening silence follows when questions are solicited.

In contrast, a high-challenge environment carries a different energy and produces very different observable signs. A challenge culture recognizes and purposefully minimizes threats to create a safe environment, both psychologically and physically. It's a culture where all involved make a concerted, continual effort to learn, grow, and increase trust.

In cultures where leaders embrace the Challenge Strategy, a few observable signs are:

- A "one-team" mindset that is lived out through collaboration and sharing insight, ideas, and information.
- People feel valued, heard, and have a genuine sense of belonging.
- Team members are empowered, energized, and take pride in being part of the team.
- Each person brings their best self and their best brain to the task.
- Tough problems and tough conversations are faced head-on, sooner rather than later, and handled with courage and consideration.
- Goals and objectives are meaningful and lead to real, impactful results.
- People laugh.
- Colleagues know each other beyond their work roles.
- Work is fulfilling and purposeful.
- Morale and engagement are high, resulting in genuine commitment and loyalty.
- Setbacks are viewed as valuable learning opportunities.

The Challenge Strategy builds a culture of trust and empowerment. Creating and maintaining a challenge culture requires leaders who identify and adopt beliefs and actions that foster an environment that activates the PFC, leaders who promote learning, experimentation, creation, communication, development, and growth.

| WITHOUT THE CHALLENGE STRATEGY | WITH THE CHALLENGE STRATEGY |
|---|---|
| • Indirect, low-quality feedback | • Direct, high-quality feedback |
| • Fake nice | • Genuine relationships |
| • Side conversations after the meeting | • Direct conversations during meeting |
| • Low morale | • High morale |
| • Apathy | • Passion and purpose |
| • Results over relationships | • Results through relationships |
| • Division and silos | • Collaboration |
| • Steppingstone to next role | • Forever home |
| • Checking boxes | • Meaningful tasks and dialogue |
| • High turnover | • Low turnover |
| • Low engagement | • High engagement |
| • Limited talent pipeline | • Constant talent pipeline |
| • Silence | • Laughter |
| • Stiff, stale environment | • Fun, celebratory environment |
| • Conspiracy theories | • Assuming good intent |
| • Waiting to be told | • Initiating action |

# BE A LEADER
# WORTH FOLLOWING

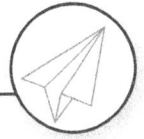

*How to live out the Challenge Strategy*

High-performance leaders actively identify and reduce threats.

We've established the negative consequences of negative threat. Challenge is the opposite of threat. While challenge turns up the activity in the PFC, threat turns it down—way down.

Think about the last time you were under physical threat (or thought you were). Maybe a person in a dark parking lot made you feel uncomfortable. Perhaps a stick on the ground looked like a snake. Perhaps the airplane dropped suddenly due to turbulence. Possibly you heard your child scream. You most likely didn't pause and consciously evaluate whether the threat was physical, emotional, or psychological—real or perceived—and adjust your response accordingly. Instead, your heart rate likely increased, your jaw clenched, you had a knee-jerk reaction, and you may have used colorful language.

A few years ago, I traveled to Boston to facilitate a workshop. I'm from Texas, which is an important detail in this story. We rarely see freezing temperatures. In Boston, it was the middle of winter. Around 3 a.m., the fire alarm in my hotel went off. I came out of a dead sleep (something I'm famous for) and reacted the way any sane person from Texas would—I ran outside into three feet of snow with no coat and no shoes.

The wait for the fire truck was miserable and a bit embarrassing. I wasn't the only person standing out in the cold, unprepared. (There must have been other Texans in the hotel that night.) But most had the forethought to grab shoes and a coat; a few overachievers even had hats and gloves.

We'll return to that story later. For now, it demonstrates some important points we can't afford to forget about negative threat.

## Our brains simply react to threat.

In that situation, my brain didn't pause to evaluate the kind of threat I was facing. I simply reacted in the same way I would if a ball flew at my head, a car swerved into my lane, or a boss screamed at me in a meeting.

Reacting to threats can cause us to "lose" our ability to exercise higher-order, thoughtful, critical thinking skills.

We lose the ability to take a different perspective, demonstrate empathy, see options, or assume good intent. Instead, we get stuck, controlling, and overly committed to being right. We become defensive, narrow-minded, and paranoid.

So, what are the most common conditions that trigger the fire alarm for threat at work?

Over the last 30 years, I've identified ten. My list of the top 10 threats lurking in the workplace includes those I have most frequently observed, coached on, and developed learning solutions for.

The potential for these threats exist in all industries. Where people are, they are.

See which ones you identify with and strategies you can use to prevent and minimize the negative results they produce.

# How High-Challenge Cultures Address the Top 10 Threats

### *Threat #10: Lack of meaning*

Meaning matters.

It matters at all ages and in all situations. In high-threat cultures, people work for a paycheck, while in high-challenge cultures, people work for a purpose.

One of the most frequently cited drivers of engagement is "meaningful purpose." This is especially true in the post-COVID world. People are motivated by making progress and contributing to something greater than themselves. They want to connect the dots between their daily work and the organization's overall mission.

One surprising discovery is how often leaders in organizations with noble missions, such as nonprofits and healthcare, overlook the importance of purpose and meaning. These leaders assume or take for granted that their teams know the importance of their daily efforts. For example, we've witnessed healthcare and non-profit staff no longer see the meaning or value of their work, despite being on the front lines with patients and interacting with the homeless and hungry.

I believe it's even more important to emphasize meaning in professions requiring high levels of empathy and regulation. When purpose gets lost, apathy and burnout take over.

We find that leaders in organizations with less inspirational products and services often do a better job of connecting the work to a higher purpose. They are more intentional about connecting the day-to-day doing with the bigger why.

Rather than a lack of meaning, challenge cultures are vision-driven. Leaders strive to ensure everyone knows the greater impact and purpose of their daily tasks. There is a clear and compelling "why" that unites the team and the organization. They care about purpose and passion as much as pay.

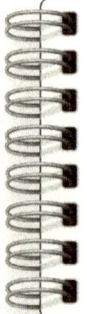

1. What is your company's purpose?

2. What about the company's purpose is important to you? to your team members?

3. How do you explicitly connect the daily doing to the mission, vision, and purpose?

## ACTIONS

- Have a compelling mission, vision, or purpose statement.
- Define clear organizational values and/or beliefs.
- Connect changes, requests, decisions, and tasks to the bigger why.
- Add the phrase—*and here's why*—to requests and changes.
- Communicate regularly how work impacts the team, the organization, the customer, the patient, the community, the world, the company's future, etc.
- Do not assume people see the connection between their daily tasks and the bigger impact they have.

## Threat #9: Favoritism

Favoritism and bias, or the perception thereof, have a debilitating impact on brain performance at any age.

My daughter played select or "club" softball from age 9 through college. Fastpitch is a wildly popular and sometimes cut-throat sport in our part of the world. I feel like we sold our souls to the softball gods for several years and am often surprised at how easily it was to get sucked into the competition and the comparing. All those years, I packed the cooler, loaded the car, and spent most weekends sitting behind the cage in a folding chair with the rest of the crazy softball moms.

But crazier than the softball moms were the softball dads. These were dads who thought that just because their daughters had the ability and desire to play ball, they had the ability and right to be coaches, a phenomenon called "daddy ball."

When tryouts rolled around and these guys posted "all positions open," they told a partial truth. They meant that all positions were open except those earmarked for their daughters. That favoritism and bias diminished the enthusiasm of the other players, hindered coaches from making objective decisions, and ultimately, held the team back from performing at its best.

The same result happens in our schools, homes, and workplaces when favoritism and bias are unchecked. This behavior shows up in multiple forms, such as who gets assigned to certain projects and who doesn't, who receives special privileges and who doesn't, and who is considered for specific positions and who isn't.

The impact of favoritism in the workplace is the same as I witnessed on the softball field. The enthusiasm of the players, especially the talented players, is diminished. Loyalty fades. The leaders' decisions aren't objective or effective. The team will never achieve its best.

Rather than favoritism, challenge cultures offer a fair chance to anyone willing to put forth the effort, aspire to level-up performance, and get the work done. Leaders recognize everyone has bias and seek feedback to mitigate their bias. Rewards and opportunities are based on performance.

## ACTIONS

- Establish a fair and equitable process with objective criteria for hiring, promoting, and giving opportunities.
- Recognize that we all have blind spots and biases. Seek feedback from others to help you see what you aren't seeing.
- Remember silence is not silent. When tasks are delegated for example, explain to the person why he or she was or was not chosen for the project.
- Be as transparent as possible in decision-making.
- Avoid over-socializing with only one person or group.
- Self-reflect. Are there multiple perspectives and backgrounds represented on project teams and in meetings? Or, does everyone think, act, and look like you?

1. When have you experienced or observed favoritism and bias?

2. What was the immediate and long-term impact?

3. Where might someone on your team perceive a decision or action as favoritism?

## Threat #8: Micromanaging

The need to control is pervasive and exists at birth.

I was once given powerful advice: You can have control or you can have growth, but you can't have both in equal proportion at the same time. Read that again. And again.

Leaders who micromanage create hard. They stunt their own growth and the growth of everyone around them.

A client of mine had a boss who asked her to take minutes in meetings, only to rewrite them before distributing them to the team. The meaning my client gave to this repeated behavior was "she doesn't trust me and doesn't have confidence in my ability." In reality, the boss lacked confidence and trust in herself.

Micromanaging frequently occurs because a person needs to control. And, people often feel the need to control when they are insecure and under threat. Ironically, we believe that micromanagers have an overwhelming confidence in their own abilities and display a superior arrogance towards everyone else. On closer reflection, however, our need to control situations, people, and outcomes is always rooted not in confidence but in fear—fear of the unknown, fear of the future, fear in our ability, fear of not being needed, etc.

One of the best movie scenes that captures true growth and learning is in *Apollo* 13.[3] The engineers realize the astronauts are slowly being poisoned by carbon monoxide gas. The lead engineer upends a box of random items the astronauts have at their disposal onto a table and gives straightforward instructions to the team. It's a literal square peg-in-a-round-hole problem.

With clarity on what winning looked like, the engineering team dove right in without guidance from any one person. No micromanagement was necessary. NASA's senior leadership wasn't concerned with charts, graphs, or reports. They never asked for a slide deck or spreadsheet. The team was clear on success, the available resources, and their expertise. Leadership gave them full autonomy to get the job done, and they did.

In a high-threat culture, leadership is suspect of others' capabilities. They delegate tasks rather than authority. In a high-challenge culture, leadership trusts that they have hired capable, resourceful professionals. They mindfully give the freedom and authority needed for the task. In turn, they grow themselves, those around them, and their results.

Rather than micromanaging, challenge cultures honor input and seek ways for people to have a choice and a voice. Leaders in these cultures are coachable and committed to learn. There is no "my way or the highway," but rather, a desire to co-create "our way." Leaders invest in building their team and empower team members to make decisions. Being rich in results is more important than being right.

1. When have you been micromanaged?

2. What was the immediate and long-term impact?

3. Under what circumstances do you tend to micromanage?

## ACTIONS

- List those situations where you can come across as micromanaging.
- Identify what those situations have in common.

- Write down your beliefs about asking for help.
- Improve your delegation skills.

## NAVIGATE TO RESOURCE

The Ultimate Checklist for Effective Delegation:
Course and PDF

## Threat #7: Humiliation

Humility and humiliation are opposite experiences. Interestingly, though, they are derived from the same word "humus", which means earth or ground.

Humility keeps you steady on the ground. Humiliation knocks you right to the ground.

Humiliation is the act of degrading, disgracing, devaluing, and shaming. It is tolerated, if not rewarded, in high-threat cultures. The physician who screams and throws a tantrum, blaming others and dismissing her own accountability. The executive who silences a direct report by reminding him of his pay grade. The construction manager who belittles the subcontractor and makes disparaging and inappropriate comments and jokes at someone else's expense. The board that doesn't manage meeting time, so the emerging leader who spent hours preparing gets bumped. The manager who schedules one-on-one meetings with her team members and repeatedly cancels at the last minute. The leader who has to have the last word, the best idea, and be the smartest person in the room. People who use humiliation as a strategy for getting results are bullies.

I've seen CEOs and Presidents tolerate this type of behavior, justifying their decision because of the bully's specialized skillset, their tenure with the company, their promising potential, or their sales numbers. Everyone is replaceable. Everyone. There are 8 billion people on the planet. Leaders must never make decisions out of fear or scarcity to retain someone who humiliates others.

***What you permit, you promote. What you excuse, you encourage.***

You may be thinking, "I would never scream, throw things, or belittle people," so I can check this threat off my list. Not so fast.

Humiliating someone is not always a blatant and intentional act. People can feel humiliated or shamed even if that is not our intention. I have had this happen a handful of times when facilitating workshops. In one instance, a group of leaders was completing an assessment. One of the leaders did not complete hers properly, so I gave her another one to complete. She called me later that night to tell me how humiliating that was for her to have made that error in front of her peers. In future workshops, I gave more precise directions. In a second situation, I used the example of losing weight as a New Year's resolution. In the post-session evaluation, someone in the workshop shared her struggle with losing weight, and my using that as an example derailed her for the remainder of the day.

Even in our attempts to foster a high-challenge culture, humiliation happens. If you talk to enough people, you will eventually (albeit unknowingly) offend someone. The point is to be as mindful as possible. Assume the social risk as much as possible by making every environment psychologically safe. Invite continuous feedback. And certainly, never tolerate or promote direct acts of humiliation, bullying, and shaming.

Rather than using humiliation as a form of control, challenge cultures use feedback and engagement to involve and motivate.

Leaders spend less time on what someone is doing wrong, more time on what someone is doing right, and how they can better leverage individual strengths to improve in all areas. Ego-driven leaders are quickly managed out.

1. Have you ever been on the receiving end of humiliation, shaming or bullying?

2. What was the immediate and long-term impact?

3. Who are people you trust to give you feedback on times when you may have unintentionally humiliated someone?

## ACTIONS

- Be culturally aware when using sarcasm.
- Give feedback in private, especially feedback which can be perceived as negative.
- Remember silence is not silent. If anyone acts in a manner that could humiliate another person, have the courage to respectfully speak up.
- Ask trusted colleagues to share ways you come across as humiliating or off-putting.
- Speak directly with someone who humiliates you.
- Use organizational resources such as Employee Assistance Programs or Human Resources if you feel you are being humiliated.
- Be mindful of your tone and body language. Though your intention may not be to humiliate, other people may experience it as humiliation.

## Threat #6: Risk of loss

Loss aversion and loss bias are intriguing psychological phenomena. Studies show that, when faced with a choice, people often prefer to stick with what they have—even if it's undesirable or risky—rather than take a chance on something better. This tendency persists even when clinging to the familiar could result in total loss or even death.

On October 13, 1972, Uruguayan Air Force Flight 571, carrying the Uruguayan rugby team and their friends and family, crashed in the Andes mountains. 29 of the 45 passengers survived the initial crash. By day 62, with sub-zero temperatures and limited food supplies, only 16 people were still alive. They were emaciated, dehydrated, suffering from frostbite, and had no hope of being rescued. Death was certain.

Even in these horrific, unimaginable conditions, only 2 of the 16 survivors were willing to leave the safety of the fuselage to risk going out into the unknown to find help. I include this story not to pass judgment on the other 14. I haven't experienced the trauma of what they endured, and clearly, I wasn't there when those decisions were made. But their story does cause me to pause and consider what a potent threat the risk of loss is. The pain of losing something is psychologically more powerful than the pleasure of gaining something.

In the workplace, loss can take many forms. Job loss, or the threat of job loss, is a common and obvious concern. A job represents much more than a literal place where a person is employed and receives a paycheck and benefits. A job is often tied to our identity and our purpose for living. Given our insatiable need to keep what we have, even when it isn't ideal, a significant loss can evoke intense emotional reactions and drive us to make decisions that focus more on avoiding further loss than pursuing potential gains.

We can experience loss when replacing old technology with new, a beloved colleague retires, or a new policy is implemented. Even setting a healthy boundary with someone can feel like a loss. I recently had to set a hard boundary with a childhood friend and felt a deep sense of loss knowing that by saying "yes" to the boundary, I was saying "no" to familiar past behaviors.

Most everyone coming to work each day is facing loss. There are personal losses such as divorce, family and friend drama, death, health issues, empty nesting, and aging. There are professional losses that could include any number of situations, such as a change, reorganization, retirement, relocation, rumors of layoffs, job loss, loss of title, loss of credibility, loss of acceptance in the group. Even something as simple as losing one's parking spot or cubicle can trigger the stress of loss.

In high-threat cultures, the impact of loss is overlooked. In high-challenge cultures, leaders are mindful of the threat of loss and help themselves and others navigate it.

In challenge cultures, leaders don't dismiss the impact of loss. They communicate directly and openly and seek continuous feedback. Instead of allowing stories and rumors to circulate in a cloud of mystery, communication is transparent—even when the message is unpopular. Leaders in these environments present a clear picture of the future. Then, they help others move methodically towards the future.

1. How have you seen leaders help individuals and teams navigate loss or change in a healthy way?

2. What was the immediate and long-term impact?

3. What are losses or changes in your immediate experience you want to be mindful of?

## ACTIONS

- Listen empathetically.
- Before saying "yes" to something that will impact you, your team, or your organization, reflect on what you say "no" to.
- Hold regular, genuine, and meaningful conversations with your team members so that you can better understand what other losses they may be experiencing in life.
- Acknowledge losses that naturally accompany change. Allow the team time to process and discuss the loss. (Remember, the brain processes information through the emotional center, the limbic system.)
- Reflect on where you are postponing a decision because of the fear of loss. Fear-based decisions leverage the threat part of our brain, not the PFC.

## NAVIGATE TO RESOURCE

Empathic Listening: Video

## Threat #5: Lack of resources

Most people will say they need more resources. I rarely hear someone walk into a room complaining about having too much support, money, energy, and time. The threat of a lack of resources refers to situations where there is a genuine shortage of resources that prevents people from doing their job. Lacking adequate resources can create a state of hopelessness and even lead to learned helplessness.

As a reminder, the three conditions that most often contribute to negative threat are confusion, a lack of choice and control, and perceived negative consequences. A lack of resources contributes to all three.

For example, one of our clients was tasked with launching a leadership program by the end of the year. She wasn't assigned staff, autonomy to make decisions, a budget, or the support of senior leaders to champion the initiative. Another client was tasked with recruiting without training, direction, authority, or a budget. Assigning responsibilities without the resources to accomplish the task perpetuates a high-threat culture.

Leaders in high-challenge cultures ensure appropriate resources are available when setting expectations or assigning tasks. Resources include everything a person or team needs to execute successfully, including direct and indirect resources, people, time, dollars, support, training, etc.

An ongoing lack of resources can create a long-term deficit, leading to systemic challenges that may culminate in a cultural crisis. Eric Jensen, one of my professional heroes and the father of brain-based learning, writes about such a situation in his book *Poverty and Equity in Mind: Succeed with the Students Who Need You Most.*[4] He advocates for children living in poverty and works with the teachers to equip them to recognize and support these students.

He explains that the poverty problem exceeds money. Instead, children living in poverty are disadvantaged because of many inadequate resources. They lack stability as they move twice as often and get evicted five times as frequently as other children. They are at a higher risk of being in pedestrian accidents than other children. They lack encouragement as significant adults, such as teachers, do not expect them to achieve as they do other children. They lack health resources, moral support resources, nutritional resources, and on and on.

The cumulative effect of resource deficiencies impacts morale and performance of all types—academic achievement, healthy relationships, individual achievement, project completion, and so forth. Once entrenched, this kind of resource deficit can be particularly difficult to reverse, as it often impacts morale, pro- ductivity, and overall organizational and societal well-being.

In high-threat cultures, leaders assign tasks with little regard for the availability of resources.

In high-challenge cultures, leaders are mindful of balancing their demands with the availability of resources. They understand that operating lean is a good business practice as it promotes accountability, stewardship, and prioritizing. However, these leaders scale accordingly when workload increases faster than the available resources. They also tend to encourage innovating without fear of failure to leverage unconventional solutions.

1. What tasks have you recently assigned or received?

2. Do you have the necessary resources (people, time, technology, authority, etc.) to accomplish these tasks?

3. How can you best leverage existing resources?

## ACTIONS

- Ask yourself and your team members directly, "Do you have the resources you need to do your job?"
- Explore creative ways to fulfill the need for resources. I remember one team needing a cart to move supplies from one end of the building to the next. By the end of the day, they had access to twelve carts simply by contacting a few colleagues in other departments and asking.
- Request the resources you need, knowing the answer may be no.
- Pose questions that spark innovation, like, "What are they doing in other industries?" "What have we tried in the past?" "What haven't we tried?" "Who could help us?" "And what else?"
- Stay flexible and willing to adapt processes, timelines, or scope based on available resources.

## Threat #4: Unclear expectations

Clarity is like a deep, cleansing breath.

When people I coach are faced with unclear expectations, they start using words like "overwhelmed," "frustrated," "discouraged," and "unrealistic." It's easy to resort to these words and the feelings behind them because a lack of clarity is a threat and causes the brain to get stuck. The threat of confusion hinders the brain from its valuable ability to think creatively, prioritize, plan, and get moving. We often don't realize that the overwhelm isn't necessarily coming from the expectation itself but from the lack of clarity about the expectation.

For example, one client was recently asked to create a corporate university. She immediately went into overwhelm and threat and severely compromised the very skills and abilities she needed to create a corporate university.

Because she understood how to work with her brain, she recognized her brain was under threat, and the fastest way out of the threat was clarity. So instead of staying stuck and wandering in the dark, she immediately made a list of where she needed clarity.

- *What does a winning corporate university look like?*
- *What are the best practices of companies that have built a corporate university?*
- *How will we know we've created a high-performing corporate university?*
- *What is a process we can use?*
- *Who do we need to involve in the beginning stages?*

Gaining clarity in these high-level questions got her moving forward and clarified the next set of questions. For the brain, the knowing comes in the going. Gaining clarity for the next step is usually all the brain needs to move from stuck to a state of momentum.

Rather than accepting unclear or unrealistic expectations as the norm, leaders in high-challenge cultures understand the power of clarity. Therefore, they make sure they are clear in their own heads before setting expectations. They clearly communicate "clear" expectations and live and model them. They also verify that the listener heard clear expectations.

## CLARIFYING QUESTIONS

- What does winning look like?
- What makes this important right now?
- If we are at the end of this project, what are we seeing, feeling, thinking, and experiencing?
- Can you repeat back to me what you heard me say?
- What are any non-negotiables we need to honor in this expectation?

- When in your career have you been given unclear expectations?

- What were the short-term and long-term consequences?

- What is an expectation you have where there seems to be some confusion?

- What questions can you use to make sure the confusion is replaced with clarity?

- Delegate intentionally and with clarity.
- Remember that people don't always hear what you say. Always take the time to have someone repeat back to you what they heard.
- Document expectations to provide clarity and accountability.
- Adopt the belief that sooner is smaller. Regularly check in with others to ensure they and you are aligned. We want to course-correct before the car drifts over three lanes.
- Provide clear examples.
- Use the WWLL ("What Winning Looks Like") framework to define success early.

## NAVIGATE TO RESOURCE

The Ultimate Checklist for Effective Delegation:
Course and PDF

## Threat #3: Change

The brain doesn't resist change; it resists confusion.

Good or bad, change presents a threat simply because it represents the unknown.

A few years ago, my dishwasher died, and I had a new one installed. It's a good change, right? It's energy efficient, less noisy, holds a larger load, etc. But the design and placement of stacking dishes disrupted my well-established method.

When a baseball player changes his swing, it can take up to six weeks for noticeable improvement.

When an organization implements a new technology system, it can take months or years to experience a measurable impact.

Change of almost any kind requires a setback before a comeback. Change causes a hiccup in the flow of life. It requires us to slow down, reevaluate, and make adjustments, unlike the automaticity that occurs when habits form.

The brain is not working in our favor when it comes to change. The brain strives for homeostasis, the tendency for processes and systems to stay stable, familiar, and consistent. This is a fantastic brain feature for our blood pressure and body temperature. However, it can present a serious obstacle when we need to change well-established behaviors and beliefs.

In high-threat cultures, the focus is on the change. In high-challenge cultures, the focus is on the process of change. The success and ease of any change is directly correlated to how well we manage the process of change.

We had one client who changed their logo, a seemingly tactical change. But the existing logo held meaning to many in the organization; a few even had it tattooed on their body. Leadership presented the why behind the change. They conducted focus groups to solicit input. They presented three drafts of the logo and allowed team members to vote. They had a reveal ceremony where they paid tribute to the old logo, which they permanently displayed in a prominent area of the building, before launching the new. Team members were given "swag bags" with items sporting the new logo.

High-challenge cultures know that change is easy until it involves humans.

Therefore, rather than ignoring the impact of change, challenge cultures acknowledge the threat associated with change and seek ways to turn it into exciting, memorable opportunities. Resistance is anticipated, expected, and processed in a healthy way. They plan for the process of change, allowing for time along with appropriate training, resources, and tools to ensure the change is successful. At every step in the process, people are involved, and wins of all sizes are acknowledged and celebrated.

- When have you seen a change implemented successfully? What made it so?

- Where are you needing to lead a change effort (no matter how small)?

- What steps can you take to manage the change process?

## ACTIONS

- Explain the "why" behind the change to give context and meaning.
- Share a story of how the change will alleviate frustration or open a meaningful possibility.
- Offer multiple ways for people to ask questions, such as in a large group, small groups, individually, in writing, through casual conversations, surveys, polls, etc.
- Involve all stakeholders in decisions that impact them.

## NAVIGATE TO RESOURCE

Stakeholder Mapping Made Simple: Video and PDF

- Create a clear vision for the change. What does winning with this change look like?
- Communicate a compelling "why" behind the change. How will this change eliminate pain? How will this change produce pleasure?
- Identify your stakeholders. Stakeholders include everyone impacted by the change.
- Discover what is important to your stakeholders.
- Communicate clearly and often the benefits of this change by building on what is important to your stakeholders.
- Provide a clear timeline for the change.
- Communicate promptly any delays or changes in the implementation plan.

## Threat #2: Low trust

The opposite of negative threat is trust.

Trust is foundational to all the CRANIUM strategies simply because our brains on threat are anything but what we want when we walk into our workplaces, schools, or homes every day.

When there is low trust, the threat brain takes over. When this happens, people struggle to collaborate, demonstrate empathy, think strategically, be creative and innovative, prioritize and plan, or have the resilience and motivation to keep moving during tough times. Instead, they get stuck, defensive, paranoid, apathetic, tired, and even sick.

And as a result, low-trust teams, relationships, and organizations pay what Francis Fukuyama calls unnecessary taxes.[5] He argues that low-trust societies pay an unnecessary tax that high-trust societies don't have to pay.

High-threat cultures are low-trust, high-tax cultures. The unnecessary taxes they pay are often in increased drama, unresolved conflict, a lack of meaningful dialogue, higher turn-over, lower engagement, and a toxic environment of blaming, finger-pointing, criticizing, condemning, complaining, dissen-sion, and sabotage. Professionally or personally, we all have witnessed the unnecessary negative consequences of low trust. Low trust is like second-hand smoke. It's poisonous, and it impacts everyone.

High-challenge cultures don't pay the taxes that high-threat cultures pay. Relationships are healthier, and results come more easily. People show up to work as their best selves, exchanges assume good intent, feedback flows, conflict is resolved quickly, and the tough conversations become meaningful conversations.

Trust is earned and extended in both high and low-trust cul-tures with one significant difference. In high-trust cultures, the mindset is that *I* am responsible for extending trust and actively earning *your* trust. In low-trust cultures, the mindset is that *you* are responsible for extending trust and actively earning *my* trust.

Threat kills, steals, and destroys. High-threat cultures pay taxes.

Trust yields life, speed, and quality. High-challenge cultures enjoy dividends. Leaders in these environments, though human, are dependable, predictable, and consistent. Their team mem-bers, clients, and peers can rely on them to be transparent; they openly admit mistakes and are willing to correct and redirect based on what's best for the team rather than what's best for their ego.

- On a scale of 1 to 10 (1 being low to 10 being high), how would you rate trust in your team and/or organization?

- What would a 10 look like? What would it take to get it to a 10?

- What is one action you can take to start building trust? (Hint: start with trusting yourself.)

## NAVIGATE TO RESOURCE

25 Simple Trust-Building Actions: PDF

## Threat #1: Social rejection

All pain is pain to the brain.

The number one threat in the workplace is social rejection, not feeling a sense of belonging.

In 2011, a study from the University of Michigan discovered the similarities between physical pain and the pain of social rejection using fMRI (functional magnetic resonance imaging scans). Participants who had experienced an unwanted romantic breakup within the last six months viewed a photo of their ex-partner and thought about their feelings. Participants had a thermal stimulation device attached to their forearms to identify the pain regions. The device either gave a painful but tolerable or a non-painful warm stimulation.

This study and other similar studies discovered that the brain regions activated by physical pain were also activated in the emotional pain of a breakup. So, while the brain doesn't differentiate among types of threat, it appears it doesn't differentiate among types of pain. Both physical pain and the pain of social rejection "hurt" in very similar ways.[6]

Human beings have a deep need for social connection, bonding, and cohesion. Spanning more than 30 years, Gallup interviewed millions of people across cultures to determine what drives employee engagement and satisfaction. What they discovered was a set of twelve questions. Employees' responses to these twelve questions on a 1-5 scale (1—strongly disagree to 5—strongly agree) can predict a number of outcomes, including productivity, profitability, customer satisfaction, quality of work, and employee satisfaction.

All twelve questions have a common denominator of feeling respected, cared for, heard, and valued.

**THE GALLUP Q12**

- I know what is expected of me at work.
- I have the materials and equipment I need to do my work right.
- At work, I have the opportunity to do what I do best every day.
- In the last seven days, I have received recognition or praise for doing good work.
- My supervisor, or someone at work, seems to care about me as a person.
- There is someone at work who encourages my development.
- At work, my opinions seem to count.

- The mission or purpose of my company makes me feel my job is important.
- My associates or fellow employees are committed to doing quality work.
- I have a best friend at work.
- Someone at work has talked to me in the last six months about my progress.
- This last year, I have had opportunities at work to learn and grow.[7]

Since the Gallup Q12 was first published in *First, Break All the Rules*, over 35 million employees across 160 cultures have answered those twelve questions.[8] The questions with the lower percentage of agreement involve recognition, development, feeling their opinion counts, and social connection.

Gallup's work highlights why fostering genuine relationships at work and creating a sense of belonging are so meaningful to the brain. COVID-19 presented a unique challenge that further impacted authentic interactions and connections. According to the Centers for Disease Control and Prevention[9] and the World Health Organization,[10] anxiety and depression spiked as much as 25% from 2019 to 2021.

While many people have returned to the office, many continue to work remotely permanently. Remote work has advantages, but leaders of remote teams must be even more mindful to create a sense of belonging.

High-threat cultures exclude. High-challenge cultures include.

Leaders who want to decrease threat by creating a greater sense of belonging can leverage formal programs like precepting and mentoring, and informal moments such as teambuilding activities, professional and personal development, one-on-one meaningful conversations, cross-functional teams, collaboration, involving people in decisions that affect them, and having fun.

---

### NAVIGATE TO RESOURCE

Hill & Wilkinson's Fun Committee: Video

---

Challenge cultures actively promote acceptance and inclusion rather than social rejection and exclusivity. People have a voice and feel valued and appreciated. All are welcome to bring their whole selves, including their differences, to every situation. You'll find more on the power of belonging in the Mosaic Strategy chapter.

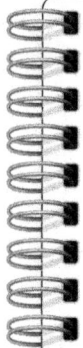

- Answer the Gallup Q12. What trends in your responses do you notice?

- How do you create a sense of belonging with those you work with?

- What small action could you start to foster a greater sense of belonging?

## ACTIONS

- Greet everyone before a meeting begins.
- Review the Gallup 12 questions individually and as a team.
- Assign new hires a mentor or buddy.
- Meet with new hires at 30, 60, and 90 days.

- Say hello to others when you walk down the hallway.
- Ask others about their lives, and genuinely listen to the responses.
- Send a text or email each morning to thank someone or share a word of encouragement.

# FINAL THOUGHTS ON THE CHALLENGE STRATEGY

Before we wrap this chapter, I want to emphasize two crucial points about threat. The greatest thing leaders can do to bring out the best in themselves and those around them is to recognize and minimize threats. We must always keep in mind that threat is all about perception. What may present threat to one brain may not to another, and not all threats are bad.

## Your threat may not be my threat.

Let's return to my experience with the hotel fire alarm in Boston. In that situation, my brain perceived the alarm as a threat, and I simply reacted out of fear and ran into the cold.

But let's explore a different response. Imagine a seasoned business traveler in the room next to mine. He may have laid out his coat, shoes, hat, and gloves before going to bed—just in case of an emergency. He may have studied the emergency exit map on the back of the hotel door. He may have been awake at 3 a.m., finishing the best novel he had ever read. He may have been waiting his whole life to be present for a hotel fire, preparing to rescue frightened people. When the alarm sounded and the light flashed, he may have recognized the situation not as a threat but as an opportunity.

Instead of scurrying thoughtlessly around, he may have gotten out of bed with an enthusiastic energy, calmly dressed, and walked out of the building looking for people to help along the way.

The exact circumstances can present themselves differently to different people. What is a threat to one brain may not be to another. In Boston, as it turns out, there never was a threat in the first place; the smoke detector in one room had simply malfunctioned.

## The brain reacts whether the threat is real or perceived.

Just because something "feels" real doesn't necessarily make it so. We must question the meaning we give the event. I had two clients apply for the same promotion but neither got it. One interpreted the event as an insult and left the company. The other interpreted the event as a challenge. She finished her degree and received the next promotion.

In most circumstances, we can choose to frame a threat however we want. By doing so, we build resilience and strengthen our ability to manage threat.

Negative threat increases problems and decreases results.

A friend of mine is an executive at a concrete company where physical safety is paramount. A sign at the entrance of the building reads, "Number of days without accident." When they reach a certain number of accident-free days, they celebrate. Clearly, we want physically safe workplaces.

But what about emotionally and psychologically safe workplaces? Are those days tracked as well? After all, a threat to the brain is a threat to the brain, regardless of if the threat is physical or psychological, real or perceived.

High-threat cultures are toxic. They carry costs. They cause damage, sometimes irreparable, damage.

The Challenge Strategy, where threat is decreased and trust is increased, is foundational to achieving what matters in a meaningful way. Reducing negative threat is essential for high-performance leadership and for becoming a leader worth following.

# WHAT MAKES A LEADER WORTH FOLLOWING?

*We asked real people. We got real responses.*

Here are just a few. Would anyone say the same about you?

- ✔ *A leader inspires their team to excel and grow by trusting them and acknowledging their effort can achieve more than anyone thought possible.*

- ✔ *A leader worth following embodies humility and authenticity. These two qualities create an environment where people feel valued, heard, and inspired to do their best work.*

- ✔ *A leader who leads by example, creates a safe and open environment, and one with effective communication.*

- ✔ *A good leader worth following inspires trust, shows competence, and genuinely cares about the people they lead.*

- ✔ *Someone who is trustworthy and empathic. They strive to make the entire team better, not just themselves.*

# THINK. DISCUSS. APPLY.

*Make it matter*

1.  Think of a season in your life when you felt overwhelmed or stressed. This may have been marked by anxiety, stress, dread, or frustration.

    Consider:
    - What were the conditions that characterized this season?
    - What was the professional impact?
    - What was the personal impact?
    - What was sacrificed because of being overwhelmed or stressed?
    - What changed for you when the overwhelm or stress was no longer present?
    - What did you learn from enduring this season?

2.  Describe a time when you responded to a challenge differently than others around you. Others perceived the circumstances as a "threat" and wanted to give up or walk away. But you perceived the exact circumstances as a "challenge" and felt energized and motivated to succeed.

    Ask:
    - What caused you to frame the circumstances differently from others?
    - How did your results compare to those of others who perceived the circumstances as a threat?

3.  What conditions lead you to see situations as threat, stress, or overwhelm? Reflect on past experiences that produced that feeling and identify what they all had in common.

4.  What conditions lead you to see situations as challenge, boosting your curiosity, enthusiasm, and attitude? Reflect on past experiences that produced that feeling and identify what they all had in common.
5.  Think about leaders in your personal experience. What role did they play in whether you perceived a set of circumstances as a threat or a challenge?

    -   Have you ever left a job because of a leader? What were the circumstances that led to that decision?
    -   Have you ever stayed at a job because of a leader? What were the circumstances that led to that decision?

6.  Review the top 10 threats. Which show up in your workplace? What are the costs? What strategies can you implement to minimize the threats?
7.  Which of the threats impact your team? What are the costs? What strategies can the team implement to minimize the threat?
8.  How can you more actively replace threat with challenge for you and your team?

## Decrease threat.
### Increase trust.

# Your Brain on Threat

1. Hijacks the Prefrontal Cortex (PFC
2. Triggers a Cortisol Stress Surge
3. Diminishes Creativity and Innovation
4. Distorts Perspective
5. Impairs Emotional Regulation
6. Reduces Learning and Memory Capacity
7. Elevates Risk of Physical and Mental Illness
8. Destroys Trust
9. Triggers flocking
10. Increases Resistance to Change

*Your current rules are creating your current results*

*You can be right or you can be rich.*

# 3 Big Deals:

1. The PFC is priceless.
2. Threat to the brain is threat to the brain.
3. Emotions run the show.

# Top 10 Threats:

1. Social rejection
2. Lack of honesty or trust
3. Change
4. Unrealistic expectations
5. Lack of resources
6. Risk of loss
7. Humiliation
8. Micromanagement
9. Perceived favoritism
10. Lack of meaningful work

**PFC** = Self-Control - motor, financial, emotional, cognitive, perspective

# 3C's of Negative Threat:

- Confusion: We have more confusion than clarity.
- Control: We feel we have little control over or say in the situation.
- Consequences: We anticipate a negative consequence.

# CHAPTER 2

# The Relevance Strategy

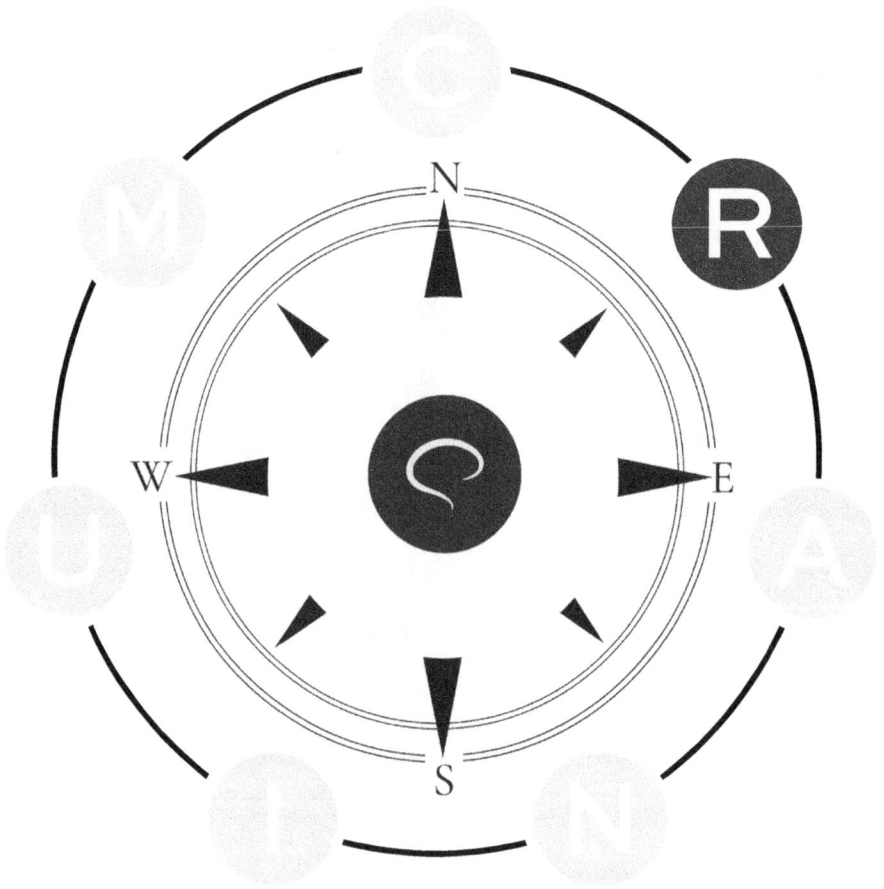

**LEAD WITH VISION.
BUILD ON STRENGTHS.**

**BIG IDEA**

Imagine a culture defined by clarity and alignment, with all team members using their individual strengths to drive a united purpose.

## BREAKTHROUGH BELIEFS

Every brain is tuned into the station WII-FM.

The brain doesn't resist change. It resists confusion.

Clarity lives on the other side of the phrase "and here's why."

# REAL LEADERS. REAL LIFE.

*Missed opportunities.*

It's a cold Wednesday morning, and daylight is just beginning to appear as Greg drives through the gates and to the front section of the parking lot. He finishes the last drops of his coffee, grabs his lunch, locks the door, and reaches for his badge. This is a familiar routine; one he has performed for nearly 26 years at a defense manufacturing facility. He says, "Hello," to the guard at the gate and briefly jokes about the game last night, flashes his badge, and walks through the turnstile. Employees are slowly filtering into the building, much like zombies, not quite awake during these early-morning hours. Greg passes through the break room for a second cup of coffee to jump-start his day and exchanges casual "Good mornings" with a few co-workers he's known for years.

His boss passes by, stops, and sticks his head into the break room. "Hey Greg, remember the training team is planning on doing some observations this morning. Are you OK with answering some of their questions and showing them around?"

"No problem," Greg replies. After all, he has the longest tenure in the quality department and looks forward to a break in the dull routine of the day.

He heads toward his workstation, where he glances at the pictures of his family. They are his pride and joy, his reason for getting up so early every morning and going to a job that is, on most days, unfulfilling. The pictures are secured by a magnet on a small whiteboard, including a daily countdown. Greg plans to work 1,195 more days before retiring. For motivation, he started this countdown, which he edits every morning. He checks his personal email quickly before the tasks on the assembly line begin.

Greg has been learning after-hours to create websites for a few small companies in his community. In the last year, he has discovered a real talent for creating impactful websites and loves that he gets lost and fully engaged when creating them. When he retires, he plans on doing web design full-time.

Later in the morning, Greg is working as the last stop for quality inspection when the training team shows up. I am a part of that team. We are there to learn from experts like Greg so we can create training modules for new hires.

We ask Greg about the part he inspects, specifically its final destination.

Greg thinks for a minute, points to the next station, and says, "It goes to packing."

My heart sinks. Greg is the last person to inspect a part critical to the Javelin missile system, a weapon with enormous military significance.

Greg doesn't know the potentially life-changing impact of his role or the value he brings to the world each day.

# YOU'RE WIRED FOR RELEVANCE

*Why your brain thrives on the Relevance Strategy*

Like the Challenge Strategy, the Relevance Strategy honors the 3 Big Deals—the three facts everyone on the planet should know about how the brain works.

Let's quickly revisit the 3 Big Deals introduced in the last chapter.

## Big Deal #1: Your Prefrontal Cortex is Priceless

The prefrontal cortex (PFC) is the seat of our being our best selves, making optimal decisions, having innovative ideas, thinking ahead, collaborating with others, and being open to new and better ways. It is the control center for all those priceless functions we want leaders and teams to effortlessly produce every day.

The secret to producing these PFC results is paying attention to the other 2 Big Deals.

## Big Deal #2: Threat to the Brain is Threat to the Brain

Threat hijacks the prefrontal cortex. Creating and perceiving negative threat is the fastest way to turn off the best version of ourselves. Negative threat occurs when we feel we have little say or control, confusion outweighs clarity, and we anticipate a negative outcome. Think COVID-19. Threat can deactivate the PFC, whether the threat is real, perceived, past, present, future, psychological, emotional, or physical.

## Big Deal #3: Emotions Run the Show

We aren't thinking individuals who happen to have emotions. We are emotional individuals who happen to think. Every action we take and decision we make involves emotion because that is how the brain processes events. Emotion is involved in everything we do. Emotion can fuel the prefrontal cortex, and we experience the best version of ourselves and others. Or, emotion can fuel negative threat, and we experience the worst version of ourselves and others.

**NAVIGATE TO RESOURCE**
3 Big Deals: Video and PDF

The goal is to meaningfully engage emotion with the prefrontal cortex (PFC) rather than escalate negative threat and shut down the prefrontal cortex.

Relevance supports this goal because it aligns with key brain facts.

## Fact #1: The brain learns best whole-to-parts.

The Relevance Strategy is about showing the bigger picture. Forest first and then the trees. Why? Because on average, the brain learns best using a whole-to-parts approach.

Consider this: I invite you to my house for puzzle night. You walk in and sit at the kitchen table. I dump onto the table a 5,000-piece puzzle.

What might your first question be?

My guess is, "Where's the box?"

How frustrating would it be to be tasked with assembling a puzzle without seeing the finished project?

Ironically, whole-to-parts is rarely how we teach and seldom how leaders lead.

In most of our educational experiences, we were handed puzzle pieces. In writing classes, the puzzle pieces were punctuation rules. In math, the pieces were formulas and function rules. We trusted that one day, these puzzle pieces would come together in time and form a picture that made sense. We learned the parts before we learned the whole, which likely meant years of confusion and meaningless effort.

I see leaders lead this way every day. A puzzle piece here, a few puzzle pieces there. Few team members, if any, know how all the pieces fit together or why their given pieces matter. Motivation turns to cynicism when team members feel they are just moving puzzle pieces in a random, meaningless way. There is no reward. People become disgruntled and inefficient as threat grows, and creativity and innovation fade. Talent leaves.

The picture on the puzzle box immediately tells you what "winning" and "done" look like. It also likely informs the process of assembling the puzzle.

The Relevance Strategy involves showing the big picture and then the details. This approach reduces confusion by providing clarity and a larger context and meaning. By reducing confusion and resistance, we activate positive emotion and the prefrontal cortex.

When we think "whole-to-parts," we start with the "big picture" or "end in mind." This approach makes it easier for the brain to see how everything fits together and why it matters. It also reduces the energy burn of anxiety and defensiveness and leads to greater efficiency and productivity.

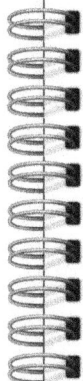

- What is a change you are asking others to make?
- What is an initiative that you are leading?
- What does "done" or "winning" look like?
- Why does the change or initiative matter?
- How can you leverage the whole-to-parts approach to communicate more clearly, lower resistance, and gain buy-in?

## Fact #2: The brain learns by building neural networks.

Neurons that fire together, wire together.

The Relevance Strategy is about building on familiar, existing neural networks by leveraging strengths and interests. This approach maximizes the brain's efficiency.

Let's compare neural networks to social networks. A vast social network is critical to growing our careers and our businesses. Getting referrals and support through one's existing social network is faster and more efficient than creating a new one because there is a well-established history. We love referrals! When we leverage referrals from our social community, the sales cycle is drastically faster.

This same concept applies to your brain. Your brain has well-established neural networks, and we learn more efficiently when we leverage these existing networks. We can activate this neural network advantage by building on what is familiar, as well as individual strengths and interests.

Neural networks are worthy of awe and a bit more explanation. Warning: This may get a bit geeky, but leaders need to know the basics of how the brain actually learns.

If you are capable of higher cognitive thought, thank your neural networks. Your brain has two kinds of cells: glial cells and neurons. Glial cells comprise about 90% of the cells, which support, protect, and nourish neurons. Neurons exchange signals with each other to form highly complex neural networks. This is the foundation of learning.

No one knows exactly how many neurons the typical brain has; estimates range from 50 billion to 100 billion. Let's just say the typical brain has an abundance of neurons.

Some scientists believe it isn't necessarily the number of brain cells you have (which is excellent news for some of us who may not have always made the most intelligent decisions earlier in life, especially during college days); what counts is the number of connections you have. I once heard one scientist predict that the number of possible connections equals the number of leaves on every tree in every forest in the world. Mind blowing.

Neurons are made up of cell bodies, dendrites, and axons. The cell body is the central mass. Dendrites receive information and carry it to the cell body. Axons transmit information and carry it away from the cell body.

Terminal buttons are like little parking spaces or key holes located at the end of each axon. They release neurotransmitters, chemicals that activate neighboring neurons. The junction or gap between one neuron's axons and a neighboring neuron's dendrites is called the synapse or synaptic cleft. The presynaptic neuron is the signal-sending cell, and the postsynaptic neuron is the signal-receiving cell.

When the cell body is triggered by an action potential (a change in the electrical potential on the cell's surface), neurotransmitter molecules pour into the synaptic cleft. When the molecules reach the postsynaptic cell, they attach to matching receptor sites. This forms a connection or network with other neurons.

One widely accepted theory about neural networks is the Hebbian theory, named after renowned neuroscientist Donald Hebb.[1] He proposed that the connection strength among synaptic cells increases as cells are simultaneously activated. Thus, the common saying "cells that fire together, wire together."

This is the science behind the power of repetition and building on strengths, interests, and the familiar. Imagine a seasoned employee who has been doing the same thing for years. Those neural networks are wired together really, really well. If you've ever thought, "I could do this in my sleep," you, too, have solid neural networks relative to that activity.

Think of neural networks like an information transportation system in the brain. There are farm-to-market roads, highways, and interstates.

When a new concept or task is introduced, our brains begin to build a neural network. At this point, that network is similar to a farm-to-market road, the winding, rocky, narrow roads far from the interstate we usually find when we are completely lost, usually at night, when it's foggy or raining.

Can you imagine traveling from California to New York on farm-to-market roads? It would be a long, arduous, and frustrating journey; you might even give up. This may be how seasoned employees initially feel when asked to do something different.

The building of neural networks is fascinating. For example, I play piano. Today, reading music and matching the right notes comes easily. But this was not always the case; just ask my poor parents. At first, my feet didn't touch the floor, my fingers were too small to reach an entire octave, and my brain struggled to read the notes and tell my fingers where to go. I was the child my parents begged to stop practicing. I had a farm-to-market neural network for piano.

Once a neural network strengthens, we are more efficient, and the task becomes easier. A more well-formed neural network is like moving from a farm-to-market road to a highway. Though we can go faster, and the trip is less frustrating, we still do not hit top speed and full efficiency. We may have two lanes on the highway, but we all know about construction backups, traffic accidents, and red lights. Those kinds of distractions, interruptions, and setbacks can cause delay.

It's similar in the brain. With practice on the piano, I could match my fingers to the correct notes with relative ease if the music was simple and had lots of repetition. My confidence and ability grew. I no longer had to pause as long when a note was a sharp or a flat, and my fingers flowed much more smoothly on the keys. The notes began to sound like music, and my parents complained less. My neural network was getting stronger.

This same process applies to us and our teams when we learn a new skill or way of doing our work.

Once a skill or subject area is mastered, our neural network becomes a superhighway. The interstate is firmly established, clear of obstacles, and has multiple lanes of traffic, which allows for higher speeds and fewer accidents. We may even hit cruise control from time to time. Such is the case when I play the piano today; I no longer give conscious thought to mechanics. I am free to "get lost" in the music.

The Relevance Strategy honors the efficiency of neural networks by leading whole-to-parts, showing the map, and building on strengths, interests, and familiarity.

## A word of warning about learning and time.

Mentally moving from a farm-to-market road to a superhighway or interstate doesn't happen overnight. Building a strong neural network can be highly time-consuming and vary from individual to individual, depending on aptitude and desire.

The brain takes much longer to master something new than most think. And, studies show that subject-matter experts are the worst predictors of how long it takes for someone to learn a new skill. We severely underestimate how long it will take for a novice to become an expert.

Sian Beilock discusses one such study in her book *Choke: What the Secrets of the Brain Reveal About Getting It Right When You Have To.*[2] She shares how a mobile phone company attempted to determine how long it would take consumers to master the new technology. The tech-savvy subject-matter experts estimated it would take the novice 13 minutes to master the phone skills. In reality, it took around 30 minutes.

Some studies indicate the brain can require as much as 10,000 hours of intentional practice to master a skill. Of course, that depends on various variables, including a person's natural aptitude. For example, I'm not sure 10,000 hours of intentional practice would enable me to master my golf game. Professional sports teams will spend 5-10 times more time in practice than they do playing in games.

The point is that mastering a new skill or adopting a new way of thinking takes time and differs from person to person.

Eric Jensen cautions that the brain requires much more processing time depending on the type of learning. He distinguishes between simple learning and complex learning.[3] "Simple learning" may be instant. For example, if I put my hand on a hot stove, I learn quickly not to do that again.

However, "complex learning," such as learning a new process or technology, may require an extraordinary amount of time. The learning time is influenced by one's natural abilities, interests, capacity, engagement, and so forth.

The critical takeaway is that the brain takes time to build a strong neural network. There is no replacement for time.

The Relevance Strategy aims to accelerate the building of neural networks. By starting with the whole and building on strengths and interests, learning is faster, more meaningful, and fun.

The best news for all of us, especially leaders, is that the brain can grow new neurons and make new connections. This is called neuroplasticity and is likely the most significant discovery ever made in neuroscience.

The hard news for all of us, especially leaders, is that making these connections takes longer than we ever thought. Leaders who move very quickly may need to slow down and grow their own neural networks of patience.

Additionally, growing new networks requires new experiences, and the brain tends to resist new experiences because they involve uncertainty. So, leaders need to anticipate resistance when people are asked to engage in the negative threat of unfamiliar, new experiences.

- What change do you need to make or are asking others to make?

- How can you build on existing neural networks by connecting the new way to the familiar and individual strengths and interests?

- What adjustments must you make to allow for more patience and time?

- How can you celebrate small milestones to encourage your team as they build new neural networks?

- As late as the 1970's, scientists believed that the brain was born with all of the neurons that a person would ever have.
- Scientists also believed that neural networks were only formed in childhood.
- By the 1980's, Michael Merzenich, the father of neuro-plasticity, along with others, proved this belief wrong.
- The brain peaks somewhere around our 30s.
- We can grow new neurons and new neural networks throughout our entire lives.
- As we age, we need to be even more intentional by learning new things and having new experiences.
- Want to learn more? Read Michael Merzenich's book *Soft-Wired: How the New Science of Brain Plasticity Can Change Your Life.*[4]

## Fact #3: The brain learns best when negative threat is low.

Clarity calms confusion.

Negative threat occurs when we feel more confusion than clarity, anticipate a negative outcome, and feel like we have little agency, choice, or control. Under negative threat, our brain doesn't pause and react differently based on physical or emotional threat. The brain doesn't even care if the threat is perceived or real, past, present, or future. Universally, negative threat lowers performance.

The Relevance Strategy minimizes negative threat and helps the brain learn and change faster by providing the big picture, which reduces confusion. It also builds on the familiar, utilizes existing neural networks, and leverages individual strengths and interests, which triggers confidence to create a positive outcome.

I remember years ago teaching an introductory class on Microsoft Word. How introductory, you ask? Let's just say we started by practicing the "double click." The class was offered to savvy administrative assistants who were experts in their jobs; however, they had never used Microsoft Word or similar software.

I knew I had to reduce threat and resistance to set this effort up for success. I wanted to quickly build their confidence and fear by proving this tool was not as foreign as they thought.

I used the Relevance Strategy. Though the assistants had never stored files electronically, they had organized files in a designated file cabinet, a drawer, and a folder with a specific name. Though they had never created an electronic document, they had drafted documents on a typewriter for years and knew the steps for formatting and making corrections. Though they had never saved a document electronically, they all knew the importance of saving a document. You get the idea.

The Relevance Strategy doesn't focus on the unfamiliar; it focuses on the familiar. This shift in focus results in less resistance and greater confidence and ownership.

The Relevance Strategy also lowers threat through purpose. By leading with a clear, compelling vision that matters and building on strengths and interests, everyone knows how what they do makes a meaningful impact. They are more likely to buy in because they see how the new puzzle pieces contribute to the picture on the box.

By incorporating relevance, learning is faster. Change is easier. Life is more fun.

We achieve more with less effort.

- What change do you need to make or lead others to make?

- How will this change help your team? How will it alleviate pain? How will it help them hit their goals faster?

- How can you introduce the change by building on what they already know and care about?

- How can you celebrate small milestones to encourage your team as they build new neural networks?

## Fact #4: The brain learns best by engaging emotion.

Emotions run the show.

The Relevance Strategy involves two leadership choices: to lead with vision and clarity and to build on strengths and interests. Both are essential if we want to truly leverage the power of the emotional brain. After all, we are emotional individuals who happen to think.

Think of emotion as fuel—premium fuel!

Emotion can fuel threat, and we become the worst version of ourselves. We get stuck, overly committed to being right, defensive, and narrow-minded. We seek out an enemy to blame, criticize, condemn, and sometimes even hate. But when emotion fuels the prefrontal cortex, we become the best version of ourselves. We are adaptable, collaborative, innovative, and more positive. We have greater willpower and are open to new perspectives and new ways of doing things.

We can use that premium emotional fuel to get results quicker and more easily by establishing a clear, compelling "why" and then building on strengths and interests to accomplish the why.

Jane's approach to a high-profile initiative is a textbook example. She and her team were tasked with planning the largest fund-raising gala the nonprofit had ever hosted. The team defaulted into confusion and overwhelm. Instead of staying there, she used the power of the Relevance Strategy.

She provided a clear and inspiring why. She assembled her team and explicitly connected the gala to their vision and values. She and the team discussed the impact this event would have on the community members they served.

Then, she showed the familiar visual of their planning process. She led the team in discovering that their proven process, which ensured success in smaller events, would also ensure success in a larger event.

From there, she delegated specific next steps based on team members' interests and strengths. By the end of the meeting, everyone knew what winning looked like. They were confident their process would get them the win, and they were empowered to use their strengths to execute.

- What is an initiative you have been asked to lead?

- How does this initiative support the vision and values?

- How does this initiative support what each team member values?

- What is a simple (ideally familiar) roadmap for getting there?

- How can you celebrate small milestones to encourage your team as they build new neural networks?

## Fact #5: The brain learns best when it is rewarded.

*Reward* is your brain's favorite drug.

Emotion is the fuel. Reward is the spark. Dopamine is the match.

Let's look at the brain's reward system as it is key to motivating ourselves, our teams, and our organizations.

The brain's reward system is a group of structures that respond to stimuli the brain finds rewarding, reinforcing, or pleasurable. Like other systems, it is highly complex. But, for our purposes, let's think about it as a stage. The leading actor on the brain stage is the neurotransmitter dopamine. Other supporting actors in the mesolimbic dopamine pathway include the ventral tegmental area (VTA), the nucleus accumbens, and the frontal lobes.

Dopamine is the secret to motivation and action. It is a neurotransmitter often referred to as the "reward chemical" or the "motivation molecule." It plays a central role in motivation, goal-directed behavior, reward, pleasure, focus, attention, movement, and learning.

When the brain's reward system is activated, the VTA releases dopamine, and the mesolimbic dopamine pathway transports it to the nucleus accumbens and the frontal lobes. When dopamine is delivered to the nucleus accumbens, we get more dopamine and are motivated to move from desire to action. When dopamine is delivered to the frontal lobes, we have a greater capacity to focus and regulate impulsivity.

I can't imagine any leader turning that down.

Think about the last time you were engaged in doing something you love, like a hobby. I'll wager you were intensely focused; you lost track of time because you were highly engaged; and you had energy to keep doing that activity. The magic of that moment was brought to you by elevated dopamine.

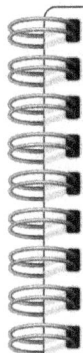

- What is a current or future project requiring a motivated team?

- What threats or resistance will you need to plan for?

- How can you activate the reward system?

# THE RELEVANCE STRATEGY IN PRACTICE

*What a Relevance culture looks like*

The Relevance Strategy involves leaders making intentional choices: to establish the *why* with a clearly defined vision, to establish the *how* by defining values, and to capitalize on strengths to accomplish the why and the how.

Leaders committed to creating a relevance-rich culture communicate and live out the vision and values so everyone in the organization owns and believes in them. They also focus on strengths rather than gaps. They leverage individual strengths to ensure the right people are in the right position, allowing them to have multiple opportunities to do what they love and what comes naturally.

In cultures where leaders embrace the Relevance Strategy, a few observable signs are:

- The organization has clearly defined an inspiring vision and values so that all have clarity on what they do as an organization and how they are expected to do it.
- Team members understand how their daily actions impact those around them and contribute to whole.
- The team grasps the "why" behind the "how" and the "what."
- The mission, vision, and values are more than posters on the wall. They serve as guidelines for making daily decisions, solving problems, and interacting with both internal and external customers.
- The values are non-negotiable, and people are held accountable to them, even when it is inconvenient.

- Leaders regularly discuss with team members their strengths, talents, and goals, and assist in creating career growth plans that align with what is important and fulfilling to the team member.
- Leaders delegate mindfully to develop the strengths of their team members.
- Leaders make strategic hiring decisions to bring the right strengths to the table.
- Team members find meaning and purpose in their daily work.

Cultures that embrace the Relevance Strategy collaborate rather than compete. The organization is aligned; individuals and teams do not operate in silos with differing visions, values, and goals. Individual strengths are recognized, valued, and leveraged to achieve the mission.

In cultures where leaders ignore the Relevance Strategy, a few observable signs are:

- The organization lacks a compelling vision or purpose.
- Individuals operate with differing views of what excellence and acceptable behavior look like.
- Teams work in silos and lack understanding of how their work impacts other teams or the overall bottom line.
- Employees feel disconnected from a sense of meaning or purpose in their roles.
- Values and standards are not clearly defined to guide decision-making, problem-solving, or interactions with internal and external customers.
- The workforce is not informed about the broader strategic direction.

- Attention is placed on gaps and deficiencies rather than gains and strengths.
- Motivation, engagement, and loyalty are low.

Relevance-deficit cultures lack the clarity, consistency, loyalty, and unity that we find in relevance-rich cultures. And the results prove it. Behavior tolerated in one department is not tolerated in another. The processes followed on one side of the house may not be on the other. It's like an orchestra with the conductor and each musician playing different songs in different keys.

This disconnect is often revealed in employee reviews on sites such as Glassdoor, where one employee leaves a stellar review while another leaves a scathing review. The misalignment certainly impacts business results.

| WITHOUT THE RELEVANCE STRATEGY | WITH THE RELEVANCE STRATEGY |
|---|---|
| • No vision or values | • Clearly defined vision and values |
| • Lack of purpose and meaning | • Collaboration |
| • Competition | • Clear purpose and meaning |
| • No standard for decision-making | • Guidelines for making decisions |
| • Inefficiency | • Efficiency |
| • No "why" or "how" guiding the "what" | • Clear "why," and "how" guiding the "what" |
| • No development conversations | • Ongoing development conversations |
| • Leaders overload self and others | • Leaders delegate to build strengths |
| • Low morale | • High morale |
| • Disconnected team members and processes | • United and aligned team members and processes |

# BE A LEADER
# WORTH FOLLOWING

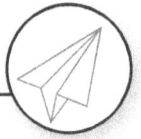

*How to live out the Relevance Strategy*

The word *relevance* comes from the Latin word *relevare*, meaning to "lift up" or "highlight" what is important.

Relevance-rich environments are those that "lift up" and "highlight" the big picture and greater purpose, a clear image of what winning looks like, and individual and collective strengths.

Leading with the Relevance Strategy begins with a clear and inspiring vision. The "why" is always guiding the "hows" and the "what." The vision is consistently communicated and kept front and center, particularly during times of uncertainty and change. Everyone can articulate how they align with and contribute to the vision.

Work is rewarding and engaging because each team member is aligned and working collaboratively to achieve a greater purpose. With a clear vision, the organization is adaptable. It can strategically determine what is no longer effective, what needs to continue, and where to make improvements.

Individual and collective strengths are leveraged to fulfill the vision. Hires are purposeful. Tasks, projects, roles, and responsibilities are a "fit" with strengths and interests. While gaps and weaknesses aren't ignored, all have multiple opportunities to do what they excel at and enjoy.

As a result, there are fewer miscommunications and competing agendas and greater efficiency. Above all, no one is hanging around until they can find their next move or waiting to retire to do something fulfilling.

Leaders who are vision-focused and strengths-centered are key to living out the Relevance Strategy.

## Vision-Focused Leaders

Vision-focused leaders follow the whole-to-parts approach. They "show the box" at the organizational and project level. Team members know where their puzzle pieces go, why they matter, and how they connect with the other pieces. This streamlines efforts, inspires, unites, and motivates.

The entire organization is in big-picture alignment. Every member is clear on what "winning" looks like, how daily work contributes to the wins, and when to adjust if the wins are not happening.

### ACTIONS

- Have a single visual stating a clearly defined mission, vision, and values.
- Regularly discuss how each effort contributes to the mission, vision, and values.

Mission, vision, and values are more than words on a page or poster on a wall. It is the puzzle box that facilitates clarity, purpose, and collaboration.

Use the mission, vision, and values:

- As a focal point in meetings and shared spaces (e.g., virtual backgrounds, break areas, entryways).
- To open every meeting.
- To guide and lead change.
- In all internal and external communications.

- To recognize and reward desired behaviors.
- To motivate individuals during challenging times.
- To distinguish between "good" and "great" decisions.
- To uphold accountability.
- To frame and focus difficult conversations as acts of service to the organization's purpose.

## Seeing the box—the end result and the big picture—matters now more than ever.

When asked why people choose a selected career path or stay loyal to a job, they frequently say it's because they want to contribute to a meaningful purpose. A common reason for remaining in a career or with an organization is that people feel they are making a difference. They desire to be a part of something greater than themselves.

Flashback to 2016. Gallup released a study explaining how millennials want to work and live.[5] One of the key findings was that millennials are among the least engaged generation in the workforce. The study revealed that only 29% of millennials were actively engaged at work, while 16% were actively disengaged. So, over half were simply showing up. One reason for this disengagement, lack of loyalty, and constant job-hopping is that they sought a job with meaning and impact. The study indicated that millennials seek more than a paycheck; they seek a purpose.

Post-COVID, the stakes are even higher. Gen Z (the generation following the millennials) reports an even greater disengagement, often called the "Great Detachment".[6] According to one study, the financial implications are estimated to be nearly $9 trillion annually in productivity.[7] The personal implications are equally alarming, as this generation reports growing mental health concerns, feeling a lack of purpose or meaning not only in their work but also in their personal lives.

The Relevance Strategy promotes purpose. One of our previous healthcare clients excels in this, and their outcomes prove it. They have a clearly defined vision to be the most trusted place in giving and receiving safe, quality, compassionate healthcare. They actively hire people whose personal values align with the hospital's values and onboard them carefully to ensure a fit. They employ their vision and values to guide day-to-day oper-ations and decision-making. The picture on their puzzle box is compelling; each sees where their pieces fit, and it unites the entire organization.

Remember, we are emotional individuals who happen to think. Therefore, having a compelling purpose is not "touchy-feely." It's how the brain works best

When we work with leaders and organizations, one of the first questions we ask is, "What is your vision?" The response often includes a list of accomplishments the leader or organization wants to *have* and *do*. But we must go deeper for sustainable growth and change. The easy work is writing down financial goals, growth plans, new market expansion, etc. The hard work, and the real game-changing work, happens by deciding who you will need to BE to accomplish these goals.

> A vision is more than what you want to *have* and *do*. It's about who you want to *be*.

Goal and vision-setting sessions can be time-consuming prac-tices with little return if we only focus on the doing and having. They can be powerful, transformational experiences when we focus on the way of being that will fuel what we want to do and have. The way of being becomes the non-negotiables, the beliefs, actions, and behaviors we will and will not tolerate.

**NAVIGATE TO RESOURCE**

Vision-Setting Session Best Practices: Video and PDF

These define your culture. And your business results will never rise above the standards of your culture.

Every brain is tuned into the station *WII-FM*. What's In It For Me?

The brain's "so what" system activates the brain's reward system. When we lead whole parts, we want each person to see a connection between the bigger vision and what is important to them.

Successful marketing and advertising companies do this brilliantly. Their campaigns either directly or indirectly answer the burning questions, "So what?" and "What's In It For Me?

Consider how powerful this approach is in getting us to change and buy. We purchase stuff to look prettier, younger, sexier, skinnier, stronger, darker, lighter, smarter, taller, and shorter. We want stuff that makes life faster, slower, exciting, predictable, less stressful, simple, and complicated.

Good or bad, it's essential to recognize that when we need to lead, influence, and motivate people, we must remember they are tuned into the station with the greatest frequency on the planet: *WII-FM*. And that means we need to lead with the Relevance Strategy.

## ACTIONS

- Identify something you are trying to "sell" right now (e.g., product, service, idea, etc.).

- Identify the stakeholders from whom you need buy-in and support.
- Schedule discovery calls or conversations with each of these stakeholders.

## Sell the destination, not the plane.

The brain is usually motivated by pain or pleasure. We want to escape Pain Island (where our problems, complaints, and frustrations are) or rush to Pleasure Island (our ideal reality). We don't care about the transportation that will get us there.

Think about going on vacation to a tropical island. You are likely motivated to leave behind the stress, problems, and grind of daily life (pain island) and long to be in a place of relaxation, beautiful scenery, favorite foods, and drinks (pleasure island). Your actions are likely not motivated by the fuel capacity or the dimensions of the seat on the plane.

Let's apply this to how most leaders present challenges or new concepts. Our default is to disregard what's important to our audience and move directly to what's most important to us, which is usually the plane.

One of my clients wanted coaching on how to lead his team into "buying into" a new technology. The presentation he created was polished, but not in alignment with how the brain works best. He had completely overlooked pain and pleasure islands and instead created an 85-slide deck on the details of the plane, the technology in this case.

My recommendation to him was that he spend no time talking about the plane (the actual technology) until he had engaged them in a discussion about the rocky cliffs of Pain Island and the sandy shores of Pleasure Island. I encouraged him to draw out the team's experience of pain and pleasure with such clarity and accuracy that they would beg him to talk about the plane.

> **NAVIGATE TO RESOURCE**
>
> Pain and Pleasure Island: Video

## Strengths-Centered Leaders

The second key to living out the Relevance Strategy is identifying, building on, and developing strengths.

We've established that the brain works most efficiently when we

- follow the whole-to-parts approach
- build on familiar, existing neural networks
- minimize negative threat
- engage emotions
- activate the brain's reward system

The great news is that we capitalize on these brain-based learning facts when focusing on strengths and interests.

The Gallup organization led the charge in the early 1990s through the work of the "Father of Strengths-Based Psychology," Dr. Donald O. Clifton. He asked, "What would happen if we stopped studying what is wrong with you and started studying what is right with you?"[8] This question changed the conversation.

Through the years, Gallup has led the most extensive studies of strengths ever conducted. By the late 90's, Gallup had interviewed over 2 million people across multiple professions to identify patterns of success. This led to the StrengthsFinder Assessment (now *CliftonStrengths*), which is used by individuals and organizations worldwide.[9] More than 30 million people have taken this assessment to identify a person's 34 strengths.

We've used it in our practice for years with individual clients and entire organizations. Organizations that use the tool report higher engagement, better hiring practices, and enhanced team performance.

While assessments are helpful, they aren't necessary. We can produce better results simply by shifting mindsets from "what is missing?" to "what is available?"

Dan Sullivan and Dr. Benjamin Hardy's book *The Gap and the Gain: The High Achievers' Guide to Happiness, Confidence, and Success* helped us see that we experience improved outcomes with less stress when we focus our attention and energy on the gains rather than the gaps.[10] The gap represents the space between our current reality and our ideal, while the gain represents our progress from where we started.

For example, you set a goal to write a book in a year. If you didn't fully accomplish that goal, it would be easy to sit in the gap, which demotivates and further slows progress. To sit in the gain means celebrating the progress you have made, which activates the reward system.

Reframing is a similar concept based on the belief that we can give an event whatever meaning we want. For example, let's say the event is that I didn't get a promotion I applied for. I can make the event mean that I'm a failure. Or, I can make the event mean that I need to grow and prepare for the next opportunity. I get to decide.

The pandemic presented many people with the opportunity to reframe their lives. I was one of them. On March 12, 2020, every speaking opportunity I had was erased from the books. If my team and I had framed that as a gap, a setback, a weakness, we may have joined the hundreds of businesses that closed forever. Admittedly, we had a brief pity party.

Thankfully, we reframed the event as an opportunity. We started asking, "What do our clients need from us right now? What can we be doing for them that we might not have had the opportunity to do under different circumstances?"

After a few calls, we created a six-part webinar series called *Stay Calm and Lead On* and offered it to our clients for free to help them navigate this difficult time. The gesture was appreciated and turned out to be very profitable for us in the following year. None of that would have been possible if we hadn't chosen to reframe.

Referencing *Apollo 13* once more, one of my favorite reframing movie scenes is when everything that could go wrong is going wrong. Unlike those who saw only the failures, Gene Kranz asks, "What do we have here that's good?" Suddenly, people saw options they hadn't before.[11]

Carol Dweck's groundbreaking research, discussed in *Mindset: The New Psychology of Success*, aligns with the Relevance Strategy.[12] She differentiates between a fixed mindset, where talents, abilities, and intelligences are fixed and static and a growth mindset, where talents, abilities, and intelligences can be developed through learning, resilience, and effort.

We can improve in any skill we dedicate ourselves to learning. Thank you, neuroplasticity.

When we maintain a strengths-centered mindset, we

- activate the brain's reward system
- build resilience
- reduce stress
- enhance our health, sleep, and immune system
- strengthen neural pathways
- boost confidence
- enhance memory
- accelerate learning
- foster curiosity and flexibility
- promote collaboration
- increase positive emotion and decrease negativity bias

One of the most valuable strategies for discussing strengths we use in our practice is a Strengths-Discovery Conversation (SDC).

An SDC is a private 1:1 conversation a leader has with each team member about their strengths, interests, experiences, and aspirations. These conversations are constructive for new leaders. However, we encourage seasoned leaders who "think" they know everything about their team members to hold regular SDCs. We typically find new and valuable information.

The goal in an SDC is to listen, stay curious, and ask powerful questions in four categories: Strengths, Interests, Experiences, and Aspirations.

Below, I've listed a few of the questions we recommend.

> ### NAVIGATE TO RESOURCE
> Strengths-Discovery Conversation Guide: PDF

**Strengths:**
- When people come to you for help, what questions are they asking?
- What would your peers identify as your greatest strengths?

**Interests:**
- What projects at work have you enjoyed the most?
- If you could retire today, what would you want to spend your time doing?

**Experiences:**
- What prior experiences have prepared you for what you are doing now?
- What formal learning experiences have been most meaningful to you?

**Aspirations:**
- If you could create a brand-new position for yourself at our company, what would that be?
- If we are having this conversation three years from now, looking back, what would you be proud to have accomplished or learned?

## A FEW TIPS ON WHAT AN SDC IS NOT

- a promise of promotion
- something you, as the leader, are responsible for implementing
- a formal document linked to someone's performance appraisal
- a time for the leader to dominate the conversation with unsolicited advice

## ACTIONS

- Hold an SDC with each employee.
- Have team members complete the *CliftonStrengths* assessment. We recommend assessing all 34 strengths and working with a certified coach to help the team integrate the results in the intended way.
- Delegate based on interests and strengths.
- When an event happens that feels like a setback, ask questions like:
  - What meaning am I giving this?
  - What meaning do I want to give to this?
  - How might this be happening FOR me rather than TO me?
  - What response will lead to the desired outcome?
- Focus on gains rather than gaps by tracking and celebrating progress.

## NAVIGATE TO RESOURCE

The Ultimate Checklist for Effective Delegation: Course and PDF

Reframing: Video

# FINAL THOUGHTS ON
# THE RELEVANCE STRATEGY

In a world of distractions, noise, and uncertainty, relevance "lifts up" and "highlights" the important by providing clarity, direction, and meaning.

When leaders consistently communicate the big picture and intentionally build on strengths, they lower threat, increase engagement, and create environments where people do their best work.

The Relevance Strategy isn't a luxury but a leadership essential. It aligns individuals with purpose, unlocks motivation, and accelerates learning by working with the brain's natural wiring. When people understand why their work matters and how they contribute, they don't just show up; they step up. That's the power of the Relevance Strategy and a mark of a leader worth following.

# WHAT MAKES A LEADER WORTH FOLLOWING?

*We asked real people. We got real responses.*

Here are just a few. Would anyone say the same about you?

✔ *The leader is human-centric and finds fulfillment in helping others discover their strengths and achieve their full potential.*

✔ *They inspire me to believe in their cause. When a leader connects with me by demonstrating that my skills and talents have a meaningful role within the team and contribute to a greater purpose, I am more inclined to follow them. It is this ability to align individual strengths with a shared vision that makes a leader truly worth following.*

✔ *A leader worth following is the one with a vision, who retains and reinforces that vision over time, who maintains a standard of excellence, and most importantly, is a coach, coaching their employees towards personal excellence in the name of the vision.*

✔ *They're clear about their vision and why it matters, so you have a sense of purpose following them.*

✔ *The leader has an idea where they're going, is transparent, and provides enough autonomy and guidance to grow those behind them to be individually successful as well as part of a successful team.*

# THINK. DISCUSS. APPLY.

*Make it matter*

1. Call to mind your organization's mission, vision, and values statements. From memory, write each out:
    - Mission statement
    - Vision statement
    - Guiding values or beliefs
        - Where are these declarations displayed?
        - How are they utilized in making decisions?
        - How are they reinforced daily?
        - How do you create opportunities to reinforce the mission, vision, values?
2. In your experience, what score would you give your organization in "walking their talk"? (1–almost never to 5–almost always)
3. How does your work and your team's work contribute to the mission and vision?
4. How consistently are you connecting the daily work to the mission and vision?
5. What percentage of time do you spend each day doing what you do best?
6. When was your leader's last meaningful conversation with you about your experience, strengths, and aspirations?
7. When was the last time you had a meaningful conversation with each of your team members about their experiences, strengths, and aspirations?
8. Would you describe the performance conversations in your organization as deficit-focused (looking at where people fall short and need to improve) or strengths-focused (looking at where people perform well and how to leverage more of that)?
9. How can you bring more relevance to you and your team?

**Relevance** comes from the word **relevare,** which means to "lift up" or "highlight"

Every brain is tuned into the station

WII-FM –
What's In
It For Me?

Your team's favorite radio station is WII-FM. If you're not speaking to their priorities, you're getting static.

# WHY FOCUS ON STRENGTHS?

- Activates the brain's reward system.
- Builds resilience.
- Reduces stress.
- Enhances our health, sleep, and immune system.
- Strengthens neural pathways.
- Boosts confidence.
- Enhances memory.
- Accelerates learning.
- Fosters curiosity and flexibility.
- Promotes collaboration.
- Increases positive emotion and decreases negativity bias.
- Motivate a more strengths-centered mindset.

Confused brains say no. Inspired brains say GO!

Neurons that fire together, wire together...and here's why:

Not "parts to whole" (puzzle piece) but "whole to parts" (puzzle box)

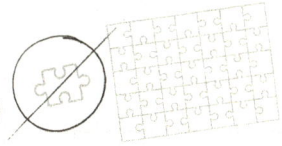

Vision Isn't a Poster - it's a GPS. Mission, vision, and values should guide every decision, not just hang in the breakroom.

*Lead with Vision. Build on Strengths.*

# USE VISION & VALUES:

- to maintain a standard of excellence.
- as a focal point.
- to begin every meeting.
- to lead change.
- to reinforce in every communication.
- to reward and recognize.
- to motivate in uncertain times.
- to make decisions.
- to hold people accountable.
- to focus tough conversations.

## And here's why...

### WWLL
"What Winning Looks Like"

**CLARITY** IS THE ULTIMATE PRODUCTIVITY HACK...

knowledge | experience
~~talent~~
attributes | aspirations

the brain doesn't *resist change,* *resists confusion.*

# CHAPTER 3

# The Action Strategy

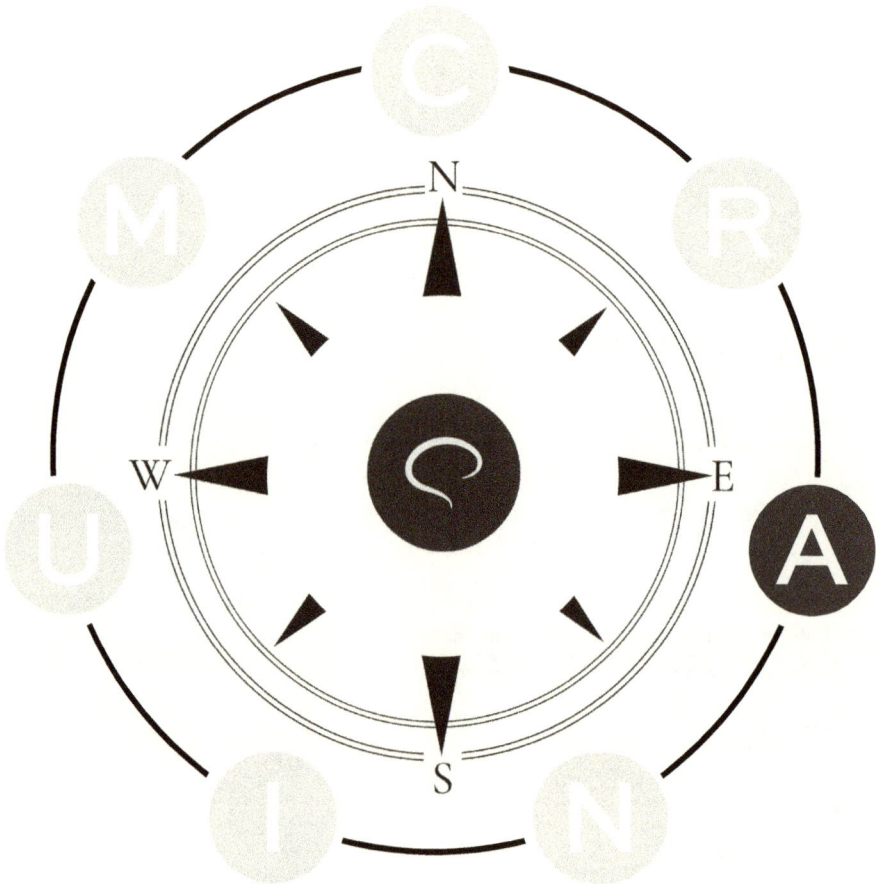

**EMBRACE LIMITATIONS.**
**DEBUNK MYTHS.**

## BIG IDEA

The cheaper, better, faster philosophy works—until you apply it to people.

The brain demands a slower, deeper investment.

## BREAKTHROUGH BELIEFS

You are human. So is everyone else. It's OK.

Wherever you are is exactly where you need to be.

Don't believe everything you believe.

# REAL LEADERS. REAL LIFE.

*Honor the brain's limitations.*

Kristin sits in her car, fifth in line at the coffee house drive thru. "Come on, people," she moans. She turns off the podcast, reaches for her phone and texts her two teenagers to make sure they are awake and getting ready for school. Lost in her cell screen, the car in front moves up in the line and the car behind her honks. She grabs her purse and digs in the side pocket looking for the protein bar she thought she threw in last night. No luck. "What the hell," she thinks as she pulls up to order. "A lemon muffin, please, and a venti mocha." She pauses, thinks about her first meeting, and adds, "Can you add two extra shots, please?"

As Kristin clumsily tackles her coffee and muffin while entering the crowded freeway, her phone rings. It's her boss who has been in the office for more than an hour. She asks if Kristin can forward a meeting invite, which Kristin does, almost rear-ending the car in front of her. Coffee splashes everywhere. Then her 16-year-old son sends her a text telling her he has to be at school early, but his 15-year-old sister won't get in the car. Kristin sends an emoji to him and then texts her daughter: "Please get in the car."

Traffic picks up, and Kristin tunes back into her podcast, which features a health and wellness coach talking about the importance of nutrition and fitness. Kristin knows she needs to make changes in her physical health but is clueless on where to begin. Since she accepted her promotion a year ago, she has packed on 20 pounds, mostly around her midsection.

The new job takes her to corporate headquarters, adding an hour to her daily commute and requiring longer working hours. She let her gym membership expire. As Kristin listens to the podcast, she remembers how much she enjoyed going to the gym each morning with one of her best friends. The workouts and conversations were life-giving.

She thinks about calling her friend that evening, but she knows all too well she won't—who is she kidding? The real work begins when she gets home. After the day's petty personnel problems, endless meetings, and a brutal commute, Kristin's evening holds fast food, school projects, laundry, dishes, teenage drama, and chaos. She has a stack of books she would like to read one day. But when Kristin finally crawls into bed, she is physically and mentally exhausted.

# YOU'RE WIRED FOR ACTION

*Why your brain thrives on the Action Strategy*

Ironically, one of the most effective ways to achieve high performance is to accept the brain's limitations.

## Cheaper, better, faster.

The cheaper, better, faster philosophy works for machines and manufacturing. This philosophy sounds incredibly inviting. Who isn't interested in better, higher-quality outcomes with less input in less time at a reduced cost? Who isn't down for these benefits? Cheaper? Sounds good. Better? You bet. Faster? Bring it! After all, we live in a world where fast is never fast enough and enough is never enough.

Here's the problem. The cheaper-better-faster dream crumbles considering what we know about the human brain. The idea that all things can be made cheaper, better, and faster—simultaneously—fails when applied to the most important piece of equipment in this universe. The equipment that drives everything we are, everything we do, and everything we will be is incompatible with the cheaper-better-faster school of thought.

## Just balance work and life, right?

For some time, we've heard the rallying cry for work-life balance. Once we realized that was an unachievable goal, we changed the language to work-life integration. I'm not sure the language makes a difference. Ultimately, whether we shoot for balance or integration, we are searching for a way to live our best lives and maximize our potential in every area of our lives.

Oftentimes, it's complicated to describe when work ends and life begins. As an entrepreneur, my work is my life's calling. For good or for bad, my life and my work are virtually one and the same. Like me, most of you are knowledge workers. The work you do is primarily in your brain. Ideas are your currency. You don't take your brain out when you leave work or home. There isn't a switch in our brain that flips from "work" to "life."

We are always doing life while we work and frequently doing work while we live life. How many have spent time on the treadmill mulling over a work-related issue? How often do we have meaningful conversations at work over personal problems involving our spouses, children, and families? How many of us have gained clarity on a work situation while we were in the shower or right before we fell asleep? We don't deduct time from our work when we discuss our personal lives on the job. We don't add time to our work when thinking about work-related issues on our personal time.

So rather than getting caught up in whether our work and life are balanced, blended, or integrated, what we are really trying to achieve in life, in this short time on the planet, is *optimization*.

We want to optimize who we are in life, and work happens to be one slice of that pie.

The goal here is to create our success and enjoy it at the same time, rather than allowing our success to eat us alive.

To live our best lives, we must be our best selves. And to do that, we must make conscious choices to sustain a great brain. Best-selling author and noted psychiatrist Dr. Daniel Amen and his team have made profound contributions to our understanding of how powerful our brain is. His work repeatedly reinforces that the effectiveness of our brain determines our effectiveness in this life. To live our optimal best life, our brains must operate at their best.

Unlike other mental health professionals, Dr. Amen and his team at the renowned Amen Clinics look at the brain. Using single photon emission computed tomography (SPECT) imaging, a functional brain imaging technique, they examine the brain to determine its overall health. With the proper intervention, the brain can get healthier. With no intervention or with the wrong intervention, the brain can get worse. They know from over 260,000 scans and decades of research that a healthy brain means a healthy life.[1]

Most people have never stopped to think about what they must do for their brain to work at its optimal level. As a culture, we have adopted brain-antagonistic practices, such as slamming energy drinks instead of getting a much-needed nap. As a workplace, we have also adopted brain-antagonistic assumptions and beliefs like glorifying multitasking, packing back-to-back meetings, and treating exhaustion as a badge of honor.

Can you imagine a company investing millions of dollars into a new technology and not using it for its intended purpose? Or deliberately working against how the technology is designed to operate so that the system breaks or wears out much earlier than it should?

Yet, we do this every day.

We do this daily with the most valuable and expensive piece of technology any company has on the payroll—the human brain. People are a company's most precious and most costly asset. When we adopt beliefs and practices that are counter to how the human brain works best, we are essentially investing millions of dollars in technology, not using it for its intended purpose, and deliberately working against how it operates best.

Let's debunk five of these myths of optimal brain performance. We'll look at why each is a myth and then at the truths and strategies we can use to optimize brain performance.

## Myth #1: My brain can multitask.

To what extent do you agree with the following?

| | Strongly Agree | | | | Strongly Disagree |
|---|---|---|---|---|---|
| I can multitask. | 1 | 2 | 3 | 4 | 5 |
| I rarely ask for help. | 1 | 2 | 3 | 4 | 5 |
| It's faster if I do it myself. | 1 | 2 | 3 | 4 | 5 |

Most of us are convinced that we are experts at multitasking, and that our productivity and quality are not negatively impacted when we multitask. I mean, it's insanity to suggest multitasking is a myth; if we really believed it was a myth, we wouldn't be killing ourselves trying to do it.

Our workplaces have stopped questioning whether multitasking is a myth or an actual ability. Most job descriptions include the expectation of multitasking.

So, let's take a moment to define what is considered a *task* and look at what happens in the brain when we attempt to multitask. The mythical phrase, "My brain can multitask," is really saying, "My brain can give equal attention to two attention-rich tasks." The truth is, "My brain can't multitask," because it can't give equal attention to two attention-rich tasks. Can you chew gum and walk? Most of us can do these two tasks because they do not compete for processing time and energy in the brain.

The brain has an elaborate attention network. Thousands of studies on multitasking conclude that the brain's complex attention system can only devote resources to one attention-rich task at a time. So, researchers believe that we aren't truly multitasking at all. The brain's attention system is not devoting equal resources to multiple tasks simultaneously; rather, it appears the brain is simply switching attention from one task to another at lightning speed.

"So what?," you ask. As a client once said, "I don't care how the brain handles all that I'm expected to do as long as it gets handled, and I keep my job and people off my back." Valid point. The problem is that rapidly switching back and forth is not how the brain works best, and when we repeatedly force it to do so, there are costs and consequences.

Multitasking interferes with our efficiency. When we multitask or suffer from an interruption, it simply takes us longer to return to the task we were previously doing, if we ever return to it at all. Some studies indicate the return time to the original task can be as high as 25 minutes. Studies have also shown that multitasking can result in up to a 50% increase in errors and a 40% decrease in productivity.[2,3]

Multitasking costs. It interferes with our overall performance and mental acuity. The prefrontal cortex, our executive control center, is highly taxed by the energy burn. Prolonged multitasking is linked to mental fatigue, stress, and diminished working memory, which impacts our accuracy, decision-making, and long-term productivity. And contrary to popular belief, the younger generation is not immune from these effects.[4]

Do we expect optimal performance from other technology we invest in? If so, why don't we have the exact expectations and give the same attention to the human technology we invest in?

Multitasking impacts performance because it affects how and where information is learned and stored in the brain. It appears multitasking causes information to be stored in the "wrong" part of the brain. When we multitask, we store information in the striatum, a part of the brain dedicated to procedure and skills rather than facts and ideas. When we focus and prioritize our attention, information is stored in the hippocampus, a part of the brain critical for long-term memory and synthesizing new information with existing information.[5]

So, why is storing information in the striatum versus the hippocampus important?

The striatum is associated with implicit, automatic, and habit-based learning, somewhat "mindless," such as riding a bike, using a keyboard, reaching for an energy drink at 2 p.m., and checking your phone fifty times daily.

The hippocampus is associated with learning that is explicit and consciously accessible, such as remembering events, learning new facts, and remembering context. Examples of this type of learning at work might include recalling historical events and conversations with an important client, responding to a new request by repurposing an existing process, or navigating a new challenge by leveraging prior experiences.

The difference is significant, given the results we want to accomplish for ourselves and through our team.

Finally, multitasking depletes the prefrontal cortex of energy and activates the reward system. This is particularly important to note. Remember all the priceless functions of the PFC from the chapter on Challenge? Multitasking compromises critical functions like emotional, financial, cognitive, and perspective-taking self-control, decision-making, planning, and empathy.

Decreased activity in the PFC means a decline in these abilities, leading to impulsivity, defensiveness, self-protection, and poor decisions. Couple this with the fact that multitasking activates the brain's reward system, and multitasking becomes its own drug. There is an increase in dopamine and adrenaline, and we can get addicted to being busy.

When we are in a multitasking frenzy, the *thinking* part of the brain is hijacked. The brain gets a "feel-good" reward and acts impulsively to do more of it. As a result, we may be busy, but we aren't productive.

You may have felt the withdrawal of this addiction if you've grown accustomed to multitasking and speed, and then it stops suddenly, such as when you are on vacation. When we are addicted to busy, disconnecting and slowing down can be very uncomfortable.

Instead of buying into the multitasking myth, let's set a higher standard. Let's schedule those weekend emails to send on Monday morning and trust our team to handle the day-to-day when we are on vacation. Let's reward prioritizing and setting boundaries.

We'll have more actions to come, but first, let's debunk a few more myths that contradict the Action Strategy

## Myth #2: I don't need sleep.

To what extent do you agree with the following?

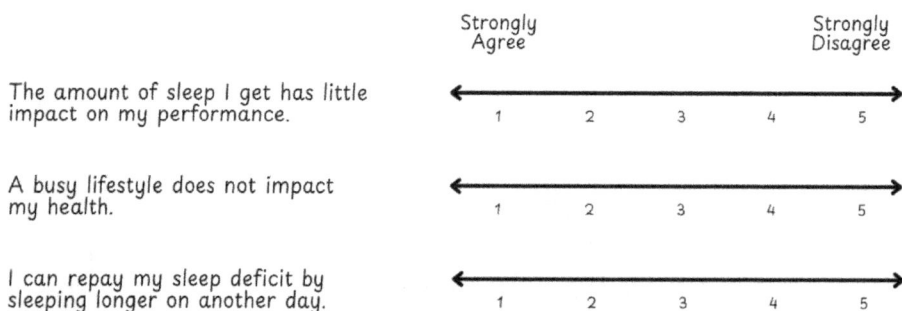

| | Strongly Agree | | | | Strongly Disagree |
|---|---|---|---|---|---|
| The amount of sleep I get has little impact on my performance. | 1 | 2 | 3 | 4 | 5 |
| A busy lifestyle does not impact my health. | 1 | 2 | 3 | 4 | 5 |
| I can repay my sleep deficit by sleeping longer on another day. | 1 | 2 | 3 | 4 | 5 |

I led a retreat once where I discussed ways to promote brain health. One of those suggestions was to get adequate sleep. One executive talked with me at every break, adamantly proclaiming he only needed two hours of sleep a night. So, was his assertion accurate, or is he living in a state of deception and denial?

I'm claiming this belief is a myth because sleep is integral to optimal performance. One of the best things we can do to optimize performance and integrate the Action Strategy in our environment is to turn everything off and go to sleep. The quality of your performance today was primarily determined by the quality of sleep you got last night.

The brain is a fascinating subject because the more we learn and think we "know," the more we are humbled by what we *don't* know. For example, how much sleep do we need? Like many of you, I grew up hearing we need anywhere between seven and ten hours of sleep, which is true for me. I often tell people I have the gift of sleep and have always needed more sleep than most of my peers and family members to be my best.

Recent research on sleep suggests that the standard of seven to ten hours may not be a one-size-fits-all approach. In fact, that executive may not have been in denial. He may have been telling the truth; though rare, he may only need two hours of sleep.

In 2015, the National Sleep Foundation conducted an extensive study to reevaluate sleep recommendations.[6] Among their conclusions was that the "standard" sleep requirement varies from person to person across our lifespans. While there is a "normal" range of sleep time, meaning the amount of time for the average person to feel healthy and well-rested, there are deviations from the norm. So, the key is to determine what sleep time is optimal for you and to be vigilant in protecting that time.

A second question of mystery about the brain, then, is, "Why do we sleep?" In years past, we thought the brain needed sleep to rest, reboot, learn, recharge, or dream. But we really don't know why the brain needs sleep. One of the most plausible reasons why sleep is critical to optimal performance is that this is a time when the brain actively processes, stores, and deletes information and experiences. One of my professors once shared that the brain performs tasks for us at night that it simply won't do any other time; one of those is to process information and memories efficiently.

The hippocampus is deep in the medial temporal lobe and straddles the right and left hemispheres. It is critical for learning and memory. Earlier, I mentioned this is the part of the brain that gets bypassed when we multitask. Through the years,

I have heard the hippocampus called the "fortress of human memory" and the brain's "surge protector." Let's take a closer look at what the hippocampus does for us and how it functions, because it can predict optimal performance, and sleep is vital to it working correctly.

Ever crammed the night before the test?

I remember driving to an exam one time and avoiding everyone I knew. I was afraid if I talked to them, the facts and dates I had memorized might leak out of my brain. I was holding these facts in the tank. After the test, a loud flushing sound could have been heard throughout the campus. It was the sound of me flushing the facts out of my head. I did fine on the test, but my cramming the night before did not result in long-term, deep-down-in-my-bones learning. Here's why.

If new information is like a large water pitcher, the hippocampus is like a small cup. For real learning to occur, at least two things must happen. First, we must be exposed to the information, hopefully in an environment with a brain-friendly delivery method. Then the brain requires time to sort, file, and selectively discard information. When does the brain sort, file, and delete? You guessed it: when we sleep. The hippocampus does its best work when we sleep. It performs crucial functions critical to learning and memory that it simply can't do at any other time.

## NAVIGATE TO RESOURCE

5 Non-Negotiables for Effective Leadership Development:
Video

> Our leadership development programs typically range from six to twelve months or longer, depending on the desired outcome. We avoid the one-and-done approach when the goals are sustained knowledge and behavior change. You may remember a time when we forced people into a room for all-day training or week-long bootcamps. Because of advances in brain-based learning, we strategically select the amount of "learning time" balanced with "processing time."

The challenge is that the consequences of a sleep deficit don't immediately surface. It's like eating ice cream before you go to bed every night; its effect on your waistline may not appear instantly, but it will eventually be revealed in a big way. The same is true with sleep. We accrue a sleep debt.

Studies have shown that the effects of a sleep debt can appear within two weeks of getting less than six hours of sleep each night. The effects can be mild, such as irritability, diminished memory, and reduced alertness. But the effects can also be life-threatening, increasing the chances of severe conditions such as Type 2 diabetes, heart disease, cancer, Alzheimer's disease, and hallucinations. An estimated 100,000 accidents on the road each year are caused by sleep-deprived drivers.[7] Fifty three percent of medical errors are attributed to sleep deprivation. In one study, sleep-deprived residents made 36% more errors than their non-sleep-deprived counterparts.[8]

The problem is that a sleep debt impairs our judgment. When our judgment is impaired, we can no longer accurately assess whether we have a sleep deficit. We may not recognize or acknowledge the impairments resulting from our deficit. So, we keep pushing forward to finish the project, drive the car, or treat the patient. In that sense, the executive mentioned earlier, the one who believed he only needed two hours of sleep a night, may have been delusional and operating under a sleep debt. Additionally, like any debt, it takes time to pay it back. We can't operate on little sleep for weeks and expect to pay it all back by sleeping longer on Saturday.

## Myth #3: I am not making myself sick.

To what extent do you agree with the following?

| | Strongly Agree | | | | Strongly Disagree |
|---|---|---|---|---|---|
| My calendar is packed most days. | 1 | 2 | 3 | 4 | 5 |
| Stress does not impact my physical health. | 1 | 2 | 3 | 4 | 5 |
| I have little control over my mental and physical health. | 1 | 2 | 3 | 4 | 5 |

It's interesting how easy it is to blame outside forces and others for making us sick. There is a reward for blaming; we don't have to take responsibility. We blame the demise of our health on everything from vaccinations and pollution to cleaning solutions and McDonald's. While these excuses have some truth, it seems the most significant culprit is us. We are making ourselves sick. The Centers for Disease Control estimate that as much as 85% of our medical expenditures are tied directly or indirectly to stress-related illnesses.[9] Other studies, targeting the workforce specifically, estimate that workplace stress is costing anywhere from $190 to $300 billion annually.[10]

Recent statistics regarding mental health are startling. Some attribute the increase and prevalence to a COVID-delayed trauma response. Lyra Health's 2024 State of Workforce Mental

Health reports 87% of US workers have had at least one mental health challenge, severe or chronic depression and anxiety are up 80% since 2021; meanwhile 65% of workers admit their mental health has impacted their performance at work.[11] Brain health challenges impact all valuable prefrontal cortex activities such as focus, thinking ahead, innovation, problem solving, impulse control, decision making, etc.

Our stress is also making us obese. According to the CDC, Americans are heavier than ever. More than 23 states have an obesity rate of 35% or more. While obesity results from a variety of reasons, stress and environment play a significant role.[12]

With healthcare costs increasing and healthcare coverage decreasing at an alarming rate, we must stop blaming external forces for our stress-related illnesses and look in the mirror.

> **WE are making ourselves sick.**

Why does stress in our lives make us sick?

The brain is directly connected to your immune system. This is the anatomical reason why, when we are under negative stress for long periods of time, we have a much higher risk of becoming sick. It's no mystery. When we are under negative stress, we should expect our health to fail and shift into becoming a self-care-taking machine!

When stressed, we experience elevated cortisol levels, a stress hormone that impacts memory, sleep, weight, and inflammation. Multiple studies have demonstrated that anxiety-reducing practices that reduce cortisol, such as yoga and mindfulness meditation, result in enhanced sleep and clarity of thought as well as decreased waist sizes, particularly in women.

Cortisol also slows the body's healing process because it disrupts the immune response. This hormone, in appropriate levels, turns off inflammation in the body. However, when excessive cortisol levels persist over time, the body becomes desensitized, and inflammation accelerates dramatically. Long-term, chronic inflammation damages blood cells and brain cells, leading to many illnesses.

Changes in life situations, even good changes, increase the likelihood of being sick because change triggers confusion which triggers negative threat. Remember Big Deal #2: All threat is brain threat? I recall the first time I completed the Life Change Index Scale, also known as the Holmes and Rahe Stress Scale or the Social Readjustment Rating Scale (SRRS).[13] In 1967, Holmes and Rahe studied if stress was connected to illness. They ranked 43 life events and surveyed over 5,000 medical patients by asking them to indicate which events they had experienced within the previous two years. A value, or Life Change Unit (LCU), was assigned to life events typically considered negative and positive. For example, divorce gets a value of 73 points, while marriage receives a value of 50 points. Marital reconciliation, a seemingly positive event, gets a higher LCU than personal injury, a seemingly adverse event. The higher the total score, the greater the likelihood of illness.

I joked as I filled out the survey. I added my points, checked the scale, and saw that I had an 80% chance of illness. In two weeks, I was in the hospital; it turns out that this scale was an excellent predictor of illness. In fact, in one study, the U.S. military used it to accurately estimate how many people would visit the ship's infirmary while on a six-month deployment.

Stress, particularly in situations we perceive as negative and out of our control, takes a toll on our performance, health, and lives.

In his book *Margin: Restoring Emotional, Physical, Financial, and Time Reserves to Overloaded Lives*, Dr. Richard Swenson tells the story of Ignaz Semmelweis, a 19th-century surgeon who practiced before the discovery of microbes.[14] Simmelweis simply made an observation: physicians who moved from performing autopsies in the morgue to treating patients in the postpartum ward were killing patients. He was one of the first to consider the possibility that there could be invisible killers on physicians' hands. Semmelweis advocated handwashing with chlorinated lime after performing the autopsies, and after that step was put into action, deaths in the postpartum ward stopped. One would think he would have been hailed a hero, but not so. The medical community crucified Semmelweis because he suggested doctors were causing the deaths. Swenson compares microbes to overload. He suggests stress and overload are also invisible killers.

## Myth #4: Long hours at work equal high performance.

To what extent do you agree with the following?

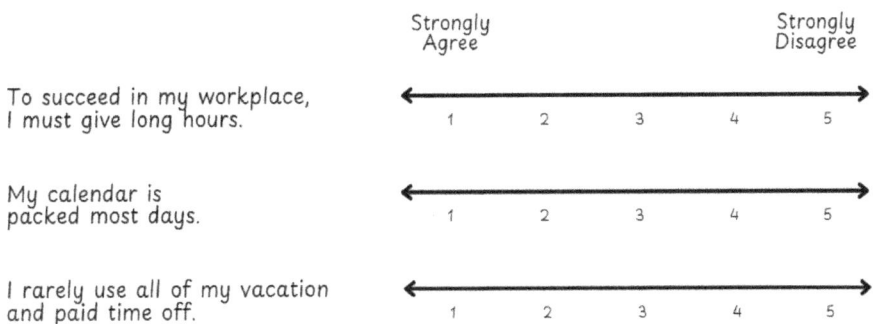

| | Strongly Agree | | | | Strongly Disagree |
|---|---|---|---|---|---|
| To succeed in my workplace, I must give long hours. | 1 | 2 | 3 | 4 | 5 |
| My calendar is packed most days. | 1 | 2 | 3 | 4 | 5 |
| I rarely use all of my vacation and paid time off. | 1 | 2 | 3 | 4 | 5 |

Leaders are frequently in the office long before their team arrives and long after they leave. They text and email into the late evening hours and on weekends. While their intentions may be to model commitment and work ethic, or just to get the work done whenever they can find the time, they often model unhealthy work habits and a lack of boundaries. They are subtly telling the team that long hours are what it takes if they, too, want to get ahead. And when we are at the office or in front of a computer or phone screen, we can't be fully present in other places that are important to a healthy life balance. Even the greatest of leaders have not figured out how to be in two places at once.

The brain has a limited amount of cognitive energy to expend during a given period. The prefrontal cortex burns an enormous amount of fuel. While the brain accounts for only 2% of your body's mass, it consumes approximately 20% of your oxygen and 20% of your energy. Much like your vehicle's gas tank, cognitive fuel runs out. We deplete fuel and energy in the PFC with every cognitively demanding decision.

*Brain Rules: 12 Principles for Surviving and Thriving at Work, Home, and School* by John Medina includes several videos to reinforce neuroscience concepts.[15] In the video on "Attention," Medina features a consultant who reaffirms that those organizations that believe they are always "on" are those organizations that are constantly distracted and inefficient. Longer hours don't necessarily translate into a stronger work ethic, better performance, or higher productivity. Longer hours simply equal longer hours. The person staying longest at the office is likely the least efficient, and possibly the least productive.

## Myth #5: The brain is not like any other organ in the body.

To what extent do you agree with the following?

|  | Strongly Agree | | | | Strongly Disagree |
|---|---|---|---|---|---|
| The brain is different from other organs in the body. | 1 | 2 | 3 | 4 | 5 |
| I would seek medical help for a physical problem faster than a mental problem. | 1 | 2 | 3 | 4 | 5 |
| I give others more grace than I give myself. | 1 | 2 | 3 | 4 | 5 |

Admittedly, this myth is tricky. After all, of course, your brain is not like any other organ in your body—it's your brain. And, if you were to remove it, no other organ could assume its functions. In many respects, your brain is entirely unique, but in different aspects, your brain is just like your heart, lungs, or bones. It requires proactive healthcare and commitment to wellness to maintain its optimal function.

At some point in our lives, most of us will either personally or by way of a family member, close friend, or coworker experience the impact of a brain health problem. The percentage of people who will experience a mental health challenge in their lifetime is predicted to be around 50%. It is even higher if you factor in substance abuse.

It is time we remove the stigma associated with this issue. A brain problem *is* a physical problem. It is no different than a heart malfunction, a lung condition, or a broken leg. And just like with these physiological obstacles, the proper intervention can improve the issue, while the wrong (or no) intervention can spell disaster.

A brain problem is a physical problem, not a character problem. You wouldn't attempt to *will* yourself out of having a heart attack; you would seek help from professionals who understand that organ. In the same way, we can't *will* ourselves out of a mental health dilemma but need to seek help from professionals who understand that precious structure. The challenge is that many doctors who treat brain problems, a.k.a. mental health issues, never look at the actual organ they are treating.

I am an avid admirer of Dr. Daniel Amen because he has led the charge in *looking* at the brain, seeing what is working too hard or not hard enough, and providing the right intervention. Unfortunately, we have a long way to go in this area. I can speak to this personally, having lived with family members who struggle with addiction and depression. We invested our hope, our time, and thousands of dollars on psychiatrists, counselors, physicians, and rehab centers; not one professional we visited over at least 10 years actually *looked* at the organ they were treating, the real source of the problem. Repeatedly, we were given prescriptions for medications and told, "Come back in six weeks, and let's see how you are doing." Six weeks! Are you kidding? In the world of someone suffering from a mental illness and their families, six weeks can seem like an eternity. More gravely, six weeks can be the end of a lifetime.

In addressing any other health problem, neglecting the organ one is treating might be malpractice. I often wondered what these doctors would have done if I had brought my family member in with a broken foot. Would they have given us medications with instructions to return in six weeks to see how the foot was feeling and healing? No, they would have taken X-rays to see the bone fracture and likely applied a cast or performed surgery. Amen has been revolutionary in that he has dared to ask those in the mental health business to look at the organ they are treating. And he has raised awareness among those suffering the consequences of mental illness to demand better treatment.

With the right intervention in the right situation, the brain can heal and improve; this is called neuroplasticity. So, a brain problem is not a hopeless problem. People with mental health challenges need to access the right help; as they heal, their performance improves and their lives get better, as do the lives of all of those around them who are impacted by the illness.

# THE ACTION STRATEGY IN PRACTICE

*What an Action culture looks like*

The Action Strategy captures the brain's dichotomy: It performs awe-inspiring functions but also has severe limitations. To accept the Action Strategy is to make friends with rather than resist the brain's limitations.

The Action Strategy fully embraces and integrates all the brain's capabilities and limitations. It accepts the brain's tremendously efficient speed and its requirement for rest and reflection. This strategy calls us to embrace the brain's inspiring, limitless capacity and demands for balance and processing time. It honors the brain's complexity and its hunger for simplicity. It evaluates when less can be more. It surrenders to the brain's unlimited potential and physical limitations. It requires designing the environment based on how the brain works best.

In cultures where leaders ignore the Action Strategy, a few observable signs are:

- Performance and productivity are prioritized over the health and well-being of the workforce.

- Quantity of results is valued at the expense of overall quality of life.
- Employees' work lives take precedence over their personal lives.
- Short-term achievements are prioritized over long-term health and wellness.
- Resources and development are directed toward organizational gains rather than helping individuals reach their fullest potential.
- Goals and objectives are measured, but individual health indicators are not.
- One-size-fits-all policies prevail, offering little flexibility in work schedules, locations, or environments.
- Long work hours are seen as a badge of success and a sign of achievement.
- Employees are discouraged from speaking up when priorities pile up.
- Leaders are rewarded for what they do rather than how they do it.
- Calendars are filled with back-to-back meetings.
- After-work boundaries are not respected.

In contrast, leaders who create cultures that embrace both the brain's strengths and limitations actively seek ways to create an environment that provides balance and encourages integration. These leaders understand that focus is balanced with rest, and one's personal life must align and integrate with one's professional life. The way one brain performs at its best does not apply to everyone. The workforce comprises highly complex and unique individuals.

In cultures where leaders embrace the Action Strategy, a few observable signs are:

- Policies are consistent yet adaptable to specific situations and circumstances.
- Resources are available to help employees integrate the demands of work and personal life.
- Leaders hold everyone to exceptional performance standards.
- People have opportunities for both personal and professional development.
- Employees are recognized as individuals with unique work styles and needs.
- Individual well-being is valued as highly as the organization's bottom line.
- Leaders set aside time in their calendars for reflection and strategic thinking.
- Communication channels remain open for raising concerns when workload affects quality of work or life.
- How leaders accomplish work is considered as important as what they accomplish.
- After-work boundaries are respected.
- Leaders regularly check in with team members in private.

Cultures embracing the Action Strategy realize that cheaper, better, faster may apply to manufacturing cars, streamlining processes, or producing widgets, but it does not automatically apply to the design of the human brain.

These cultures "get" the fable tradeoff.

You may recall Aesop's fable of a countryman's goose that laid the golden eggs. A favorite of mine, this tale is a powerful reminder of what happens when greed and a scarcity mentality override the natural design and order of things. To get more golden eggs, the countryman kills his very source of wealth: his goose.

Action-rich cultures are all about golden eggs. However, they recognize that people are their most valuable resource, so they take excellent care of their geese.

## WITHOUT THE ACTION STRATEGY

- Performance is valued over health and well-being
- Win-at-any-cost mentality
- Quantity over quality of life
- Work trumps personal life
- Personal problems are not permitted or tolerated
- Short-term gain and long-term pain
- Resources and growth are limited to work contributions
- Productivity goals supersede employee feedback
- Strict adherence to all policies, regardless of the situation
- "Leave your personal problems at home" mindset
- Long hours and sacrifice are rewarded
- Disrespected boundaries
- Meeting-packed calendars

## WITH THE ACTION STRATEGY

- Mindfully designed physical space
- Flexible work schedules and locations
- Adaptable policies when appropriate
- Organizational and individual well-being equal to profits
- Bountiful employee resources
- Leadership seeks unconventional talent
- Abundance of growth and developmental opportunities
- Employees are treated as individuals
- Uninterrupted time to think
- Open communication channels
- Leaders model the values
- After-work boundaries are respected
- Continuous formal and informal talent development conversations
- Feedback is sought out and welcomed

# BE A LEADER
# WORTH FOLLOWING

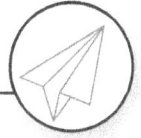

*How to live out the Action Strategy*

What does it take to see sustainable changes in results?

Let's talk about beliefs.

We are fortunate to have many brilliant resources accessible today on habits and actions that improve performance.

But what we find our clients miss is the order in which real, lasting change happens. On any desired change, we can become lifetime podcast listeners and collectors of actions (tips, tools, strategies, etc.). But that doesn't mean we integrate that change in the long term.

When it comes to genuine change, we must shift our beliefs.

Consider this model, we call the Beliefs Model.

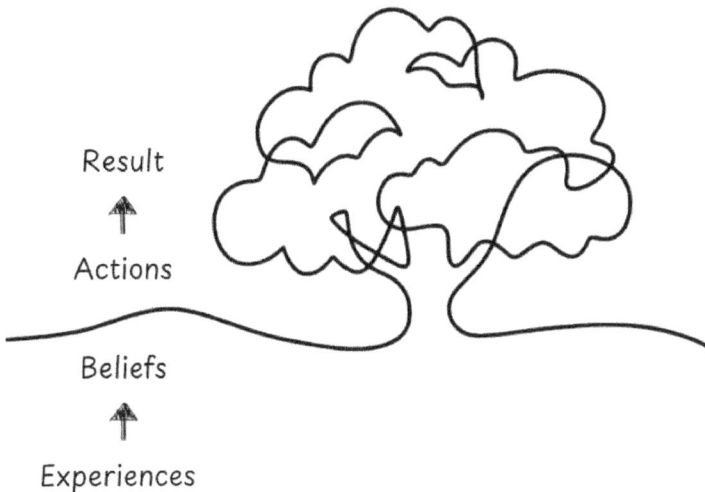

Result
↑
Actions

Beliefs
↑
Experiences

While different actions lead to different results, actions and strategies alone will not sustain results. We must change our beliefs to produce sustainable changes in our results.

## A few facts about beliefs:

Beliefs are tricky because they are like water to the fish. They have often been with us for a very long time. They may have been in our families for generations long before we entered the scene. Some of the spoken and unspoken beliefs I inherited include you'll always have a car payment; attending church is a priority; don't get too big for your britches; as long as you work, you'll always have money, and on and on.

We aren't born with beliefs. A baby doesn't come into this world with its own beliefs. We adopt beliefs over time both consciously and subconsciously from what we learn, read, see, etc.

Beliefs feel familiar and comfortable. Because they feel "right," letting go of beliefs may seem like a loss or a risky entry into an unknown world. As we established in previous chapters, loss, uncertainty, and confusion present negative threats that impair our best thinking and cause us to get defensive.

I tell the leaders I coach that beliefs can be like the old clothes we keep in our closet. We refuse to part with them, even though they may no longer fit or may not be something we would wear today.

But be warned: we will never see sustainable results unless we change beliefs. Focusing on different actions is as reliable as New Year's resolutions. A small percentage (8-10%) gets implemented, but 90% or more are forgotten in a few weeks.

New beliefs are formed through new experiences. And new experiences, the gateway to new beliefs, will seem uncomfortable and confusing, triggering threat. But just knowing to expect discomfort helps us remember that we are moving in the right direction.

NAVIGATE TO RESOURCE

Beliefs Model: Video

**This model of sustainable change applies to how we lead.**

# Delegation

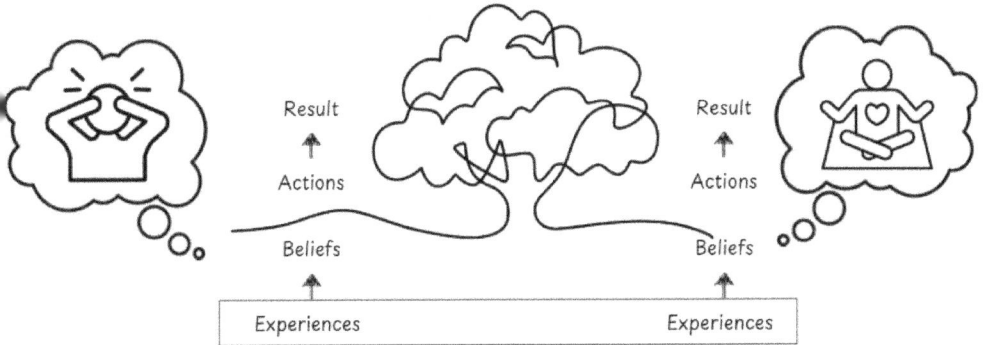

Example:

On the left side of the visual, the leader's results are stress and overwhelm. Why? The leader's actions include taking on too much work and failing to delegate. The belief fueling those actions is one we hear often. "If you want something done right, you have to do it yourself." That belief may have been handed down from a previous leader. Alternatively, it may have been formed and reinforced by an experience in which the leader ineffectively delegated a task.

On the right side of the visual, the leader's results are peaceful and balanced. Why? The leader's actions include delegating often and having more time to plan and think. A different belief fuels these actions. "Delegating is an effective way to build my team and my capacity." This belief may have been instilled by a previous leader or through effective delegation and achieving success.

## This model of sustainable change applies to how we live.

# Wellness

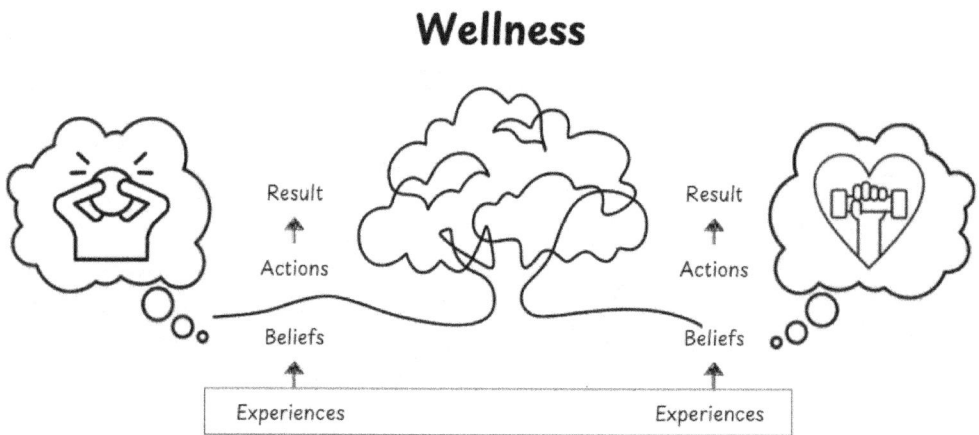

Example:

This model represents my journey towards health and wellness. I was unhappy with my results, which included weight gain, fatigue, and brain fog. These results stemmed from my unhealthy eating habits, lack of exercise, and failure to take time for self-care. The beliefs fueling my actions included thoughts like, "It's selfish to take time for myself," "I can outwork a bad diet," and "I can't lose weight no matter how hard I try." This belief originated from various sources in my life but was reinforced by past failed attempts to get healthy.

The right side represents the result I wanted instead: to be the healthiest version of myself. The actions leading to that result included working with a health and wellness coach, eating lean and green, exercising regularly, and getting adequate rest. The belief shifts that fueled these actions was "It's selfish to NOT take time for myself," "I can eat healthy and still enjoy life," and "I can lose weight given the right program." New experiences have reinforced my new beliefs, actions, and results. It's just reordering the list.

A single Google search for *"how to minimize distractions at work"* elicits nearly a million hits. If the answer were "more actions," we'd all be productivity geniuses.

> **Critical reminder: Lasting change doesn't start at the action level. It starts at the belief level.**
>
> **To achieve sustainable results, we must shift beliefs and engage in experiences that reinforce those beliefs.**

Sustainable results come when we change the belief first and then reinforce that belief with experiences that hard-wire it. That's when actions stop feeling forced and start feeling familiar.

## Belief #1: My brain cannot multitask.

If the multitasking brain is distracted and reactive, then the uni-tasking or prioritizing brain is focused and proactive.

If we want to be high performers, let's study what high performers do.

In *Uncommon Genius: How Great Ideas Are Born*, Shekerjian explores the common traits of forty winners of the prestigious

MacArthur Fellowship.[16] The MacArthur Genius Grant is awarded to exceptionally creative individuals who demonstrate originality and dedication to their field. Perhaps more important to me is what she *didn't* find when she studied their habits. These high performers did not give into distraction. They didn't rush and bounce around from one unrelated idea and task to another. Instead, they committed to a vision with unrelenting focus, purpose, determination, courage, discipline, and commitment over the long haul.

## ACTIONS

**Take 100% ownership of your time.**

As you go through these strategies, if your first response is, "There is nothing I can do about that," think again. There is always something you can do. It may be a micro change, or it might be extreme, uncomfortable, expensive, or unfamiliar. But there is always something you can do.

**Identify your common distractions.**

Make a chart with three columns.

In the first column, write down your distractions in a single day.

In the middle column, write down all the actions you can take to minimize or eliminate those distractions. Then ask, "And what else? And what else? And what else?"

In the third column, write down the beliefs you will need to hold to support the actions.

**Block out distractions on purpose.**

One of my clients and her team established a "Sacred 60" each week. Each team member is expected to take 60 minutes each week to "disconnect" and direct their focus on a specific task of their choosing. They use police crime scene tape to close off their cubicles when exercising their Sacred 60. Even better, their teammates and leader respect their request for no interruptions.

**Integrate intentional "think" micro breaks.**

Think breaks can be mindful moments. Set an alarm reminding you to breathe. Take a walk, stretch, or juggle (a skill I learned this year).

**Tell your day where it is going to go.**

Let's tell our day where we want it to go before it tells us where it went.

Brendon Burchard, founder of the *High-Performance Institute* and author of *High-Performance Habits: How Extraordinary People Become That Way* offers a unique approach to prioritizing each day.[17]

Inspired by his ideas, I grab a spiral notebook and spend about 15 minutes telling my day where to go.

I write *Projects*. I list the top three projects I'm working on that day and the three next steps I need to take to move those projects forward.

Next, I write *People*. I list people I need to contact or meet with.

Third, I write *Priorities*. These are the tasks that are important to me personally—my "no matter what" tasks, such as making a doctor's appointment, paying a bill, or buying a birthday present.

Fourth, I write *Praise*. I either write down a few wins or gratitudes, or I send someone a quick text or email expressing my appreciation for something they've done or what they mean to me.

Lastly, I review my list, and at the very top of the page, I write *Presence*. As I look at the day I've planned, I identify the way of being I want to maintain for the day. I write, "Today, I will be (focused, confident, bold, etc.)."

The key is to do this BEFORE I OPEN MY EMAIL.

Burchard says your inbox is other people's plan for your life. So, the idea behind this daily habit is to set the direction before someone else does.

**Warning: If you wake up in the morning and immediately open your phone to check the news or email, stop now!**

### DETERMINE YOUR GREEN, YELLOW, AND RED ZONES OF ENERGY.

Energy management is a very individualized art and skill. Each morning, our brain wakes up with a precious commodity: our energy. We must direct (not deliberate) where that energy goes and who gets it. We don't want every day to be Halloween, where we open the door with our energy bowl and let whoever walks up take as much as they want.

A strategy I find helpful is to identify my green, yellow, and red zones throughout the day. My green zone is my brain's best and most efficient time zone. This is when I experience the best version of myself, optimal mood, lots of focus, and creativity. My green zone is between 6 am and 11 am and returns between 7 pm and 9 pm.

My yellow zone is when my brain processes more slowly. It's the ideal zone for reflection and implementation. My yellow zone is between 11 am and 3 pm and returns between 5 pm and 7 pm.

My red zone is my brain's slowest processing zone, where I may feel more sluggish and "brain dead." This is the zone where my brain tells me to rest so it can actively recover. My red zone is between 3 pm and 5 pm and returns between 9 pm and 6 am.

After you've determined your zones, align your calendar accordingly.

For example, I avoid heavy thinking work at 3 pm. I ideally schedule my classes and writing time in the early morning during my green zone.

---

### NAVIGATE TO RESOURCE
Green-Yellow-Red Zone: Template

---

## Leverage the Eisenhower Box

Popularized by many authors, this is a powerful tool for reflecting, focusing, planning, and delegating. President Eisenhower supposedly created this tool, which reportedly helped him become the high performer and producer he was. I use this time management matrix to plan a day, a week, a month, or a project. It is also an ideal tool to identify what tasks to delegate.

As shown below, the matrix or box contains four sections. The horizontal column marks things that are "Important" because they are aligned with your priorities. The "Not Important" row contains activities important to someone else. The vertical column marks the "Urgent" tasks, those screaming for your attention and time bound. The "Not Urgent" tasks are those things that quietly wait in the background.

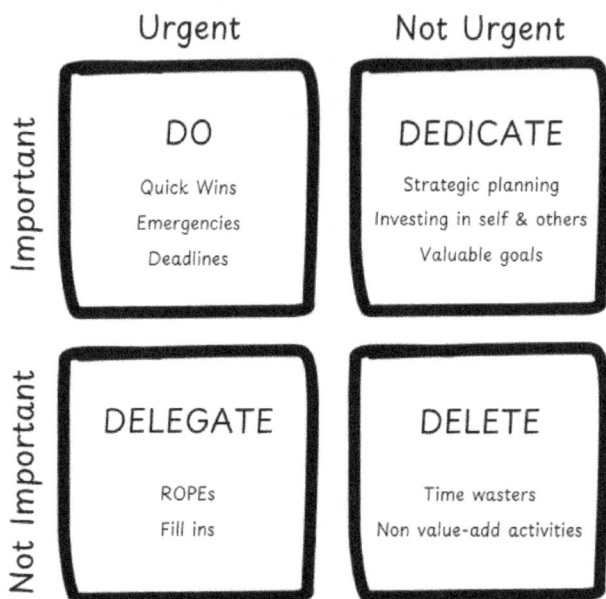

|  | Urgent | Not Urgent |
|---|---|---|
| **Important** | **DO**<br><br>Quick Wins<br>Emergencies<br>Deadlines | **DEDICATE**<br><br>Strategic planning<br>Investing in self & others<br>Valuable goals |
| **Not Important** | **DELEGATE**<br><br>ROPEs<br>Fill ins | **DELETE**<br><br>Time wasters<br>Non value-add activities |

## Quadrant 1: Important & Urgent

These are activities that are aligned with your goals and values and are time-bound. For example, if someone ran into the room bleeding and screaming while you were reading this, I'm certain you wouldn't tell them to wait a second while you finished the page. The incident would demand your immediate attention.

We should DO these things, remembering that 100% of what we do now gets done!

Note: Quadrant 1 activities activate adrenaline and the reward system; they give us a rush, so it's easy to get addicted to the feeling of being busy. Quadrant 1 can also become the "heart attack quadrant" because these activities can elevate the stress hormone, cortisol.

## Quadrant 2: Important & Not Urgent

These are proactive activities, like going to the gym, eating healthy, investing quality time in a relationship, and completing preventative health screenings. Quadrant 2 is like fueling or charging your car: you don't always feel like you have time to stop and refuel or charge, but if you don't, you end up on the side of the interstate with much bigger problems. For an organization, a Quadrant 2 is investing in their leaders.

We should DEDICATE time for these tasks and protect that time at all costs. Unfortunately, this is the time that we all-too-quickly give away to Q1 and Q3 tasks.

Note: Most activities that lead to busyness and stress in Quadrant 1 could have been avoided if we had dealt with them responsibly in Quadrant 2.

## Quadrant 3: Not Important & Urgent

These activities are important to others but may or may not be important to you. I call this quadrant ROPES (Responding to Other People's Emergencies). This is the primary quadrant for most meetings, emails, projects, and volunteer opportunities we agree to before fully considering the commitment.

This is the quadrant where we can identify what to DELEGATE. If we say "yes" to Q3 tasks, we say "no" to Q2 tasks, the important but not yet urgent tasks.

Note: One person's Quadrant 1 crisis can become another person's Quadrant 3. When we fail to be proactive, we don't just burn our own time and energy. We hijack the focus, sanity, and performance of everyone around us.

### Quadrant 4: Not Important & Not Urgent

These activities are timewasters. This is the quadrant of procrastination, social media scrolling, or binging reality TV.

Study your calendar. Review the last two weeks and identify which tasks belong in which quadrant.

The goal is to spend most of your time and tasks in Quadrant 2, the proactive, intentional, power section. The more time you spend in Quadrant 2, the less time you spend in the other three. Your energy, results, and performance improve, and you impose fewer problems onto others.

---

## NAVIGATE TO RESOURCE

Eisenhower Productivity Matrix: Video and PDF

---

## Belief #2: My brain needs sleep.

As we established earlier, sleep requirements vary among individuals and at different times in our lifecycle. The key is self-awareness and accurate self-assessment.

- How much sleep are you getting?
- What is the quality of your sleep?
- Are you experiencing any symptoms of sleep deprivation?
- How much sleep do you need to feel healthy and rested?
- Do the people closest to you agree with how you've answered these questions?

There is an ebb and flow to our brain's ability to be "on." We must unapologetically honor and lean into that rhythm rather than resist it. By getting sleep and scheduling cognitively demanding tasks accordingly, we think better and more efficiently. This cascades into a higher-quality work and personal life. Rather than push through the fatigue, we need sleep and periods of rest and reflection.

### Set an alarm.

A recent coaching client was suffering severe symptoms of sleep deprivation. She decided that if an alarm helped her wake up, it could help her go to sleep. So, at 9 p.m., her alarm goes off. That's her cue to close the computer and follow a bedtime routine to ensure she falls asleep on time.

### Connect today's evening to tomorrow's day.

Try this brain hack. "Tomorrow" starts "today." Tomorrow's success doesn't begin at 5am, it begins at 9pm when you go to bed.

Remember, your brain has limitations. One of those is that it will believe whatever you tell it. It's easily tricked and manipulated. Let's use that to our advantage.

### Take a nap (or a nappucino.)

Not only is sleep important at night, but many studies indicate the benefit of bringing sleep into the day. The reason is that the body naturally craves sleep at least twice in 24 hours. The primary craving hits between midnight and 7 a.m., and the second occurs in the afternoon, usually between 1-4 p.m. The National Sleep Foundation says that a nap of 20-30 minutes during the day can improve mood, alertness, and performance.

Daniel Pink suggests a nappuccino, an afternoon coffee followed by a brief nap. The science here is that caffeine takes

20-30 minutes to kick in.[18] So, if we can fall asleep immediately and take a 20-minute power nap, we get the full benefit of the nap and the caffeine.

### Get ready for bed.

We "get ready" to exercise and "get ready" for work, so how about we "get ready" for bed? A nightly getting-ready-for-bed routine signals the brain that it is about to engage in one of the day's most important activities. My routine involves a bath or shower, changing into pajamas, brushing teeth, prayer, etc.

### Use the power of deep breathing.

Deep breathing activates the Anterior Cingulate Cortex (ACC). This part of your brain is essential in regulating moods and emotions, balancing the parasympathetic (rest and digest) nervous system with the sympathetic (fight or flight) nervous system, and modulating attention and focus.

Deep breathing focuses the mind, reduces chatter, relaxes muscles, and increases oxygen to every part of your body.

## Belief #3: I am making myself sick.

We must take ownership of our health to the best of our ability. As the saying goes, a healthy person has a thousand wishes, a sick person has one.

Our company's founding belief is this: God has given you a message and a way of delivering that message that hasn't been given to anyone else. Honor and protect that gift. No. Matter. What.

Prioritize your health and the health of your family, team, and organization so that you and they can fulfill all they are here to accomplish.

*Evaluate the health of your organization and make changes (even if they aren't popular).*

I consulted with one of the nation's largest health insurance providers for many years. During that time, they surveyed the physical health of their workforce, measuring and tracking specific health markers such as lifestyle habits, eating habits, weight, body fat, etc. Their survey revealed that their company was the unhealthiest organization they insured.

So, they began to make changes: no smoking on the property, healthier food choices in the vending machines and cafeteria, walking programs, health education training, and financial incentives for workers to lose weight, reduce body fat, lower cholesterol and blood pressure, and free annual screenings. Within two years, they moved from the unhealthiest to the healthiest company they insured.

*Make your health a priority, set non-negotiables, and get help.*

Know your health markers. Ensure your doctor's visits are prioritized on your calendar. Block the time needed to make healthy food choices and exercise and refuse to give that time away to anyone.

I highly recommend working with a health and fitness coach. After all, you hire professionals for their expertise where you have none (accountants, financial planners, plumbers, mechanics, etc.). If your health is not optimal, you need an expert. Quit trying to figure it out on your own.

### Research best practices from other industries and companies.

There are healthy initiative programs that are best practices across multiple industries and companies. We serve a variety of clients. We've seen many innovative initiatives, including walking and standing meetings, movement challenges, creative therapy rooms, massage rooms, on-site yoga for line manufacturing workers, office meal-prep classes, mindfulness and meditation moments, standing and treadmill desks, pet therapy days, on-site gardening, and free fitness watches.

### Ask your team.

Involve your team. Create a special committee to identify and champion healthy initiatives that your unique culture will embrace.

Our country is facing a health crisis that is impacting the quality of our lives, both personally and professionally. The good news is we are capable of changing this result. If our beliefs and actions make us sick, let's choose different beliefs and actions.

## Belief #4: Productive hours at work equal high performance.

The world of productivity is rich in resources, encompassing everything from Lean, Six Sigma, and Agile methodologies to numerous books, apps, and podcasts. I don't want to tackle that topic, but below are a few tried-and-true best practices that work for my clients.

### Study and compare calendars.

Your calendar tells the story.

During coaching calls, we often ask clients to share their calendars with us. Review your calendar and see what it reveals. Have your team members regularly study their calendars and share insights.

Compare your calendar with other people in your organization. If there is someone at your level who is a high performer, compare your calendars.

- What are they saying "yes" and "no" to that you aren't?
- How do your beliefs compare?
- How do your actions compare?

If you are new to a role, find someone excelling in that role and ask to compare calendars.

### Choose productive over busy.

Implement the Eisenhower matrix or any other proven productivity tool and choose productivity over busyness.

Have the Cartesian Questions visible and use them to guide your choices throughout the day:

- What will happen if you say YES?
- What will happen if you say NO?
- What won't happen if you say YES?
- What won't happen if you say NO?

On April 14, 1912, Jack Phillips, the senior wireless operator for the Titanic, was sending messages on behalf of passengers to their friends and family updating them on their cruise experience, such as "thinking of you," "weather fine," "lovely dinner," and "looking forward to reunion."

When a nearby ship sent an iceberg warning, Phillips replied, "Shut up, shut up. I'm busy."

Busy sank the Titanic, and it will sink you, too.

### Give choice and voice whenever possible.

The brain doesn't buy into what it's told to do. It buys into what it helps build. When we tell people what to do, we get compliance. However, we gain loyalty and commitment when we involve people in decisions that impact them and empower them to make choices.

Whenever possible, give others a choice and a voice in matters such as work schedule, work location, work environment, project selection, and project execution.

### Make decisions.

Not deciding is deciding. Procrastinating when making decisions hinders everyone's productivity.

The words *decision* and *scissors* come from the root word *cis*, which means "to cut."

Visualize using scissors to cut the choice. Then make the cut.

A wise leader I coached once told me, "If you aren't making some 'bad' decisions, you aren't making enough decisions." If we make a decision that doesn't get us the desired result, we can make another decision.

Build your decision-making muscles. As you advance in leadership, you will be faced with making more decisions in less time and with less information, impacting more people and having higher stakes.

**Ask for help.**

Most leaders I've worked with over the years have limiting beliefs about asking for help. I've heard:

- *It's just faster if I do it myself.*
- *If I want something done right, I'd better do it myself.*
- *I don't want to burden other people by asking for help.*
- *I don't want others to think I don't know what I'm doing.*

High performance requires utilizing all our resources, especially the expertise of others. Asking for help and delegating are the #1 ways to increase your productivity, develop others, and build trust.

> **NAVIGATE TO RESOURCE**
>
> The Ultimate Checklist for Effective Delegation: Course and PDF

**Make friends with your doubt.**

I once heard Oprah share the common characteristics of the thousands of celebrities and world changers she had interviewed throughout her 25-year show. One interesting observation they had in common was that after the interview, they looked for some form of validation by asking, "How did I do?" "Was that OK?"

Doubt never entirely goes away. Doubt creates negative threat that impairs our ability to make decisions, prioritize, and act. So, let's make friends with it. Trust yourself.

## Belief #5: My brain is like any other organ.

Your brain is the driver of everything you do. Dr. Amen, in his 2013 TED talk, reveals what he has learned from studying thousands of brain scans.[19] One of his key learnings is that the brain influences every part of who we are and what we do, from our abilities and talents to our likes and dislikes.

### ACTIONS

*Acknowledge that the brain is the most important technology you have.*

If your company is investing millions in new technology but ignoring the technology that people have between their ears, speak up. Make a change. It's unfathomable to me that a company budgets for technology and equipment but not people development.

*Accept the brain's constraints and the limits of willpower.*

If we (or someone in our care and influence) has a brain problem, let's take action.

Sometimes the intervention may be as simple as a flexible work schedule for a period, exercising, rescheduling travel, or adjusting work responsibilities. Sometimes the solution may require medical intervention.

What we can't do is ignore it or rely on willpower to fix it.

Like any organ, the brain needs its owner to make choices and take actions to maintain its health. When the brain needs help, get help. It's not a willpower problem; it's simply a brain problem. And brain problems, like any other health problem, get worse with neglect but improve with the right help.

As I've mentioned, one of my go-to resources is Amen Clinics because they look at the brain through SPECT imaging and create a holistic path for healing. You can find out more information about their locations and methodology at www.amenclinics.com.

NAVIGATE TO RESOURCE

Amen Clinics BRIGHT MINDS: PDF

# FINAL THOUGHTS ON THE ACTION STRATEGY

When it comes to the brain and the quality of our life, small changes produce big results.

To achieve balance, integration, and optimal lives, we must follow the framework of how the brain works best. It's time we rewrite some long-held, familiar beliefs.

- Rather than believing the brain can juggle without cost, focus on one priority at a time. Guard attention like the precious resource it is.
- Rather than dismissing the need for sleep, honor the brain's natural rhythm and fiercely protect the hours that restore it.
- Rather than outsourcing responsibility for health, own it and choose habits and lifestyles that keep your brain and body at their best.
- Rather than worshiping long hours, measure what matters. Trust people and let results, not chair time, be the proof.

Finally, we need to remove the mystery of the brain. While there is a great deal we need to learn, we know that the brain, like any other part of the body, must be treated with respect and given attention when it is not working correctly. Let's put aside the stigma of mental health, for that is often the most significant barrier to getting help and getting better.

Cultures that embrace the Action Strategy are smart. They pay attention to the brain's needs, strengths, and limitations, and adapt accordingly. The mantra of "cheaper, better, faster" may have transformed manufacturing, but it malfunctions when applied to the most advanced technology on the planet: the human brain.

# WHAT MAKES A LEADER WORTH FOLLOWING?

*We asked real people. We got real responses.*

Here are just a few. Would anyone say the same about you?

- ✔ *They know my kids' names and care about my family.*

- ✔ *Creates a relationship with individuals and the team where people don't have to do something for the leader "because they have to" they get the task done because they want to.*

- ✔ *Someone that takes an interest in learning from others.*

- ✔ *A great leader supports you, has your back and has your best interests in mind.*

- ✔ *Provides autonomy and respects work/life balance.*

# THINK. DISCUSS. APPLY.

*Make it matter*

1. List 10 activities you performed yesterday. Don't concentrate too hard, just write out the first 10 things that come to mind. Plot them into Quadrants 1, 2, 3, or 4. What do you notice?

2. Who is someone in your life who seems to have struck a balance with work and life? What do they say "yes" to? What do they say "no" to?

3. Review the statements under each of the 5 myths. Where can you make improvement?

4. What is one action you can take to influence a more brain-friendly culture?

*Embrace limitations.*
*Debunk myths.*

Result
↑
Actions

Beliefs
↑
Experiences

☑ **Trade Multi-Tasking for Uni-Tasking**

LONG HOURS ≠ HIGH IMPACT

If your brain works right, you work right. If your brain doesn't work right, you've got problems.
- Dr. Daniel Amen

## Multitasking Is a Myth
### Stop the Brain Drain

Your brain isn't juggling; it's just switching (badly). Multitasking = more mistakes, less memory, and one cranky PFC.

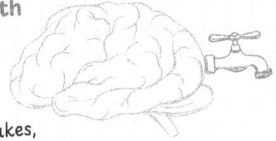

**Sleep Is Your Superpower!**
**Sleep isn't lazy - it's brain fuel.**

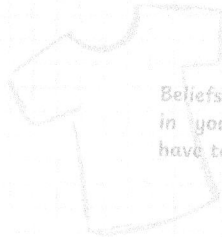

Beliefs are like the clothes in your closet; you don't have to wear them forever.

Green Zone: Pedal to the Metal
Peak Focus. High Output. Strategic Work.
Best time to tackle hard tasks
This is your brain's high-performance gear - use it wisely.

Yellow Zone: Cruise Control
Reflect. Organize. Brainstorm.
Ideal for planning, processing, light collaboration, or creative thinking.
Let your brain wander and connect the dots.

Red Zone: Pull Over
Low Energy. Foggy Focus. Time to Rest.
Schedule breaks, admin work, walks, naps, or brainless tasks.

*Don't believe everything you believe.*

# CHAPTER 4

# The Novelty Strategy

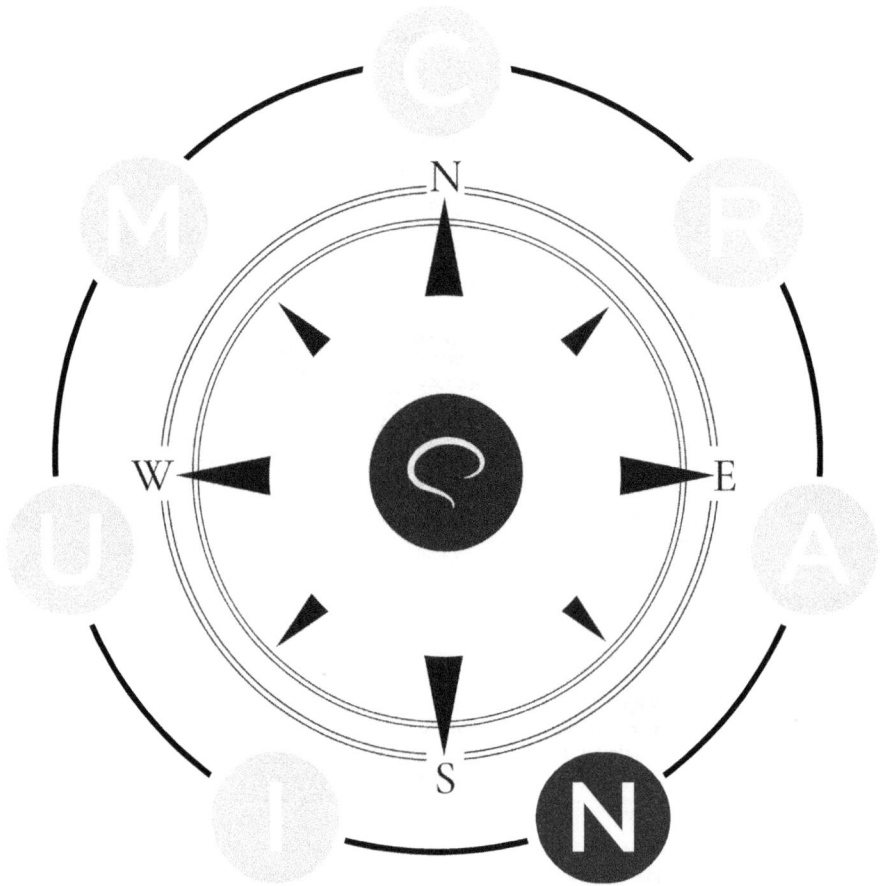

**CHALLENGE CONVENTION.**
**NUDGE IMAGINATION.**

## BIG IDEA

Think big. Think differently. Think deeply. Think forward.

Novelty is not a luxury; it's a brain-based necessity for attention, learning, motivation, and innovation.

## BREAKTHROUGH BELIEFS

Curiosity didn't kill the cat. Certainty did.

Novelty isn't a "nice to have." It's a "must-have."

Ask the magic question: "Even better if...?"

# REAL LEADERS. REAL LIFE.

*Two stories. Two results.*

"Can you grab my backpack?" Sara asks Tom as they leave for work—an everyday ritual. Married for nearly 18 years, both work in IT. Sara changed jobs a year ago; her new office is just a few miles from Tom's.

"Make it a great day," Tom says as he drops her off. She kisses him and heads into her building. Tom drives into his usual parking spot, checks social media, flashes his badge at security, and walks past sleek signage for the "Innovation Lab."

In Tom's building, employees move quickly, eyes on phones. Words like "innovation" and "collaboration" cover the walls, echoing the company's recent rebrand.

Tom arrives at his open cubicle, puts in earbuds to block the growing noise, and scans his schedule—an overstuffed calendar filled with back-to-back meetings. His only blocked work time has been hijacked by a meeting with a manager he dreads spending time with.

His first meeting begins: a vague PowerPoint-heavy presentation on a proposed testing change. With no agenda and unclear ownership, debate breaks out. Tom, like several others, slips out early for his next meeting.

Meanwhile, Sara starts her day with a coffee and a friendly nod to coworkers. She settles at a table, plans her day using a tool from a recent productivity workshop, and checks email. Today she's leading the team's design session—a highlight of her week.

Passing a community board, she signs up for a "future of work" focus group. A senior leader thanks her for her help on a project and invites her to pick up a resource about the company's lean initiative.

Arriving at the "collaboration zone," she hears music playing. Her leader has arrived early, posted a hand-written agenda, rearranged tables for group work, and placed a goody bag and a water bottle at each seat. Sara smiles. She couldn't have imagined this environment at her old company.

She chats briefly with her leader about an upcoming call, and soon the team trickles in, exchanging high fives. The leader opens with a funny, on-topic story, aligning the group with a shared purpose. With energy and applause, Sara takes the lead.

As she thanks the team for last week's progress, she wonders how Tom's day is going.

# YOU'RE WIRED FOR NOVELTY

*Why your brain thrives on the Novelty Strategy*

Innovate or die. Innovation is the currency of success and longevity.

No one wants to be the next Blackberry, Blockbuster, Sears, or Kodak. COVID gave us all a crash course in the value of innovating.

Innovation is among the top five words in companies' mission, vision, and values statements. We all get why innovation (or novelty, as we call it in CRANIUM) is good for business.

Now, let's look at why it's good for the brain.

## Novelty wakes up the brain.

Have you ever driven a familiar route, and when you arrived, you didn't remember one detail of the trip? That's a phenomenon called "highway hypnosis." Your brain goes into a trance. You can thank your basal ganglia. This is the part of the brain responsible for automation and habit formation. The basal ganglia automate the familiar to make your brain more efficient. When the basal ganglia take over, we don't have to pay attention.

The problem is when the trance accompanying automation takes over in situations where we should pay attention: meetings, making decisions, etc. Our brains are inundated with information and stimuli in a very noisy, busy world. It's easy for this deluge of input from so many platforms to lull our brains into a stupor similar to "highway hypnosis." There is so much to pay attention to that we stop paying attention to anything.

The brain doesn't pay attention to the familiar or the boring.

## Novelty engages emotion.

Ever had someone introduce themselves and ten seconds later, you couldn't remember their name?

Big Deal #3 is that emotions run the show. There is little chance of learning and remembering if emotion isn't involved, such as remembering someone's name. There is rarely emotion involved. The name may mean something special to the person's mother or father. But outside of that, it's just a name. We typically remember a name only when it engages emotion of some sort. The name may be the same as someone special to us, or it may be unique. So, drop the shame of being bad at remembering names. It's not your fault; it's how your brain is wired.

Emotion is critical to grabbing attention and being memorable. We've all experienced this thousands of times in our lives: that one presenter who stands out among the thousands of presentations we've sat through; that one professor, or one classroom moment, we remember even though we've endured thousands of hours of lecture; that one image we remember; that one stranger; that one moment on a vacation...and the list goes on. A novel event—a name, a face, or an experience—activates the brain, emotions, and memory in a way that sticks. It imprints itself so profoundly that it returns to us again and again. The routine, the expected, the boring? They rarely do.

## Novelty transforms routine moments into memorable experiences.

Novelty for novelty's sake is just noise. It's not about being flashy or distracting; it's about being intentional. Novelty must serve a purpose. The Novelty strategy should highlight meaning, reinforce a message, meet a need, or deepen a learning experience.

I often work with trainers and teachers to help them design learning experiences that are engaging and memorable, essentially aligned with how the brain learns best. We harness the power of novelty when trainers face the challenges of teaching important yet dry content, covering boring yet required material, or working within limiting formats such as e-learning. These very constraints offer the richest opportunities for transformation. Together, we brainstorm bold, even outrageous, ideas to shake things up and do something different and completely unexpected. Novelty is a brilliant strategy to use in design to turn the mundane into something memorable.

The same technique turns necessary but dreaded, unproductive meetings into memorable ones that people look forward to. When I work with leaders and influencers who suffer from unengaging meetings, we intentionally "flip" them simply by using the power of novelty. Incorporating novelty in classrooms and meeting rooms yields better results and higher engagement.

One of my past coaching clients was also the president of her HOA (Homeowners Association), a responsibility she couldn't wait to step away from. The meetings she chaired were tedious, unproductive, and a burden that caused her a great deal of anxiety. She literally had a bottle of wine waiting at home for when the meeting ended and joked about wanting to sneak a flask into the gathering to help her get through the two hours of torture. I got a Mayday text from her, and we jumped on a call to discuss an upcoming meeting she was particularly anxious to lead.

In our discussion, we turned to the power of novelty. We identified the parts of the meeting she dreaded and integrated the unexpected and different.

When members walked into the room for the meeting, they were greeted with a bowl of candy and the sounds of Motown. She started the meeting with a compelling story about a couple in the neighborhood, struggling with an illness, who were able to relocate and be near their family primarily because of their home's property value. She displayed a "scoreboard," a flipchart page labeled "Decisions." Each time a decision was made, a sticky note went up on the flipchart, and everyone did the "wave." She ended the meeting by showing a cartoon about HOAs. The members left laughing, feeling accomplished and valued, having much less dread of next month's meeting. No flask required.

In *The Power of Moments: Why Certain Experiences Have Extraordinary Impact*, Dan and Chip Heath explore how some moments stand out and stay in our memories forever.[1] He identified four characteristics of such moments: elevation, insight, pride, and connection. Elevation happens when the experience rises above the everyday and triggers a positive emotion. Insight refers to when the moment provides an aha or profound realization. Pride occurs when the moment gives a feeling of accomplishment or appreciation, and connection results when the moment strengthens a bond with others. Engaging emotion is the common denominator to all of those characteristics.

## Novelty motivates the brain.

In addition to having the power to capture attention and shift the energy of an entire group, novelty holds the secret to changing behavior. The Volkswagen auto company supported an initiative called "The Fun Theory," essentially an experiment to motivate people to change their behavior simply by making things fun.[2] In one of my favorite videos from the campaign, the company wanted to see if they could encourage more people to take the stairs instead of the escalator. The experiment involved converting a set of stairs at Stockholm's Odenplan subway station into working piano keys.

What was the result of shifting the expected to the unexpected? Station-goers chose the stairs over the escalator 66%. Conclusion: People tend to change their behavior with less resistance when something is fun and engaging.

In other "The Fun Theory" experiments, people were likelier to use their seatbelts if the in-car entertainment system played only when they were fastened. People were almost 100% more likely to recycle bottles using a bottle bank when inserting the bottle mimicked a video game experience. And people were more likely to obey speed laws when the speed camera lottery was implemented; those who disobeyed the speed laws were caught by the camera, fined, and contributed to the lottery, while those who obeyed the laws were caught by the camera and were entered for a chance of winning the lottery.

As this exercise demonstrates, novelty and fun can grab attention, enhance memory, and change behavior for the better. The presence of novelty activates the PFC, triggers the brain's reward system, engages emotion, promotes brain plasticity, and elevates important brain chemicals.

## Novelty lowers negative threat.

In previous chapters, I've mentioned the priceless functions of the PFC. This is the seat of abilities such as creativity and innovation, willpower, character, empathy, collaboration, and cooperation. If these are the outcomes we are looking for in our own lives and in the lives of those we influence, it is in our best interest to do everything possible to stimulate lots of activity in the PFC.

Negative threat dramatically deactivates this part of the brain. Of course, some level of anxiety or threat in the brain is positive and motivating. What is perceived as positive threat and negative threat can be different for everyone. But when any kind of negative threat (something we perceive as confusing, having an adverse outcome, or out of our control) is present, the PFC's functions are compromised. The goal, then, is to minimize negative threat so we don't compromise the functions of the PFC.

NAVIGATE TO RESOURCE

3 Big Deals: Video and PDF

Novelty can reduce negative threat by bringing a sense of play, curiosity, and fun. Novelty holds the potential to turn up the volume on the better part of who we are and new possibilities by turning down the volume of negative threat.

## Novelty enhances performance.

Leveraging novelty by doing the unexpected even under the most stressful conditions has many benefits. Physicians who see humor in everyday situations are less prone to depression and burnout and receive higher patient satisfaction ratings. Patients who use humor sleep better, remember more information told to them during their medical care, have reduced pain, and heal faster. Teachers who use novel classroom learning approaches gain better engagement, improve test scores, and experience fewer behavior problems. Military personnel who laughed more reported reduced combat stress and enhanced group cohesion. Professional athletes who focus on the joy they feel while playing the game, particularly the happiness they experienced as a child playing the game, perform better on the field.

## Novelty increases dopamine (albeit temporarily).

Novelty also enhances brain function by impacting essential chemicals. Exposure to surprise and a novel environment releases a rush of dopamine, a chemical necessary for heightened attention, focus, motivation, and goal-directed behaviors that activate the brain's reward system. When novelty triggers the brain to release dopamine, we are motivated to explore in search of the reward.

I experienced this firsthand while on vacation in Mexico with my two adventurous, thrill-seeking teenagers. We went on an excursion to a cenote (cave) and were invited to jump in. That sounded fine until I looked down and realized the fall would be at least 50 feet. My son and daughter jumped without hesitation.

I, on the other hand, summoned the power of novelty. Fear, too, showed up big-time, but not negative fear. The novelty of the moment activated dopamine, arousing my reward system and motivating me to crave the reward of jumping. I envisioned conquering my fear, free-falling, plunging into the beautiful water, and bragging to my friends for the rest of my life. So, I took a deep breath and jumped!

Warning: novelty is short-lived. Things that were once novel (ex: PowerPoint) can quickly become familiar. Much like the effects of a drug, novelty can leave the brain craving greater dopamine release to activate the reward system. It can propel us to seek more novelty. In the case of the cenote, after my kids jumped several times, they discovered a higher platform that would increase the drop by 10 feet. In time, even the novelty of jumping from the higher platform became boring. I drew the line when they considered doing backflips.

## Novelty rewards the brain.

The brain's reward center is located deep in the midbrain and regulates reward and motivation. It responds best to absolute novelty—completely new things or experiences—rather than relative novelty. The brain is a tough sell and not easily entertained for long. We seem to be hard-wired to seek out novelty, and when absolute novelty becomes relative novelty, we crave more novelty.

The reward center is also closely linked to two brain areas critical to emotion, memory, and learning—the hippocampus and the amygdala. I mentioned the hippocampus in the Action chapter; it sorts, files, and deletes information, especially when we sleep at night, to enhance memory and learning. This may be one reason why novelty is such a powerful teaching tool. In one study, the plasticity of the hippocampus (the ability to create new connections between neurons) was increased by the influence of novelty. Not only did the plasticity of the hippocampus increase while exploring a novel environment or stimuli, but the plasticity continued to increase for up to 15-30 minutes after the novel exposure. Therefore, one effective learning and memory strategy is to set aside time to reflect and process information after taking in novel stimuli.

## Novelty releases several beneficial chemicals.

Novelty also activates the amygdala, an almond-shaped structure in the midbrain responsible for powerful emotions, especially fear. A great deal has been published on the amygdala, largely because of its predicted role in PTSD. The amygdala has been referred to as the integrative center for emotions, emotional behavior, and motivation. It appears that the release of dopamine triggered by the novel stimuli reduces anxiety in the amygdala, activating rather than hijacking the prefrontal cortex, which enhances learning, memory, and overall performance.

If we can choose to make it fun and love the 'play' of the game, we perform better.

Other vital chemicals that novelty activates in the brain are serotonin, oxytocin, and endorphins. Serotonin, a chemical produced by nerve cells, fuels the brain, sparks curiosity, and impacts virtually every area of the body. Serotonin stabilizes mood, reduces depression, affects sleep and sexual function, and contributes significantly to overall health and happiness. Oxytocin, also known as the "hug hormone," facilitates bonding and triggers emotional responses that enable us to relax and trust. And finally, novelty elevates endorphins, the neurotransmitters that help block pain and induce pleasure and a sense of satisfaction.

## Novelty impacts neuroplasticity.

Research has shown that a depressed brain can begin to shrink or atrophy. A happy brain, on the other hand, has greater neuroplasticity, the ability to heal and form new neural connections. When we have happy brains, we are more open to change, more flexible and adaptable, have a greater ability to see situations from various perspectives, and can more easily synthesize new experiences and information with existing ones. Good Think co-founder Shawn Achor, in his brilliant and popular TED talk, calls this the "Happiness Advantage."[3] More on that in the upcoming chapter on Using Emotion.

## Caution: Novelty means risk.

We must also be mindful that novelty can introduce risk, as it disrupts the familiar. It can stir up discomfort, a sense of loss, or even a fear of rejection, especially when it challenges group norms or deviates from what is familiar. Novelty introduces the unexpected, and that can lead to confusion or uncertainty.

For some brains, this disruption is perceived as a positive challenge; it sparks curiosity, ignites engagement, and activates the prefrontal cortex (PFC), the area responsible for higher-order thinking.

However, for others, the same novel event may be perceived as threat. When novelty feels unsafe or too far outside the comfort zone, it can trigger resistance and shut down the PFC, limiting access to reasoning, reflection, and learning.

Understanding this variation in response is essential for using novelty to stretch and motivate without overwhelming. We need to use novelty mindfully. Novelty should always contribute to rather than distract from the desired purpose or outcome.

# THE NOVELTY STRATEGY IN PRACTICE

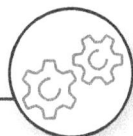

*What a Novel culture looks like*

The Novelty Strategy encompasses three related concepts: creativity, innovation, and novelty. These three concepts are often used interchangeably, but they have subtle but important differences.

## Create

The word *create* means "to bring into existence," to create something that didn't exist before. Think of creating the universe, capturing the first written language, instituting democracy in Ancient Greece, and writing a book. We create and exercise creativity when we start with a blank page or with nothing at all and produce something.

## Innovate

The word *innovate* means "to nudge or alter" something that has been created. So, in that sense, it's much easier to innovate than create. You may have noticed that everyone is an innovator once someone else has created.

## Novel/Novelty

The word *novelty* means "new." Novelty exists in both creating and innovating.

The Novelty Strategy can be about creating or simply nudging. It is about thinking bigger, slightly differently, subtly deeper, and marginally forward. The Novelty Strategy is at work when we create from a blank page or take something that already exists and ask, "Even better if?"

All three of these ideas, *creativity*, *innovation*, and *novelty*, involve growth and change. Growth and change mean facing the unknown and taking risks, which can trigger challenge for some and negative threat for others. Therefore, to reap the rewards of novelty, we must create a psychologically safe environment where people feel supported to experiment, to show vulnerability, and to risk failure.

> **Talking innovation is one thing. Living it out is another.**

I led workshops at a global company that touts itself as innovative. The word is in their mission statement and is one of their values. An entire wing of their corporate headquarters is named The Innovation Center. Sounds impressive and progressive. Yet, I remember thinking the first time I was in their building, "If innovation happens here, I'm looking for unicorns in the parking lot." Why? Because the culture they created was completely counter to the kind of culture where one finds innovation, creativity, and novelty. Team members rarely acknowledged each other, even when passing in the hall. People were fearful of questioning decisions or bringing forth new ideas. Numerous stress-related heart attacks had occurred in the office.

Novelty is about meeting a need by imagining differently than before, above and beyond what has been or what is. Novelty is about alternative thinking, a willingness to take action that veers from the expected and differs from conventional, accepted methods.

Novelty is about diving deeper, strategically considering and analyzing motives, rewards, risks, and returns. And novelty is about looking ahead and taking a positive, solution-focused approach. It requires a culture that can view past decisions not as failures but as valuable learning for the future. It's about questioning beliefs and patterns.

The fruits of novelty require a safe, healthy culture.

In cultures where leaders ignore the Novelty Strategy, a few observable signs are:

- More time is spent talking about innovation than taking action.
- Risk-taking is discouraged.
- Few individuals maintain a sense of wonder, curiosity, and fun.
- Best practices are not explored beyond the boundaries of their industry.
- New ideas are adopted slowly, if at all.
- The environment is characterized by high threat, low trust.
- The fresh perspectives of new hires are dismissed.
- Egos drive the need to be right and take credit.
- Bureaucracy stifles interest and enthusiasm.
- Novel ideas are met with the response, "That would never work here."
- Difficult conversations are avoided that could drive individual and team growth.

- Collaboration is mandated through forced initiatives rather than cultivated through culture.
- The workforce is composed of like-minded individuals.

The consequences of such an environment impact not only individual lives but also the overall health and sustainability of the company. The speed of change in today's workforce is on overdrive. Novelty, innovation, and creativity are game changers. They determine who adapts and survives and who becomes obsolete. Every day, we either reimagine the future or risk losing it.

In cultures where leaders embrace the Novelty Strategy, a few observable signs are:

- Innovation is consistently supported and lived out.
- Risk-taking is encouraged and rewarded.
- Leaders actively seek and value input.
- Differences are welcomed and leveraged.
- Wonder, curiosity, and fun are intentionally cultivated.
- Contributors seek best practices from outside their industry.
- New ideas are embraced and tested.
- Bureaucracy is minimized to protect engagement and efficiency.
- The perspective of new hires is actively sought out and valued.
- Collaboration occurs naturally.
- All team members have a clear sense of purpose.
- Tough talks are embraced as opportunities to grow and strengthen the team.
- Leaders seek to develop individual strengths, interests, and passions.

- Problems are framed as challenges and opportunities for growth rather than threats and obstacles.

All are encouraged to ask, "Even better if?"

The Novelty Strategy in a culture is not a nice-to-have. It's a must-have. I've mentioned the typical Hall of Famers who, for many reasons, did not innovate: Blackberry, Blockbuster, Sears, Kodak, etc.

Novelty has a bottom-line return. Just ask Amazon, Google, Zappos, Apple, Uber, Airbnb, and many other companies that have revolutionized their respective fields. Study the small businesses that had to innovate or die virtually overnight due to the pandemic. We saw heroic examples. Restaurants that changed their menus and expanded their outdoor seating, grocery stores that offered personal shopper services and home delivery, retailers that transitioned to online sales, consultants like us who provided virtual workshops at no cost, physicians who adopted telehealth, and personal service providers like salons that offered in-home services.

At the heart of the Novelty Strategy is the curiosity to ask, "What if?" and "Even better if?" followed by the courage to try something new.

| WITHOUT<br>THE NOVELTY STRATEGY | WITH<br>THE NOVELTY STRATEGY |
|---|---|
| • More talk than action<br>• Punish risk-taking<br>• View curiosity and fun as time wasters<br>• Do not look beyond their industry<br>• Late adopters<br>• High threat and low trust<br>• Driven by egos<br>• Committed to being right<br>• Silence new perspectives<br>• Have a "that-won't-work-here" approach<br>• Force collaboration<br>• Seek out like-minded people<br>• Believe they will always be relevant | • Walk the talk<br>• Encourage risk-taking<br>• Value curiosity and fun<br>• Seek best practices and ideas from other industries<br>• Early adopters<br>• Minimal bureaucracy<br>• Seek new perspectives<br>• Genuine collaboration<br>• Clear sense of purpose<br>• Challenge each other's ideas<br>• Continuously learn and develop<br>• Approach problems as challenges, not threats<br>• Continuously ask, "Even better if?" |

# BE A LEADER WORTH FOLLOWING

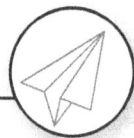

*How to live out the Novelty Strategy*

After more than thirty years of working with leaders and teams and studying the brain, learning, and behavior change, I'm convinced that beliefs, not actions, drive results. Actions alone are not enough. Real, sustainable change requires a shift in our beliefs. This is especially true when it comes to embracing and fostering anything new.

NAVIGATE TO RESOURCE

Beliefs Model: Video

## Shift

A few years ago, Nissan had a series of commercials that conveyed a powerful message with a single word: *shift*. The ads sold the concept of shifting...style, freedom, creativity, desire, evolution, and exhilaration. They wanted viewers to see Nissan as novel and different, and I loved the idea. Like Nissan's message, when it comes to implementing the impact of the Novelty Strategy, we simply need to shift.

If we want to unleash the potential of the Novelty Strategy, we must *shift* beliefs and behaviors.

Innovation and creativity are essential for generating solutions, products, and services that today's consumers need. Most organizations are in a whirlwind of change and increasing competition. Innovation and creativity are essential to meeting the demands of a rapidly changing, fiercely competitive world. Many companies incorporate innovation and creativity into their mission, vision, and value statements. But while it's easy to talk the talk, far fewer are willing or know how to walk the walk.

If novelty, and therefore creativity and innovation, are ever to become a reality, we need to evaluate the beliefs and behaviors that must shift. A culture's beliefs and behaviors can either awaken the brain and spark curiosity or threaten it and maintain the status quo. It is not technology alone that advances or hinders innovation; it is our beliefs and behaviors.

Novelty demands we...shift.

## Shift...from sick to healthy

First and foremost, novelty requires a healthy brain, a healthy body, and a healthy lifestyle. While this may sound basic, an organization seeking innovation must prioritize health.

American workers face multiple health obstacles. The Centers for Disease Control and Prevention reported that today's average American female weighs the same as the average male in the 1960s, and today's average American male weighs one and a half times what the average female weighed back then.[4] That's an 18.5% increase for women and a 17.6% increase for men. According to the study, 69% of adults over age 20 are either overweight or obese, as are nearly one-third of children between the ages of 10 and 17. Obesity increases the likelihood of heart disease, diabetes, strokes, and a host of other costly illnesses and life-limiting circumstances.

In addition to weight gain, Americans are growing in stress, overload, distraction, lack of sleep, and mental illness. Though Americans are using more of their vacation days than they did in previous years, they still leave more than 650 million days on the table, with women typically taking 10% fewer days than men.[5] Gallup's Life Evaluation Index indicates 58% of workers are "struggling," indicating a poor work-life balance and burnout.[6]

American workers suffer from email and technology addiction. One study found that American workers check their email a whopping 15 times daily, spending more than six hours doing it.[7] While the recommended amount of sleep for adults is 7-9 hours a night, 30% of American workers get under 6 hours. That percentage of sleep deprivation increases to 40% for those working a night shift.[8] To top it all off, at least 50% of adults will develop a mental illness in their lifetime.[9]

America has little "health" care because today's focus seems to be on providing "sick" care. Our nation is sick, our workplaces are sick, and our schools and homes are sick. Healthy bodies and brains are essential to healthy lives, healthy workplaces, and certainly to novelty.

This concept is not difficult, and it is sometimes not popular. Nonetheless, it is critical, especially when it comes to promoting innovation. Innovation requires a high-functioning brain, and a high-functioning brain is a healthy brain.

## ACTIONS

- Model a healthy life.
  - Healthy starts with you. Model a healthy lifestyle for your team, including workouts, nutrition, and self-care.
- Invest in health and wellness plans.
  - The characteristics of a healthy workplace plan are multidimensional. They begin with a baseline assessment and are supported by several solutions, ranging from healthy eating options in vending machines and the cafeteria to gym memberships to financial incentives for participating in health screenings and weight loss initiatives.
- Monitor work hours
  - While Elon Musk is rumored to work 120 hours a week and believes that 80-100 hours is necessary "to change the world," there does seem to be a point of diminishing returns. Productivity and hours worked have a direct correlation. According to a 2024 Stanford study conducted by economics professor John Pencavel, productivity drops significantly when a person works more than 50 hours per

week, and those working 70 hours a week aren't getting any more accomplished than those who put in 55.[10,11]

## Shift...from threat to trust

An organization that seeks innovation must have healthy individuals and a healthy culture.

If I could share with the world the greatest leadership choice that can ever be made, I would say to be proactive in minimizing threat and building trust.

In all my years studying how the brain learns, the most powerful message we all need to hear is that threat kills, steals, and destroys. It kills our ability to perform at our best. It steals from individuals the ability to reach their full potential. And it destroys organizations, preventing them from the engagement, passion, ownership, and innovation essential to surviving in a highly competitive, fast-paced world that is growing increasingly complex every day.

Negative threat, which we perceive as harmful, uncertain, and over which we have little control, damages the brain. Negative threat increases cortisol, which makes us more prone to illness and disease; diminishes the priceless functions of the PFC; compromises our ability to learn and remember; and even causes parts of the brain to shrink or die.

The brain is our greatest asset, the very equipment driving retention, engagement, survivability, profits, and innovation. Why, then, would we tolerate anything less than a brain-healthy culture? The priceless returns we crave, especially those of innovation, cannot exist and grow in a high-threat environment. Threat hijacks creativity, impairs judgment, and erodes trust. If we want breakthrough performance, we must stop normalizing brain-antagonistic cultures and build CRANIUM cultures where the brain and people flourish.

We cannot expect novelty (innovation and creativity) to happen in an inhospitable environment.

Culture precedes novelty. An optimal culture paves the way for true innovation and lasting results.

Let's talk about plants for a moment. I don't have a green thumb; I don't even have one living plant in my house. But plant experts say that some plants, like the snake plant, can grow anywhere and under almost any conditions. Other plants require particular conditions and attention. According to plant experts, the Boston Fern is the hardest indoor plant to grow and keep alive. The temperature must be just right, as does the amount of sunlight, the direction the plant faces the light, the amount and frequency of water, and fertilizer. The plant may even need a humidifier in the winter. But if you get those conditions right, it thrives.

The desired results require the right environment.

This analogy is appropriate to the Novelty Strategy. To grow novelty (creativity and innovation), we need to create the optimal environment, one of low threat and high trust.

In a high-trust environment, people feel safe exploring, sharing, experimenting, learning, failing, and growing. *How* someone does something matters as much as *what* they do. People and relationships are valued as much as bottom-line results and monetary returns. Leaders in high-trust organizations never lose sight of the fact that *people* are their most valuable resource. They know and live out the belief that their company is only as strong as its people.

Trust is a common denominator on Fortune's "100 Best Companies to Work For" list. In companies that make this list, employees trust management to inform them of important issues and changes with direct, transparent, and honest communication. Employees believe leadership is honest and ethical in business practices, delivers on promises, and consistently "walks the talk." Their employees are flourishing along with profits. Trust is the number one theme from the thousands of responses we've collected to our one-question survey, "What makes a leader worth following?"

The trust gap is growing. Most leaders overestimate how much their people trust them and how much their people feel trusted.

In a PricewaterhouseCoopers study, 93% of business executives agree that building and maintaining trust improves the bottom line, and 86% of those business executives reported high employee trust in leadership.[12] Only 67% of these executives' employees highly trusted their leader. In that same study, 86% of executives say they highly trust their employees, but only 60% of employees feel highly trusted. A great example of how leaders can intend one thing, but the team experiences something quite different. A 2024 Gallup study revealed that only 23% of US employees strongly agree that they trust their leaders.[13]

So, while there doesn't seem to be a problem in realizing the importance of trust, there does seem to be a problem in recognizing how wide the gap is and how to close it.

---

**ACTIONS**

- Minimize negative threat.
  - Review the top ten threats and strategies for minimizing those threats discussed in the Challenge Strategy.

- Trust starts with you.
  - Trust yourself. You didn't achieve your success by accident. And if you are reading this, you are 100% successful in making it through tough days. Your inner sense of knowing has developed over time through experience. Trust it.
  - Trust others. Don't wait for other people to earn your trust. Be proactive in taking actions that earn the trust of others.

## NAVIGATE TO RESOURCE
25 Simple Trust-Building Actions: PDF

## Shift...from busy to breathe

As mentioned earlier, your calendar tells the story. Are your days stacked with back-to-back meetings? The likelihood of innovation is low with a calendar that looks like a jar of jellybeans.

Packed schedules often result in busy, shallow work. As the Action Strategy reveals, the brain's output, unlike a machine's output, can rarely be made cheaper, better, faster.

The brain needs a balance of focus and reflection.

Brain waves, patterns of electrical activity in the brain, correspond to different mental states. You can remember the main brainwaves by using the mnemonic BATD. Beta is the brain wave associated with a focused, active mental state during cognitively demanding tasks. Alpha is the brain wave for relaxed, daydreaming reflection, and Theta is the brain wave when we enter light sleep. Both are optimal for reflection, finding innovative solutions to problems, and generating ideas. Delta is the brain wave we experience during deep sleep, and it is the ideal time for our brain to process information received throughout the day.

Our brain needs the cycle of brain waves. It cannot stay in Beta all day. Our brain needs time and space to breathe, and it simply won't get that if each day is a hustle and grind, hopping from one meeting to the next.

Many studies have shown that allowing people to block time on their schedule to think can increase productivity, even with a four-day workweek.[14] The amount of time that should be spent in meetings depends on several variables, including the quality of the meeting. Rogelberg draws on survey data and organizational research to offer evidence-based recommendations for effective meeting practices. Among his findings, professionals should spend no more than 25% of their working hours in meetings to sustain productivity. For leaders, meeting time should not exceed 50% of their work schedule.[15]

Taking time to stand, breathe, and move supports the natural brainwave cycle and resets neural rhythm. Standing for 10-15 minutes increases oxygen and blood flow to the brain, gently shifting it from high beta (stress) into mid or low beta (focused and alert). A brisk 30-minute walk activates alpha and theta waves, which enhance creativity, idea generation, and problem-solving. Movement can also help release stuck energy if we are in a hyper-aroused beta state. Intentional breathing slows the heart rate and stimulates the parasympathetic nervous system, encouraging a transition from beta to alpha waves—a calm yet alert state that is optimal for learning and creativity.

- Set a reminder.
  - Set reminders throughout the day to stand, stretch, and breathe. Even better if...you move outdoors and integrate a 20–30-minute walk or workout.
- Audit your calendar.
  - Review how you are spending your time using the Eisenhower Matrix tool discussed in the Action Strategy.
- Evaluate the quality of your meetings.
  - Are they organized?
  - Is there an agenda?
  - Do they start and end on time?
  - Should someone else be facilitating or attending them?
  - Could the outcomes be accomplished through an email or a quick video?

## NAVIGATE TO RESOURCE

Effective Meeting Tips: PDF

## Shift...from weaknesses to strengths

While focusing on strengths has gained greater acceptance over the last several years, our culture remains fixated on closing gaps. We test little Johnny at an early age to identify his weaknesses, often assigning him a diagnosis and adjusting our expectations of him accordingly. Throughout Johnny's childhood, we continue to focus on closing his gaps, testing him regularly to ensure they are still there. Johnny will likely be exposed to that same deficit-focused mentality when he participates in sports, attends church, and attempts to please his family and friends. When Johnny enters his career, he faces the annual performance review, during which his manager will continue to help him identify his ongoing gaps.

I'm not saying we should never work to improve where we are not strong. We can; that's the beauty of neuroplasticity. But we kill the human spirit when the norm is focusing on gaps and improving in the things we struggle at, don't enjoy, and aren't gifted to do.

One poignant example of this is the fable, "The Animal School," written in 1940 (long before brain imaging) by George Reavis, superintendent of the Cincinnati Public Schools:

> *Once upon a time the animals decided they must do something heroic to meet the problems of a "new world" so they organized a school. They had adopted an activity curriculum consisting of running, climbing, swimming and flying. To make it easier to administer the curriculum, all the animals took all the subjects. The duck was excellent in swimming. In fact, better than his instructor. But he made only passing grades in flying and was very poor in running. Since he was slow in running, he had to stay after school and also drop swimming in order to practice running. This was kept up until his webbed feet were badly worn and he was only average in swimming. But average was acceptable in school so nobody worried about that, except the duck. The rabbit started at the top of the class in running but had a nervous breakdown because of so much makeup work in swimming. The squirrel was excellent in climbing until he developed frustration in the flying class where his teacher made him start from the ground up instead of the*

*treetop down. He also developed a "charlie horse" from overexertion and then got a C in climbing and D in running. The eagle was a problem child and was disciplined severely. In the climbing class, he beat all the others to the top of the tree but insisted on using his own way to get there. At the end of the year, an abnormal eel that could swim exceedingly well and also run, climb and fly a little had the highest average and was valedictorian. The prairie dogs stayed out of school and fought the tax levy because the administration would not add digging and burrowing to the curriculum. They apprenticed their children to a badger and later joined the groundhogs and gophers to start a successful private school.*

It seems absurd to set up a school that punishes students for obvious weaknesses at the expense of developing their obvious strengths. And yet, doesn't that look a lot like our current learning environments? It seems ludicrous to put people in jobs that aren't the right fit and then evaluate and compensate them for accomplishing tasks they never had a propensity or passion for in the first place. And yet, doesn't that look a lot like our current work environments?

If we want to reap the rewards of novelty, such as innovation, creativity, and peak performance, we must stop the trend of closing gaps and shift to finding strengths. In "The Animal School," if the focus had shifted to strengths, the rabbit would have avoided a nervous breakdown and years of counseling that most likely ensued, and the duck may have gone on to establish an international swimming school and mentor thousands of troubled ducklings.

Organizations that identify and build on strengths enjoy better results with less effort. A Gallup study found that organizations with leadership that focused on strengths enjoyed 73% engagement, as opposed to 9% engagement at those organizations where leaders ignored strengths.[16] Engaged employees are not only happy, but they are also contributors who are loyal, more productive, quicker to learn new roles, and more creative and innovative. In addition, they cause fewer problems and stir up less drama.

Shifting from weaknesses to strengths is an inexpensive leadership tool that elicits an immeasurable impact on both the individual and the organization.

## ACTIONS

- Hold strengths-discovery conversations (SDC)
  - As explained in the Relevance Strategy, an SDC is a private 1:1 conversation you have with each team member about their strengths, interests, experiences, and aspirations.
  - These conversations are helpful even if you "think" you know everything about your team members. When we ask different questions, we find new and valuable information about what matters most to each team member.

### NAVIGATE TO RESOURCE

Strengths-Discovery Conversation: PDF

- Delegate based on interests and strengths
  - Delegation is the optimal way to develop talent. However, we must set our team members up for success by matching the delegation task and

approach to the individual's strengths, interests, and capacity.

### NAVIGATE TO RESOURCE

The Ultimate Checklist for Effective Delegation: Course and PDF

- Give freedom to explore and experiment
  - Give freedom to explore new ideas and try new approaches.
  - Other companies have implemented similar policies, such as Google's 20% Time policy, which allows employees to use 20% of their time to pursue personal interests. A company we partner with honors meeting-free Fridays for the same purpose.

## Shift…from confusion to clarity

Just like the brain craves novelty, it also craves clarity and knowing the *why*. This is one of the first questions children ask: "Why, Mama? Why, Daddy?" And the hunger for the answer seems to haunt us from cradle to grave.

We all crave purpose, meaning, and fulfillment, and often spend much of our lives in pursuit of the why. Knowing the why is critical to all 7 CRANIUM Strategies, especially novelty. People are motivated and inspired to think bigger, deeper, forward, and differently when there is a clear, motivating purpose and a clear sense of what winning looks like (WWLL). Clarity in expectations and purpose activates the prefrontal cortex; confusion shuts it down.

We improve performance and buy-in when we are clear on the "why" and the "win" or vision.

One example is NASA's Apollo 13 mission. The mission's goal was clear: to safely land a man on the moon. When unexpected problems happened, the goal abruptly changed to get the astronauts safely home.[17]

Having a clear vision encouraged immediate innovation and engagement.

Years later, another NASA initiative had a clear goal: to reduce the weight of the tanks to increase payload capacity and efficiency. With that clarity in mind, one of the engineers had the novel idea to test if the paint on the tank was necessary for protection. When it was discovered that this wasn't the case, they stopped painting the tanks, freeing up another 600 pounds.[18]

Communicating a clear "win" applies to every endeavor.

Erik Weihenmayer and his team climbed Mount Everest. Erik was the first person to climb the world's tallest peak, blind.

They had a clear win (get Erik to the top of the mountain) and a clear why (to model living a life without limits). This team's heart and passion for innovation are inspiring. Confusion was widespread due to the uncontrollable variables that any team faces when climbing Everest. However, because there was absolute clarity in the end goal and the why, they collaboratively thought deeper, bigger, forward, and differently throughout the climb. They changed communication systems, adapted to adverse circumstances such as sickness and weather, and adjusted approaches in the moment. The result of their constant innovation? The entire team, including Erik, reached the summit.[19]

- What is the WWLL? (What Winning Looks Like)
  - What does winning look like in a project you are currently leading? Or in your company? Communicate the WWLL so everyone is clear on what success looks like.
- What is the why?
  - What is the "why" of a project you are currently leading? Or in your company? Communicate a compelling "why" so threat decreases, PFC activity increases, and innovation is set up for success.

## Shift...from despair to hope

Once you provide a clear vision and clear why, lead with confidence and inspiration so the team has no doubt it can and will be done. Trust and believe in yourself.

Several years ago, I saw a powerful example of this with one of the healthcare organizations we support. While healthcare always faces external challenges, this was a particularly uncertain time in our nation's history for the healthcare industry. Leaders in this field were confused, stressed, and stuck.

I attended a town hall for healthcare leaders to share ideas and strategies on navigating these uncertainties. One leader after another stood at the podium before a crowd eager for answers and delivered a despairing message: "We will just have to wait and see what Washington does."

Except for one leader.

When this leader's turn came, he adjusted the mic and emphatically stated, "I represent the XYZ health system, and we aren't waiting on Washington." The crowd broke out in applause. He laid out a plan for how the system would continue and adjust, explaining how these adjustments would likely impact and benefit local business owners and individuals, as well as how others could get involved. He operated with the same unknowns as every other healthcare leader in the room that night.

The difference was his ability to shift. He shifted his focus from despair to hope. He clearly stated his vision and explained why, giving people the confidence they needed.

This same strategy saved a team I was on early in my career from a significant layoff.

I worked for a defense company that was acquired by a global organization. Restructuring and layoffs were inevitable. Rumors were flying, and people were scrambling to update resumes and rebuild long-neglected networks. Most leaders were paralyzed and took the 'wait and see' approach.

Our leader called our team together, as we were clearly on the verge of being cut. She directly addressed the grim reality of the situation, then shared her inspiring vision and why for our team: "This is our current reality, and this is what we want our reality to be. Let's create a plan on how to do it." We did.

Enthusiastically, the team collaborated to determine novel ways and ideas that would help us get the win. In the end, not a single team member was cut, and through the purchase, our leader successfully positioned our services as vital to the company's new direction.

As an executive leadership coach, I partner with clients who are facing some degree of uncertainty and confusion. Most of the time, we work together to navigate uncertainty. They may be making or experiencing a change, trying to solve a problem or make a decision, leading a team, etc. They are seeking clarity and a path forward. Threat looms when there is a perception of confusion, limited control, and anticipated adverse consequences.

An effective coach meets people where they are (which is often a state of despair), helps them clearly state where they want to go, and then assists them in moving forward, ideally to take action. When we can shift that despair to hope by assisting the client in identifying what winning looks like and the bigger why, an unlimited number of creative and innovative options suddenly become available.

Lisa is a past client in a director role who wanted to move into a VP role. Her counterpart was offered the VP position only a few weeks into our coaching. Despair. By thinking bigger, she identified what her goal was and her why. This shift to hope and forward thinking allowed her brain to move out of threat mode, where the focus becomes the problem, and into possibility mode, activating the prefrontal cortex, where multiple solutions become accessible. Today, she is the CEO.

## ACTIONS

- Create a Stuck to Success Continuum
  - The fastest way out of stuck is to generate options. When feeling despair, draw a continuum. On one end, write Stuck. Describe reality, including what you are feeling, thinking, seeing, and projecting.
  - On the other end, write Success. Describe what winning looks like and why it matters.
  - In the middle, brainstorm all possible solutions that can move you from the Stuck State to the Success State.
  - Don't judge any of the ideas; write out as many as you can. Keep asking "and what else?," "even better if?" and "yes...and."

- Generate options
  - When the brain is under threat (feeling despair), it's hard for us to see options because our PFC is compromised. Our brain goes into a narrow tunnel. The quickest way to reactivate the PFC and move out of the tunnel is to generate more and more options by asking, "and what else?," "even better if?" and "yes… and."

---

### NAVIGATE TO RESOURCE

Stuck to Success Continuum: Video and PDF

---

## Shift…from silos to collaboration

Innovation seldom happens in isolation. Innovation is not a solo act.

Our belief that innovation is a single Eureka moment is often portrayed in cinema. We've all seen movies with the mad scientist in a basement on a dark and stormy night or Chuck Noland in *Cast Away* stranded on an uninhabited island. However, in real life, innovation often requires collaboration with others, particularly those who think differently from us.

Most real-life examples of innovation occur when people with diverse skills, thought processes, perspectives, life experiences, and approaches come together to create something greater than anyone could have achieved on their own. For example, in 1969, the Apollo 11 mission, which successfully landed two people on the moon, resulted from the efforts, talents, and expertise of approximately 400,000 people.[20] Organizations, work teams, and individuals who reap the most significant benefits from novelty are those who seek out and value differences.

The digital age has provided us with more tools for collaboration than we can comprehend, along with access to the talents of anyone, anywhere in the world. Freelancers have access to multiple platforms to showcase their skills and find projects. Entrepreneurs can leverage the power of sites such as Etsy, Pinterest, Craigslist, and eBay. Small business owners can level up with powerhouses such as Amazon. We have crowdfunding platforms, shared workspaces, shared living spaces, and more social media outlets and groups than I could begin to list here. There are more forming even as I write.

One gift of collaboration is that the whole is greater than the sum of the parts. However, a second (and perhaps more powerful) gift of collaboration is a sense of ownership. When we are involved in creating, we have a piece of ownership and accountability. This fuels emotion, engagement, and commitment.

The most significant barrier to the collaboration required for novelty is not the lack of tools and technology. The most significant barrier to overcome is the human factor, specifically changing familiar beliefs.

To leverage differences, we must first value them. Valuing differences means moving past our biases, both conscious and unconscious.

Collaboration is an issue of trust; to truly accomplish it, we must trust each other and the process. It is also an issue of communication, requiring that we communicate with extreme clarity and in continuous, calculated ways. Finally, collaboration is a matter of unconditional positive regard and inclusion.

Genuine collaboration occurs when we wholeheartedly embrace and truly value the backgrounds, experiences, opinions, skills, cultures, and perspectives of people who are different, sometimes drastically different, from ourselves. Without a doubt, collaboration is a highly sophisticated ability. If we want to harness the power of novelty, our actions, behaviors, and beliefs must shift from solitary to collaborative.

## ACTIONS

- Create a Perspective Wheel
  - Place the problem to be solved in the center of the wheel. What perspectives are necessary to gain a 360-degree view of the problem and the solution? What stakeholders should be involved in the process?
  - Create a spoke on the wheel for each of those perspectives.
- Become diversity aware
  - Review the perspectives that are listed on the wheel. Continue to ask, "What perspectives are missing? And, do all perspectives have equal representation?
- Become participation aware
  - Are all voices heard? Is there a pattern of certain perspectives dominating others? Don't assume; ask. And keep asking throughout the process.
- Track participation
  - Write out the contributors' names during meetings or keep the perspectives wheel available. Place a tick mark beside names each time that person speaks or is referenced. If you are recording meetings through virtual platforms, review the transcript to identify who spoke and

**NAVIGATE TO RESOURCE**

Perspectives Wheel: Template

> who didn't. Continuously evaluate to ensure all per-
> spectives are seen and heard.

## Shift...from idea to implementation

A great idea doesn't sell itself.

A new idea is one thing; getting people to adopt the new idea is another. We need stakeholder buy-in. Innovation means change. Change means uncertainty. Uncertainty means threat. Threat means resistance. Expect it and plan for it.

When we involve people in the novelty process, we have greater buy-in and less resistance.

In our leadership workshops, we run a fun but powerful and competitive simulation in which teams are given an innovative idea and compete to see which team can get enough stake-holder buy-in for the simulated company to adopt the idea.

In just 90 minutes, the simulation teaches powerful lessons about influencing stakeholders, lessons that might other-wise take years to learn through costly mistakes and frustrat-ing setbacks.

The simulation incorporates the Diffusion of Innovation Theory (DOI), developed by E.M. Rogers in 1962.[21] This theory pro-vides valuable insight into how new ideas and technologies are adopted (or stalled) in organizations.

The DOI alerts us to four very important factors leaders of inno-vation need to be mindful of:

> **The innovation itself.** How impactful is the innova-tion? Is it a vitamin (a nice-to-have) with longer-term payoff? Or, is it a painkiller (a must-have) with imme-diate payoff? Does it connect with people's WIIFM

(What's In It For Me)? How does it move the intended user from pain island to pleasure island?

**The communication channels.** What is the communication plan for each stakeholder? How will the information about the innovation spread?

**The social system.** Does it align with the cultural norms and beliefs? Does it challenge them? Is it sustainable in the culture? Does leadership support it, and are they committed to the project's duration?

**The time factor.** How long will it take for people to adopt the idea? Should the innovation be phased in? What kind of adopters are your stakeholders?

The DOI also warns us that there are specific kinds of adopters:

**Innovators**: Innovators are those who quickly and easily adopt any innovation. They will camp in the parking lot to buy a new phone. According to Rogers, innovators comprise less than 3% of the average population. But it's worthwhile to find those 3% because they can help get the momentum going.

**Early adopters:** Although not as eager and risk-seeking as innovators, early adopters have little resistance. They may pre-order the phone. DOI predicts that this group accounts for approximately 14% of the population. Targeting this group is wise, particularly if it includes key decision makers and influencers.

**Early Majority:** The early majority, roughly 34% of an average population, is the group that uses a little more caution and needs a few more answers than the early adopters, but they don't want to miss out.

They will buy the new phone a month or two after its release to ensure all the bugs have been worked out.

**Late Majority:** The late majority, also roughly 34% of the average population, are those who use even more caution and require more time and information. They buy the phone just before the next version is released.

**Laggards or Resistors:** Approximately 16% of the population will adopt innovation only when it is necessary or mandatory. They will buy a new phone when their existing phone breaks or is no longer supported.

One of my favorite examples of mindfully implementing innovation is discussed in *The Power of Habit: Why We Do What We Do in Life and Business.* [22] The story is about the product Febreze, which was first advertised as an odor eliminator. This now billion-dollar product initially struggled. People resisted the product because it required a change in their beliefs and a change in their habits. It was unfamiliar.

There was no similar product on the market to compare it to, so the concept was foreign. It also challenged a long-held belief: my house has no odor. If no one believed their house had an odor, there was no market for an odor eliminator.

After repeated failed attempts at messaging and marketing, the product gained traction after the team got the four factors right (the innovation, the communication channels, the social system, and the time factor) and enlisted innovators and early adopters.

Febreze took off when Procter & Gamble repositioned the odor eliminator as a source of fresh, clean scent. Consumers were encouraged to use it to integrate into their cleaning process.

Febreze was positioned as the final step, spraying a satisfying spritz over a clean room. Brilliant. Instead of challenging existing beliefs and habits, Febreze built on them. And as a bonus, that burst of freshness delivered a rewarding hit of dopamine satisfaction to the consumer's brain.

## ACTIONS

- Map your stakeholders
  - Stakeholder mapping is a concept introduced by R. Edward Freeman in his book *Strategic Management: A Stakeholder Approach* as a framework for ensuring a strategic approach to managing the interests and needs of any person or group impacted by an initiative, especially one that involves change.[23]
  - There are many variations available, differing in complexity. We use a simple model inspired by Mendelow's Matrix.[24]

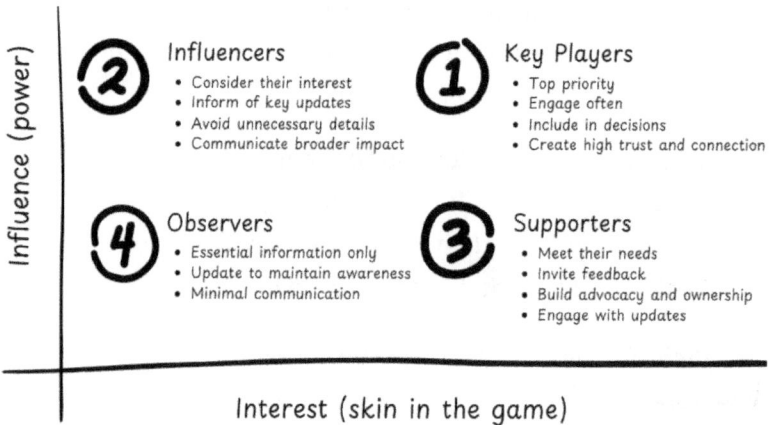

Influence (power)

**② Influencers**
- Consider their interest
- Inform of key updates
- Avoid unnecessary details
- Communicate broader impact

**① Key Players**
- Top priority
- Engage often
- Include in decisions
- Create high trust and connection

**④ Observers**
- Essential information only
- Update to maintain awareness
- Minimal communication

**③ Supporters**
- Meet their needs
- Invite feedback
- Build advocacy and ownership
- Engage with updates

Interest (skin in the game)

### NAVIGATE TO RESOURCE
Stakeholder Mapping Made Simple: Video and PDF

- Compare with the Perspectives Wheel
  - Stakeholder mapping is a method to ensure that the Perspectives Wheel encompasses everyone involved in and affected by an initiative.

## Shift...from grand to granular

Just a few more necessary shifts before we leave the Novelty Strategy.

Although exceptions exist, novelty (in the form of innovation and creativity) is rarely a grand, world-changing idea or a wildly new initiative. It's typically about small nudges or tweaks to the everyday tasks.

Dallas-Fort Worth International Airport, the third busiest airport in the world, recognizes the impact of minor improvements, empowering all its employees to be everyday innovators. They have found that the return on innovation is in the small efforts each person makes daily.

### ACTIONS

- Even better if?
  - When things are going well, ask the magic question, "Even better if?" When things are time-consuming or frustrating, ask, "Even better if?" If someone tells you, "Great job!" Ask, "Even better if?" At the end of meetings, tasks, and projects, keep asking, "Even better if?"

## Shift...from ego to exploration

If you, as a leader, must be the smartest person in the room, if you must have the first word and the final word, you will never see the fruits of the Novelty Strategy.

Innovation is change. Change is uncertainty, and therefore, threat. Threat compromises the brain.

Don't compound threat with your ego, the need to be right, and the need to take credit.

Avinash Kaushik's 2007 book *Web Analytics: An Hour a Day* introduced the term HiPPO (the Highest Paid Person's Opinion). Just as a real hippopotamus can kill a person, the HiPPO can kill a great idea.[25]

His findings support what we have all likely experienced. The HiPPO can overpower decision-making, buzz kill a great brainstorming session, and intimidate others, so it isn't safe to question or bring new ideas to the table.

---

### ACTIONS

- Speak less, speak last.
  - If you are the HiPPO, speak less than anyone and speak last when ideas are brewing. When possible, have others facilitate so you can be an equal participant.
- Be more interestED than interestING.
  - If you always have the answers, you stunt your team's growth and lose their trust. Stay curious. Ask generative questions that begin with "how" or "who" instead of leadersplaining.
- Give credit.
  - John Wooden, one of the greatest coaches in history, was often asked how he achieved his winning record. He would always answer that he didn't get those wins; his players did.
  - Allow your team to shine. Like John Wooden, a successful team is a leader's greatest legacy.

> ○ Suspend the need to be right, take credit, or be in control. Seek, instead, opportunities to encourage, reward, and recognize.

## Shift...from certainty to curiosity

Many leaders we work with have a disease we call FOBU. Fear of Being Uncertain. Uncertainty and the unknown can trigger our brains to create all sorts of meanings and crazy stories, threat ensues, and we become the worst version of ourselves.

Truthfully, curiosity is the best state for learning, exploring, creativity, innovation, and collaboration. Curiosity didn't kill the cat; certainty did.

Embrace that novelty (innovation and creativity) is all about the unknown and the uncertain. If you're committed to certainty, you forfeit the benefits of novelty.

### ACTIONS

- Face your FOBU.
  - ○ What does uncertainty mean to you?
  - ○ How would other people describe your relationship to the unknown?
  - ○ Where are you resisting something because of a lack of certainty?
  - ○ How can you mitigate your fears of the unknown and uncertainty?
- See leadership as a series of micro experiments.
  - ○ We hold free monthly sessions, which we call the LEADing Lab. The idea is to come together once a month to learn and experiment with new ideas. We believe leaders are researchers who must

continually create hypotheses, test them, learn, and adapt based on what they discover.

## NAVIGATE TO RESOURCE

Monthly LEADing Lab Mastermind

# FINAL THOUGHTS ON THE NOVELTY STRATEGY

As the saying goes, "It is not the strongest or the most intelligent who will survive, but those who can best manage change."

Along the same line, the companies and schools that will survive and win will not necessarily be the ones with the most funding or the best technology; they will be those that change and adapt more quickly than their competitors. They will be those who invest in their people and their culture. They will be those where it is celebrated to "nudge and alter," go deeper, think forward, and disrupt patterns to create new possibilities.

# WHAT MAKES A LEADER WORTH FOLLOWING?

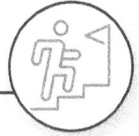

*We asked real people. We got real responses.*

Here are just a few. Would anyone say the same about you?

✔ *A leader needs to be in the front, working towards the change they want to see. They need to be dependable, reasonable, and get results.*

✔ *Someone who challenges the uncertainty in difficult situations and inspires others to achieve greatness in difficult situations.*

✔ *Willingness to listen and support the team. Showing appreciation and occasionally getting in the trenches to see what the challenges are and areas of opportunity without being asked to do so after a problem has been submitted to solve.*

✔ *Continuous learning and professional curiosity, and empathetic care of people.*

✔ *Someone who works hard to perfect their craft, someone who is willing to follow standards and push others around them while pushing themselves.*

# THINK. DISCUSS. APPLY.

*Make it matter*

1. How do you respond when faced with uncertainty? What are the beliefs or actions you can take to address your FOBU (Fear Of Being Uncertain)?
2. List three opportunities for you and your team to innovate. Where can you ask, "Even better if?"
3. In your experience, what interferes with novelty? How can you reduce the interference?
4. Rate how frequently you do the following?

As a leader I...

|  | Almost Never | | | | Almost Always |
|---|---|---|---|---|---|
| 1. Make time for fun. | 1 | 2 | 3 | 4 | 5 |
| 2. Allow team members to think differently without repercussion. | 1 | 2 | 3 | 4 | 5 |
| 3. Value all team members' ideas and opinions. | 1 | 2 | 3 | 4 | 5 |
| 4. Take the time to think strategically about what's next. | 1 | 2 | 3 | 4 | 5 |
| 5. Ensure my team is well positioned for the future. | 1 | 2 | 3 | 4 | 5 |
| 6. Invest in my and my team's professional development. | 1 | 2 | 3 | 4 | 5 |
| 7. Continuously seek to bring in new practices from different industries. | 1 | 2 | 3 | 4 | 5 |
| 8. Clearly communicate with the team. | 1 | 2 | 3 | 4 | 5 |
| 9. Recognize and effectively address conflict. | 1 | 2 | 3 | 4 | 5 |
| 10. Build on the strengths of each team member. | 1 | 2 | 3 | 4 | 5 |
| 11. Give team members continuous, real-time feedback. | 1 | 2 | 3 | 4 | 5 |
| 12. Consistently reward and recognize. | 1 | 2 | 3 | 4 | 5 |
| 13. Don't have to be right. | 1 | 2 | 3 | 4 | 5 |
| 14. Involve people in decisions that affect them. | 1 | 2 | 3 | 4 | 5 |
| 15. Seek feedback from others on how I can improve. | 1 | 2 | 3 | 4 | 5 |
| 16. See opportunities where others see setbacks. | 1 | 2 | 3 | 4 | 5 |

## CHALLENGE CONVENTION.
## NUDGE IMAGINATION.

Curiosity didn't kill the cat.
Certainty did.

### Shift...from

- Shift...from sick to healthy
- Shift...from threat to trust
- Shift...from busy to breathe
- Shift...from weaknesses to strengths
- Shift...from confusion to clarity
- Shift...from despair to hope
- Shift...from silos to collaboration
- Shift...from idea to implementation
- Shift...from grand to granular
- Shift...from ego to exploration
- Shift...from certainty to curiosity

- The word create means "to bring into existence."
- The word innovate means "to nudge or alter."
- The word novelty means "new."

FOBU
*Fear of Being Uncertain*

**CAUTION:
NOVELTY MEANS | RISK**

The brain doesn't pay attention to boring things.
**If the brain is bored; it's ignored.**

Novelty isn't a "nice to have."
It's a "must-have."

### Your Brain on Novelty:

NOVELTY: wakes up the brain.
engages emotion.
transforms routine moments into
motivates the brain.
lowers negative threat.
enhances performance.
increases dopamine.
rewards the brain.
releases a flow cocktail.
impacts neuroplasticity.

memorable
experiences.

The Magic Question:
## Even better if?

# CHAPTER 5

# The Interaction Strategy

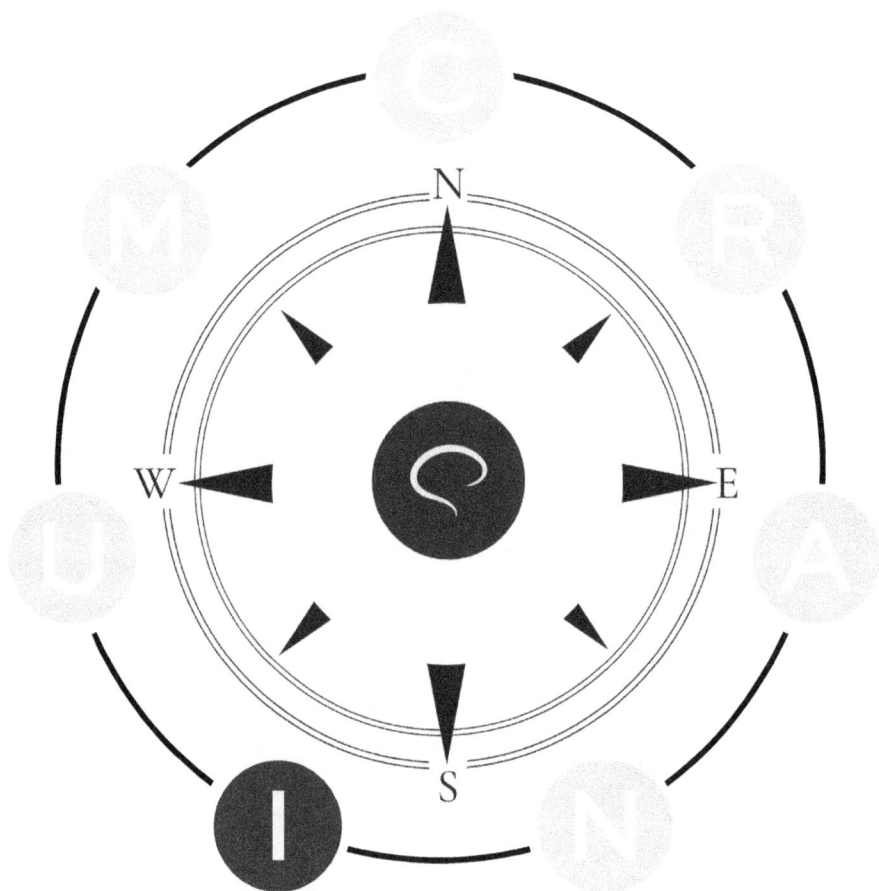

**GIVE CHOICE AND VOICE.
LET GO AND GROW.**

## BIG IDEA

When we stop telling and start involving, we turn compliance into commitment and scale capacity—in ourselves, our teams, and our organizations.

## BREAKTHROUGH BELIEFS

You can have control, or you can have growth. But you can't have both in equal proportion at the same time.

Just because you CAN do it yourself doesn't mean you SHOULD.

Be more interestED than interestING.

# REAL LEADERS. REAL LIFE.

*Be lazy. Stay curious.*

"I can't stay here anymore. I've made a huge mistake." That's how Laura began her Thursday morning coaching session.

Laura, a confident research manager, had recently accepted a director role at a new healthcare system. It meant relocating, overseeing 80 employees, and stepping far outside her comfort zone.

Just thirty days in, Laura felt overwhelmed. The teams she inherited came from three separate mergers and refused to collaborate. They physically sat in separate sections, missed work without notice, and failed to complete assignments. Laura spent her days mediating conflicts and solving problems. She wasn't sleeping and was battling headaches. But worst of all, she felt like a failure.

She hired a professional coach.

Her coach listened calmly and asked, "Out of all these challenges, which would you like to focus on?"

"I'm tired of feeling like the parent of rebellious children," Laura replied. "All I do is fix everyone's problems."

"What's the impact of that?" the coach asked.

"I'm exhausted and resentful," she admitted. "It's keeping me from doing what I love—leading research."

"And what's the impact on your team?"

"They've come to rely on me to fix everything," she said. "One research manager came to me three times in one day."

"So what other approaches could you take?" the coach prompted.

Laura paused. "I could've told her to speak to the team member herself...or find a mentor...or simply asked her what she thought we should do."

"Which of those feels best now?"

"The last one," Laura said, laughing. "She's a seasoned manager. She's capable. Handing the problem back to her would show I trust her—and help her grow."

"And if you shifted from solving to asking?" her coach asked.

"I'd sleep better. My headaches might stop. And I'd finally get back to what I was hired to do. I've probably sent the message that I don't trust them."

Her coach asked, "What are your next steps?"

"The next time someone brings me a problem, I'll pause, ask questions, and support them in finding their own solution."

"And how do you feel now?"

Laura smiled. "Relieved—and excited. Like a weight's been lifted."

# YOU'RE WIRED FOR INTERACTION

*Why your brain thrives on the Interaction Strategy*

The Interaction Strategy facilitates high-performance results because it aligns with how the brain functions most effectively. It's a simple plan, really. Work with how the brain works best and enjoy consistently better results, often faster and easier.

Learning is rarely a spectator sport. I may learn from watching if someone places their hand on an open flame and gets burned. But overall, transformational learning requires effort, time, and trial and error. I can't watch you lift weights at the gym and expect my body to transform. And, you can't lift the weights for me and expect transformation in me. I must pick up the weights and put in the reps.

Reflect for a moment on your own transformational learning experiences, those experiences that involved exponential and sustainable learning, change, and growth. What moments on the timeline of your life have made the most profound differences in your intellectual and emotional development? My guess is it wasn't the times when you were sitting in a classroom, observing a demonstration, or told precisely what to do and how to do it. They are likely the times when someone trusted you with an assignment, you struggled with the unknown, and you came out on the other side wiser.

In this section, let's examine why interaction is necessary for true transformational learning and growth. Let's uncover how leaders miss big opportunities to grow their internal talent and their individual capacity, and why companies waste their time and dollars on "one-and-done" development programs that don't stick. Let's see what the brain requires for real, lasting change.

**DID YOU KNOW?**

On average, US companies spend just over 100B annually on training.[1]

If we want to inspire, empower, and maximize our most precious (and expensive) resource—our people—we must focus on the Interaction Strategy. Four key areas from brain research reinforce the significance of this CRANIUM Strategy: it empowers and builds trust, it is necessary for long-term behavior change, it accelerates learning and memory, and it is the primary way for leaders to develop others and scale results.

## Building Trust

When it comes to maximizing the brain's performance, the importance of creating an environment of trust (or psychological safety) cannot be overemphasized. Interaction is essential in building trust.

The brain may welcome being told what to do in a crisis or when first learning a skill. If the building is on fire, I welcome someone taking charge and telling me the fastest way out. Or, if I've never hit a golf ball, I welcome someone telling me how to stand and hold the club.

Outside of a crisis or new learning, the brain pushes back when told what to do.

Telling is not optimal if we aim to develop advanced thinking skills, empower, grow, and inspire ownership.

As established in previous chapters, our brains are compromised under negative threat. Negative threat typically involves three characteristics: confusion and uncertainty, an anticipated adverse consequence, and little choice or control. When those characteristics exist, our brain is hijacked by negative threat. It cripples our ability to think strategically, synthesize new information with existing information, see from different perspectives, stay fluid and adaptable, and find new and different ways to solve problems.

The Interaction Strategy minimizes, if not alleviates, all three characteristics that spur negative threats. By intentionally being interactive, we involve rather than tell. When we engage by asking thoughtful, generative questions, we connect with others through meaningful conversation and collaboration. We seek and value others' opinions, ideas, and insight. We are purposeful in being more interestED than interestING. As a result, we lower negative threat and build trust.

The brain doesn't buy into what it's told to do; the brain buys into what it helps build. When the brain is told what to do, it resists and shuts down. There is a lack of ownership and buy-in. However, when people are respected partners in discovering solutions to problems or making decisions, the brain sees "challenge" rather than "threat." Involvement through interaction sparks curiosity, a sense of value, and increases responsibility, ownership, and accountability.

Interaction also has a critical chemical component. When we tell, control, and strip others of choice, we induce negative threat, elevating the stress hormones cortisol, adrenaline, and nor-adrenaline. These hormones impact memory, sleep, the immune system, and our ability to see options and think creatively.

When we involve, respect, and collaborate, we elevate chemicals such as dopamine, serotonin, and oxytocin. Dopamine increases motivation, heightens focus and drive, and rewards the brain. Serotonin improves mood, reduces anxiety, enhances impulse control, and gives the brain a sense of well-being and confidence. Oxytocin increases bonding and cooperation, promotes loyalty and connection, and reduces stress.

The chapter on the Challenge Strategy lists the ten most common negative threats in the workplace. These everyday situations are those most likely to cause people to perceive confusion, predict a negative outcome, and feel a loss of agency. The Interaction Strategy significantly reduces each of these threat situations by involving people, welcoming and valuing their input, and giving them a sense of control. The result? Trust over threat.

| Interaction lowers the threat of | | by providing |
|---|---|---|
| Social rejection | ⟶ | a genuine sense of belonging. |
| Low trust | ⟶ | participation in the process. |
| Change | ⟶ | clarity on the "what" and the "why" behind the change. |
| Unclear expectations | ⟶ | an opportunity to get clear on what winning looks like. |
| Lack of resources | ⟶ | a chance to ask early on for what is needed to be successful. |
| Risk of loss | ⟶ | a voice to take a stand for what is important. |
| Humiliation | ⟶ | a feeling of equality and respect. |
| Micromanaging | ⟶ | ownership of tasks and decisions. |
| Favoritism | ⟶ | an equal chance for everyone. |
| Lack of meaning | ⟶ | connection to a shared purpose. |

Trust happens when negative threats are lowered or eliminated. When trust exceeds negative threats, the brain learns more easily and quickly, retains more information, engages in advanced thinking, and welcomes rather than resists behavioral change.

## Learning and Retention

Every brain is as unique as its owner's fingerprint and constantly changing. Your brain is different now than at the beginning of this chapter. We still have much to discover about how the brain learns, but we do know a great deal. So, let's start by putting what we know into practice. Namely, the more interaction with something, the greater the retention and the greater the likelihood of lasting behavior change.

> **NAVIGATE TO RESOURCE**
> 5 Non-Negotiables for Effective Leadership Development: Video

Training is a multi-billion-dollar industry. Shouldn't we design and deliver this investment the way the brain learns best?

The Interaction Strategy has a rich history revealing the connection between the *what*, the *why*, and the *how*. *How* we learn best is tied to *what* we want to learn and *why* we are motivated to learn it.

For centuries, before the advent of brain research and imaging, educators and philosophers sought teaching methodologies that delivered an impactful and genuinely transformative learning experience. The early educators would be appalled by what higher education has become. We have abandoned the deeper purpose of learning and reduced it to a means of earning an income. What was once a pursuit of wisdom is now a chase for credentials.

The classical thinkers viewed education as a means to elevate the mind and soul—not just the paycheck. These educators and philosophers believed higher education was a noble and divine privilege. Their goals for learning were to inspire people to lead a self-examined life, seek truth and virtue, think deeply and critically, and pursue knowledge for its own sake. They emphasized acquiring ethics and wisdom over learning facts. These early educators viewed education as the path to developing enlightened individuals who could virtuously transform and lead a more evolved world.

Their desire for learning was not to produce more and make more money, but to see lasting change in thought and behavior. They discovered that involving students through asking questions was more effective than lecturing. The well-known Socratic method was one such method. Through thoughtful interaction, they successfully stimulated critical thinking, expedited learning, and deepened understanding, which changed behavior.

Continuing this tradition, the influential 20th-century educator Edgar Dale developed the Cone of Experience to illustrate the progression from abstract to concrete learning.[2] While widely cited claims that we remember 10% of what we hear, 20% of what we see, and 90% of what we hear, see, and do are often attributed to Dale, these figures likely emerged later as over-simplifications. But the point is more about the principle than the exact percentages. The greater the interaction, the faster and deeper the learning, and the greater the retention.

Influential educational psychologist Edward J. Bloom theorized that increased interaction improves retention, processing, and thinking. Bloom's Taxonomy is essentially based on the premise that the more we engage in the learning process, the more we move from basic levels of knowledge to more sophisticated levels of analysis, synthesis, and evaluation. The greater the engage-ment and interaction, the deeper the thinking and ownership.[3]

Granted, sometimes our reasons for learning in the workplace are often less about changing the world and more about an immediate return, such as becoming proficient in a software. But even then, more interaction and repetition increase learn-ing and retention. Much like the earlier gym analogy, I will only experience different results when I lift the weight. I will never change if I only listen to you tell me about lifting. The same is true with the brain and learning.

## Learning is not a spectator sport.

Two other elements are essential to the Interaction Strategy: feedback and time.

Dr. Eric Jensen, the father of brain-based learning, states that the type of feedback we receive when interacting with material and the duration of our interaction with it are crucial. Jensen's research shows we don't learn as fast with only positive feed-back. It is equally important that we receive corrective feedback that is specific rather than general.[4]

For example, let's say you have a team member facilitate a meeting. Hearing "great job" doesn't contribute to their growth and explains why they may continue to miss small opportunities to improve. A more productive approach would be to say great job with setting the agenda, clearly communicating, and redirecting unproductive discussions. One improvement is ensuring everyone speaks; I noticed two team members who were quiet the entire meeting. This type of feedback increases awareness and improves future facilitation.

In addition to specific feedback, time is critical. There is no substitute for time when it comes to transformative learning. That's why "one and done" training events may be convenient and entertaining but are rarely effective for long-term results.

When the goal is transformation in thinking and behavior, purposeful interaction that integrates engagement, feedback, and time is non-negotiable.

## Changing Behavior

Behavior change is the Holy Grail of interaction.

Influencing genuine, lasting change in how people respond, act, think, and lead is tricky. It certainly doesn't happen on accident any more than a winning football team "accidentally" wins the Super Bowl. It happens on purpose.

In our practice, we are frequently asked how to motivate someone else to change. I wish I could develop a pill, a patch, or a vaccine for that. The truth is we can't. But what we can do is set a person up for the greatest success by applying the CRANIUM methodology.

In the chapter on the Action Strategy, we introduced the beliefs model, which we frequently use in coaching and development.

This model is based on the premise that our current rules create and perpetuate our current outcomes. Our current results are simply the outcome of our current rules. Our rules are our actions, beliefs, and experiences. To change the results, we must change the rules.

We mistakenly believe that behavior change comes from changing actions.

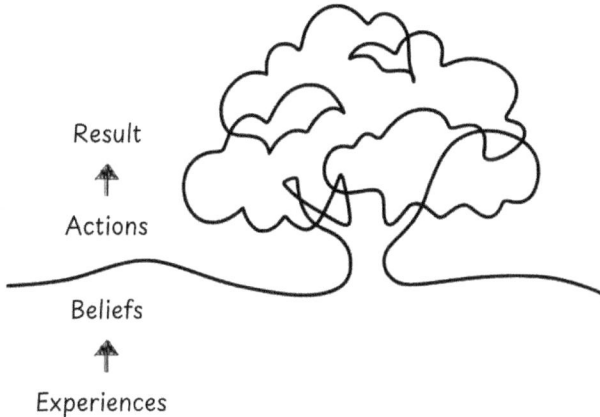

Result
↟
Actions

Beliefs
↟
Experiences

For example, a leader may aspire to establish trust. With "trust" as the desired result, the leader may take the action of listening.

However, actions alone do not lead to real, sustainable change. That result requires much deeper, self-reflective work. We must identify the beliefs that will drive the desired actions and the subsequent desired results.

We must ask, "What does my new leader need to *believe* to be true to motivate the actions that lead to the desired result?"

In this example, the real shift happens when the leader adopts the belief that high-trust relationships are important and worth the investment of time and attention.

Once we align beliefs, we must actively create consistent *experiences* that reinforce those beliefs in ourselves and in others we seek to influence and lead. Therefore, in future interactions, the leader is fully present and actively listens.

Behavior change happens when we can clearly identify our desired results and intentionally align our "rules" (actions, beliefs, and experiences). This is difficult to do independently because our long-held beliefs are hard to identify. Often, it means engaging with a 1:1 certified coach, a mentor, or a mastermind group to help us see, evaluate, and revise the rules.

As programs such as Weight Watchers and Alcoholics Anonymous have proven, it's rare for real behavior change to happen in isolation. Willpower and self-determination are not enough. They require a community to provide encouragement and accountability.

A 2013 study by Weight Watchers found that more people lost weight with Weight Watchers (an average of 10.1 pounds at six months) than in a self-help group (an average of only 1.3 pounds in the same period). The study then determined who was most successful in the Weight Watchers group. It concluded that a client's level of interaction with the program correlated with the weight lost. Those who had a high degree of interaction, attended 50 percent of the meetings, and used the website and mobile app twice a week, lost an average of 19 pounds.[5] Other change programs, such as Alcoholics Anonymous, show comparable results. The greater the interaction with the program and community, the greater the likelihood of sustainable change.

Research in behavioral psychology also suggests that increased interaction and accountability lead to greater behavioral change. One model proposes the following progression:

### 16% chance of success if I hear an idea and like it.

I hear an idea and like it, I have about a 16% chance of changing behavior. For example, I liked the idea of becoming the healthiest version of myself.

### 25-30% chance of success if I consciously decide to adopt the idea.

Then, after a health scare, I decided to adopt the idea to get healthy. My chances of successful behavior change increase to 25-30% because I made a conscious decision and commitment.

### 50-60% chance of success if I decide how I will do it.

My success jumps to 50-60% if I create a concrete plan for my wellness journey.

### 90-95% chance of success if I have someone to report to and hold me accountable.

Accountability is the real accelerator. The likelihood of changing behavior spikes significantly when we must report to someone we committed to. In my situation, I met with my health and wellness coach every week for an entire year. Each week, she was waiting for me. As a result, I adopted healthier beliefs and actions that have helped me maintain healthy results.[6]

## The brain doesn't resist change; the brain resists confusion.

The brain craves clarity. It says "no" when faced with confusion caused by too many choices or not offered enough choices. The optimal number of options is usually three, which is why we often see three choices: basic, standard, and premium.

## The brain craves a sense of belonging and ownership.

Interaction is effective because it involves others in creating the choices. This engages the emotional brain by valuing input and fostering a sense of belonging, thereby enhancing buy-in.

> ▶ **We can involve, release control, and grow capacity; or we can dictate, control, and grow stale.**

Some limited tactical skills may be learned by observation or hearing alone, such as screwing in a light bulb. However, there's no substitute for hands-on engagement when we desire deep learning and genuine "aha" moments.

Leaders worth following expand their own capacity by developing the capacity of others. That means they must let others do, which means they must let others fail at times or accept that others may not complete the task exactly as they would.

Think about those experiences that have had the most significant impact on your development. I guess your answer is similar to those I've heard from thousands of other leaders: comments like, "I learned and grew the most as a leader when...

- *I was given a project and had to figure it out on my own."*
- *I worked with a mentor."*
- *I failed at first but was given a second chance to correct a mistake."*
- *I asked for help with something I didn't understand."*

The 70/20/10 rule is frequently used as a guideline for designing and delivering training programs.[7] The 70/20/10 rule generally reflects what we hear when we ask leaders to share what has contributed most to their growth: training, relationships, and/ or experiences.

70% of the time, leaders attribute their growth to challenging and new experiences. Often, this was something that someone delegated to them, and they had to figure out how. They asked for help and involved others.

20% of the time, leaders mention a valuable relationship in the form of a boss, a mentor, or a coach. One study revealed that individuals with a mentor are five times more likely to be pro-moted.[8] Another study reported that individuals who engage with an executive coach experience a median return on invest-ment of 7 times their initial investment in areas such as promo-tion, productivity, and wellness.[9]

Only about 10% of the time do leaders report formal learning events as the most significant contributor to their growth. While formal training is important, it pales in comparison to relation-ships and experiences in terms of transformational moments.

The 70/20/10 rule reinforces the heart of the Interaction Strategy. The more we are engaged and involved, the greater the impact.

Discoveries in neuroplasticity also reinforce the Interaction Strategy. The brain learns by leveraging neural networks. Breakthrough research in neuroplasticity has proven these neural networks can grow and evolve throughout our lifetime. That's exciting, hopeful news.

But how do our brains continue to grow neurons and neural networks? It seems largely through the Novelty Strategy and the Interaction Strategy.

In his book *Soft-Wired: How the New Science of Brain Plasticity Can Change Your Life*, Dr. Michael Merzenich emphasizes the importance of "new." New neural networks are formed when we encounter new challenges, stimuli, and experiences.[10]

The irony is that the brain often resists "new" because it means uncertainty, risk, and effort. For these reasons, we see adults choose routine. How many professionals do you know who go to the same conferences, hang out with the same people, read the same kind of books about the same topics, order the same thing at the same restaurant, and even return to the same vacation spot each year? To grow capacity and brain plasticity, we must challenge ourselves and others in new and innovative ways.

# THE INTERACTION STRATEGY IN PRACTICE

*What an Interaction culture looks like*

We can unleash the power of the Interaction Strategy by involving others, increasing ownership, and growing capacity.

One of the most challenging shifts for leaders is the shift from telling to involving. Committing to the team's growth may not be easy or comfortable. A coaching client recently shared that he was in his office with the door slightly cracked open. He could hear his team, sitting just outside his office, discussing how to solve a problem. He had encountered this problem many times and could have solved it for the team in under five minutes. He admitted he put his head in his hands and mumbled, "For the love of God, this is how you solve it." But he stayed in his office and let the team figure out the solution. Unsurprisingly, they were highly motivated to implement what they had collectively discovered.

Involving instead of telling is a struggle for all of us in one role or another—whether as parents, friends, educators, or leaders.

For most of us, telling and solving is the factory default. You know the answer, and you genuinely believe you are helping by giving it. However, what you may actually be doing is creating *learned helplessness*.

Learned helplessness is a term coined by Martin Seligman, often referred to as "the father of positive psychology," to describe what happens in severe situations where people have lost hope of escaping their stress and pain.[11] It can result in severe depression and dramatic brain decline. We've all heard the cruel stories of this condition impacting people in unthinkable situations, such as those in concentration camps or those held against their will. In time, they lose their sense of agency.

But learned helplessness can also affect people if they fall victim to a toxic learning, work, or living situation. A well-meaning parent can perpetuate learned helplessness by doing everything for their child. A servant-hearted leader can perpetuate learned helplessness by doing too much for their team. Although the intent may be to help and protect, what that parent says to their child and the team leader to the team is, "I don't think you are capable." Learned helplessness stunts growth and confidence.

Learned helplessness can trigger stress damaging enough to interfere with memory, learning, and our natural defense systems. Elevated stress hormones caused by learned helplessness can literally shut down our natural defenses, particularly when exposed to prolonged or extreme stress.

Interaction is the opposite of learned helplessness. When leaders follow the Interaction Strategy, they have "power with" rather than "power over" those they lead. They suspend the need to be right and to rescue by staying curious, asking questions, valuing ideas, and welcoming input. Interaction empowers rather than stifles growth by giving others a choice and a voice. Interaction is about involving others and not telling them what to do. It is about wholeheartedly collaborating, engaging in meaningful conversations, and working together sincerely to discover optimal solutions.

Leaders and the cultures they shape see sustainable returns and increased capacity when the Interaction Strategy is activated. When it is not activated, leaders disempower others and foster a victim mindset.

In cultures where leaders ignore the Interaction Strategy, a few observable signs are:

- Training is treated as a "check-the-box" exercise rather than a transformational experience.
- Leaders feed their egos by solving everyone's problems and double-checking their work.
- Leaders prioritize control over growth.
- HR functions as an organizational babysitter, dealing with petty and avoidable conflicts.
- Employees learn quickly that their thoughts, experiences, and opinions are unwelcome.
- Team members spend countless hours reliving past grievances and criticizing others.
- Productivity halts until someone with the authority makes a decision or addresses the root cause of the problem.
- Interpersonal conflict builds until it causes costly consequences.
- Blaming, finger-pointing, and criticizing are more common than ownership and accountability.
- Leaders tell, micromanage, and stunt motivation and growth.

- Leaders operate under the false belief that sustainable results come from providing solutions rather than enabling employees to discover them.
- Learned helplessness, a state of profound powerlessness, manifests as apathy, paralysis, and attrition.

A scene from the animated movie *A Bug's Life* perfectly captures this kind of culture. The scene and our daily routines are dangerously similar.

As the ants carry out their regular, monotonous routine, a large leaf appears out of nowhere and falls in front of one of the ants, blocking the path and causing a pile-up in the single-file line. The ants are terrified, frozen in fear, and stuck. One ant nervously screams in sheer panic, "I'm lost!"

In the moment of crisis, a "leader" ant comes quickly and calmly to the rescue. He confidently marches down the hill to the distraught ants, saying, "Do not panic. Do not panic." He announces that he is a trained professional and has everything under control. He solves the problem by telling the ants what to do: go around the leaf. He makes eye contact with the trembling ant, claps his hands in reassurance, and guides them around the leaf.

The leaf, of course, is not so different from a process that needs refining, the schedule that needs reimagining, or the organizational change. The leaf represents confusion, a problem to solve, or a decision to make. The leader can be the savior who solves the problem and saves the day. However, that doesn't guarantee that the team has learned or is committed to following through. It only ensures that the next time the team faces a similar situation, the leader must continue rushing in to save the day. It ensures that the leader can't go on vacation without being interrupted. It ensures that when the leader is out, the team doesn't have the ability to decide or solve. It ensures that the leader will never scale their capacity beyond the current state.

Leaders who drive cultures that embrace the Interaction Strategy are less about solving and telling, and more about involving, developing, and empowering.

In cultures where leaders embrace the Interaction Strategy, a few observable signs are:

- Training is highly interactive and engaging.
- The intended outcome of all learning experiences is to transform thinking, performance, and behavior rather than check a box.
- Leaders spend most of their time helping others think through their challenges and discover solutions.
- Leaders find their worth and contribute to the team's overall growth by helping others identify the best possible solutions and strategies for implementing them.
- HR is a resource center, providing growth and development opportunities to help leaders and individuals achieve their goals.
- Employees grow, develop, and advance based on the value they add to the organization.
- Team members hold each other accountable and redirect conversations toward solutions rather than staying stuck in problems.
- Individuals at all levels are empowered to show initiative and take action.
- Conflict is embraced as an opportunity for growth.
- Ownership, accountability, and follow-through occur more frequently than blaming, finger-pointing, and criticizing.
- Leaders believe that better solutions emerge through collaboration.

- Multiple stakeholders are involved in exploring the problem, identifying potential solutions, and selecting the most effective option.
- Learned helplessness, a state of perceived powerlessness, is neither expected nor tolerated.

We often think it's faster or cheaper to tell and solve. After all, who has time to ask all these questions? Who has time to wait while less experienced people try to figure it out? Many people in leadership think it is their job to be the chief problem solver. They feel they aren't adding value if they don't have all the answers. Others believe they are the smartest person in the room and that their way is the right and only way.

The problem is that this approach is only faster and cheaper in the short term. Those of us who have made the shift know the "tell and solve" approach is neither faster nor cheaper because compliance is short-lived. We know that a different approach is needed if we want sustainable returns, which happen when we grow and develop ourselves, others, and relationships.

To do that, we must leverage the Interaction Strategy. We meet people where they are, without judgment, and with a mindset of "power with" rather than "power over." We co-discover and co-create solutions to empower, elevate thinking, and increase ownership. The return for increasing interaction is the team's development, the ownership each person takes, and the loyalty that results. By involving, we change the subconscious message of "I don't think you're capable" to "I think you are more than capable, and we are better together."

It is true: tell people, and they will comply, but involve them, and they will commit. High-performing leaders are interested in genuine commitment.

| WITHOUT THE INTERACTION STRATEGY | WITH THE INTERACTION STRATEGY |
|---|---|
| • Leaders are primarily problem solvers and fire fighters | • Leaders assist others in thinking through solutions |
| • Leaders feed their egos by being right | • Leaders find their worth as supportive mentors |
| • Control trumps growth | • HR is a resource center |
| • HR becomes the organizational babysitter | • Employees are rewarded based on the value they add |
| • Original thought is discouraged | • Accountability is everyone's responsibility |
| • Decision making is hierarchical | • Original thought is sought out |
| • Conflict is ignored until it becomes a crisis | • Initiative and action are expected |
| • Blaming, finger-pointing, criticizing, and condemning overshadow accountability | • Conflict is seen as growth |
| • Leaders are the smartest people in the room | • Accountability overshadows blaming and criticizing |
| • Learned helplessness is prolific | • Leaders have space to think |
| • Leaders are over-tasked and lack time for strategic work | • Problems are addressed promptly |
| | • Learned helplessness isn't fostered or tolerated |

# BE A LEADER
# WORTH FOLLOWING

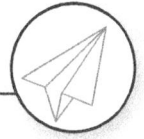

*How to live out the Interaction Strategy*

If you were constructing a building, would you want access to only a hammer or Home Depot?

A high-performing leader is a lot like a general contractor. They must manage several complexities and variables outside of their control. They must maintain the big picture while attending to the details. They can't complete the job alone. They must involve, communicate, and inspire subcontractors and partners while holding them accountable. They must ensure that the final building meets the goal, is built with integrity, and will last for years to come.

Just like a general contractor builds buildings, leaders build people. Both need and know how to use multiple tools.

## Employ a variety of leadership roles and leadership styles.

Leaders fulfill many roles, including counselor and advocate, friend, boss, mentor, coach, mediator, and more. They may flex each of those roles within a single conversation. These roles require different leadership styles. The commanding leadership style is necessary when a leader needs to act as a boss in charge, such as in a crisis. The affiliative style may be appropriate when the leader is counseling or mediating a conflict within the team.

High-performing leaders are intentional about developing the skills to successfully flex leadership styles. We all have a default leadership style, a style with which we are most comfortable. However, the goal is to be confident and effective in multiple leadership styles, even those outside our comfort zones. Just because a style isn't comfortable doesn't mean it isn't essential in certain leadership situations. We need more than a hammer; we need Home Depot.

My favorite resource on leadership styles is *Primal Leadership: Unleashing the Power of Emotional Intelligence.*[12] Authors Goleman, Boyatzis, and McKee present six distinct leadership styles and posit that emotionally intelligent leaders use all of them to drive performance and promote emotional resonance.

The six styles include:

### Visionary

*Moves people toward a shared dream.* It is helpful during times of change and uncertainty and inspires others by setting a clear direction and purpose.

### Democratic

*Builds consensus through participation.* It boosts engagement and trust by inviting input and collaboration.

### Affiliative

*Creates emotional bonds and harmony.* It helps boost morale and heal rifts by addressing conflict and prioritizing relationships and team cohesion.

### Coaching

*Develops people for the future.* It focuses on individual growth by connecting personal goals with organizational objectives.

### Pacesetting

*Sets high standards and expects excellence.* It is helpful in creating urgency to meet challenging goals but causes burnout if overused.

## Commanding

*Demands immediate compliance.* It is effective in crises but often kills morale if overused or if the leader lacks the team's respect.

High-performing leaders can adapt their leadership style to suit the team and organization's culture, the stakeholders involved, their own credibility and strengths, and the desired outcome.

- How is your default leadership style helping you and hindering you?

- Which of the styles is outside your comfort zone? Where do you have opportunities to experiment with this style?

- What is a leadership challenge you are facing? Use the following variables to make a mindful leadership style choice: stakeholders, leader strengths, company culture, and desired outcome.

## NAVIGATE TO RESOURCE

Choosing Leadership Styles: PDF

**STEP ONE: Summarize a leadership challenge you are currently facing and the ideal outcome you would like to achieve.**

Example:

*I lead a seasoned team of estimators. I have been in my role for less than six months. The company is facing a 50% increase in work over the next year, and I'm concerned that our current processes will prevent the team from delivering accurate numbers on time.*

**STEP TWO: Consider the following variables using the following questions**

### Stakeholders

- Who are your most important stakeholders?
- Describe in detail each stakeholder in terms of readiness, maturity, sophistication, rank, trust, interests, and concerns.

### Leader strengths

- What are your strengths as a leader?
- What is your default leadership style?
- What is the level of trust and credibility you have with each stakeholder?

### Company culture

- What are the interests and needs of the company?
- What are your company's values?
- What is the current state of the company? (financials, reputation, etc.)

### Desired outcome

- What does winning look like?
- Which style(s) would likely have the most positive results and why?
- Which style(s) would likely have the most negative results and why?

# Lead like a coach.

Of all the leadership styles, coaching is the most versatile and impactful for leveraging the Interaction Strategy, building capacity, empowering others, and promoting accountability and ownership. It is also the one that is most misunderstood.

The International Coach Federation (ICF) is the gold standard for coaching certifications. In 2014, I wanted to respond to a proposal request but lacked the required ICF certification. Reluctantly, I enrolled in an accredited training program because I thought I was a coach. How many more initials did I need after my name? In my arrogance, I showed up for the first day of training. Thirty minutes into what would be a life-changing experience, I was humbled. I realized I had not been coaching at all. At best, I had been consulting and giving people advice that wasn't very useful and they probably didn't want.

What does it mean to lead like a coach? It isn't what I thought, and probably isn't what you think either.

Coaching is unlike any other leadership role you will fulfill.

A coach possesses a unique set of beliefs and distinct skills, including the ability to be keenly aware, listen attentively, and ask transformational questions.

ICF defines coaching as "partnering with clients in a thought-provoking and creative process that inspires them to maximize their personal and professional potential."[13]

Notice that the definition does not include words like tell, give advice, solve, or own. It uses words like "partnering," "thought-provoking and creative," "inspire," and "potential." These words reveal an important difference in beliefs from those we hold when consulting, mentoring, and commanding. These are core beliefs of the Interaction Strategy.

The etymology of the word *coach* is interesting and sheds light on what sets this role and leadership style apart. The word *coach* comes from the French word for *carriage*. Since most of us do not use a carriage or stagecoach for transportation, think of coaching as calling a ride-share service or taxi.

First, the *passenger* calls the ride-share service and willingly gets into the car. The driver doesn't just show up unexpectedly and push the passenger in.

Second, the driver meets the passenger where *they* are and comes to a complete stop so that the passenger can safely get in.

Third, the driver confirms where the *passenger* wants to go. The driver doesn't decide the destination. The driver is less concerned about where the passenger has been and more focused on where the passenger has an interest in going.

Fourth, the driver utilizes his familiarity with the territory to help the passenger arrive as safely and quickly as possible.

Similarly, in coaching, coaching is optimal when initiated by the coachee. The coaching leader meets the coachee where she is emotionally, physically, and mentally by setting aside distractions and listening with intense curiosity. The leader, like the driver, confirms where the coachee wants to go. And finally, like a ride-share driver, the leader uses their knowledge and experience to help the coachee reach their desired destination.

There is one key difference between the driver and the leader as a coach. Unlike the driver, the coach "switches seats" with the coachee and lets her drive. Together, the two partner on a thought-provoking journey of discovery.

# Believe like a coach.

A coach holds a unique set of beliefs about the coachee and the growth process. Here are 10 of my favorites. In the field of Neurolinguistic Programming (NLP), these beliefs are often referred to as presuppositions. A presupposition is a statement or belief you act on as if it were true.

**Belief #1:** Better solutions result when we come to a conversation in a state of not knowing.

**Belief #2:** People respond to their view of reality, not to reality itself.

**Belief #3:** The more choices we generate, the more control and ownership we feel.

**Belief #4:** People are whole, resourceful, capable beings.

**Belief #5:** People are more motivated by a compelling vision.

**Belief #6:** The presenting problem is usually not the real problem.

**Belief #7:** There is a reward for all choices, behaviors, and actions.

**Belief #8:** Tell them, they comply. Involve them, they commit.

**Belief #9:** There is no failure, only feedback.

**Belief #10:** The meaning of communication is the response you get.

### *Belief #1: Better solutions result when we come to a conversation in a state of not knowing.*

If we act as if this were true, we stop giving advice and suspend our need to know, control, and be the most intelligent person in the room. In his 2019 TEDx talk, *How to Tame Your Advice Monster*, Michael Bungay Stanier warns that our advice is not as good as we think it is and is likely not even wanted.[14]

Effective coaches are a little on the lazy side. Instead of rushing to solve, they observe and stay curious. They don't enter a conversation with a predetermined solution, but rather, partner with the coachee to discover possibilities.

### Belief #2: People respond to their view of reality, not to reality itself.

First and foremost, a coach meets the coachee where they are, remembering that their view of the world makes sense to them. A coach stays curious to better understand the coachee's view of reality—not agree with it or change it. A coach strives to see through the coachee's perspective without judgment.

### Belief #3: The more choices we generate, the more control and ownership we feel.

A coach involves rather than tells, knowing that the coachee takes greater ownership and accountability of the ideas, options, and solutions that they generate. Instead of giving advice and recommendations, a coach might ask, "What are your next steps?" A coach knows that the brain can develop tunnel vision when experiencing negative threat, so the coach can open more possibilities by asking the AWE question: "And what else?" "And what else?" "And what else?"

### Belief #4: People are whole, resourceful, capable beings.

Coaches do not see the coachee as someone who is broken or needs fixing or saving. They believe that the coachee is the expert of their life and has everything they need to solve the challenge in front of them. This empowering belief is the opposite of learned helplessness. A coach believes that if a coachee created an undesirable outcome, they are fully capable of creating the desired outcome.

### Belief #5: People are more motivated by a compelling vision.

Like a taxi driver wouldn't drive backwards for miles, coaches don't need to know the entire backstory to a situation. A coach looks ahead to where the coachee wants to go. Coaching is not about the coach. It doesn't matter what the coach wants. All that matters is what the coachee wants.

One of the fastest ways to reactivate the prefrontal cortex (PFC) when it has been compromised by confusion or threat is to shift focus toward a meaningful goal or project that the coachee wants to pursue. By zeroing in on what the coachee truly wants, the brain begins to reengage. This simple shift can reignite the PFC, unlocking the creativity, clarity, and willpower that naturally follow purposeful direction.

### Belief #6: The presenting problem is usually not the real problem.

Coaches know the first problem is rarely the real problem. They resist taking the bait of the first problem and risk solving the wrong problem. Often, coaches find that if they stay curious a few seconds longer or ask even one more question, the real problem will surface.

Recently, a client began our coaching session by stating, "My team keeps missing deadlines." Further investigation revealed that she didn't feel respected by the team. With even more probing, we discovered she had not given the team clear directions.

If I had rushed the process, we would not have solved the real problem.

### Belief #7: There is a reward for our choices, behaviors, and actions.

This belief doesn't imply that the reward is always positive or empowering. In fact, the reward may be toxic and disempowering. For instance, the reward for someone who frequently blames others may be a sense of superiority. Likewise, a chronic complainer might benefit from avoiding responsibility—nothing is ever their fault. As coaches, it's essential to recognize that a reward always exists and to stay curious about what that reward might be.

### Belief #8: Tell them, they comply. Involve them, they commit.

This belief is a cornerstone of the Interaction Strategy. Outside of a crisis or a direct request for help, the brain does not like being told what to do. We trigger resistance when we give unsolicited instructions, opinions, or advice. People push back when their autonomy is threatened. While others may comply—especially if we hold a title or authority—the cost is high: we lose genuine commitment. Telling is faster in the short term, but involving others builds lasting ownership, trust, and loyalty. When we pause to invite input and let go of the need to be right, we activate engagement rather than resistance.

### Belief #9: Failure is feedback.

Failure hurts. Failure is grief. It's the loss of a desired outcome, and the confusion that comes with navigating the real consequences that often accompany it. But we can deepen the pain by the meaning we attach to it. Failure wears many faces: being passed over for a promotion, losing a job, receiving a disappointing performance review, or hosting a webinar no one attends. And sometimes, it strikes harder—a misdiagnosis, a failed business, or a mistake that causes real harm.

The belief that failure is valuable feedback invites us to lean in, not away. Failure, no matter how painful, holds seeds of insight. When we're willing to examine the result without judgment, we can shape a wiser future.

### Belief #10: The meaning of communication is the response you get.

What you say isn't always what others hear, and sometimes, it's not even what *you* hear. In communication, intent matters less than impact. We tend to evaluate ourselves based on what we *meant*, while we judge others based on what we *experienced*. The truth is, people respond to what they heard and how you made them feel, not what you intended to convey.

Communicate comes from the Latin *communis*, meaning "to connect." That's the true measure of communication: Did you connect? It's not about how polished your message was, but how it landed. Pay close attention to how others respond. Their reaction is your clearest signal of whether communication or connection truly occurred.

## NAVIGATE TO RESOURCE
Coaching Beliefs: PDF

# Listen like a coach.

Leaders who act as coaches operate on specific beliefs and hone two powerful skills that work in tandem: listening and asking questions.

### Coaches listen FOR...not TO.

Most of us are somewhat effective at listening *to* the words people use. Coaches listen *for* repeating words, metaphors, analogies, tone, cadence, sighs, pauses, laughter, and silence.

### Coaches listen for agreement rather than disagreement.

Most of us have spent thousands of dollars and thousands of hours learning how to listen for disagreement. This skill enables us to be great problem-solvers and analytical thinkers. But listening for disagreement can interfere when seeking to view the world through the coachee's eyes without judgment.

### Coaches listen for insight rather than answers.

The goal of coaching isn't to rush toward finding solutions. The goal is to engage in the deeper work of uncovering insight, clarity, and self-awareness that reshape how the coachee sees themselves, their future, and the world around them. A successful coaching engagement isn't measured by how many answers are found, but by the depth of insight gained.

Just like I thought I had been coaching before I enrolled in an accredited coach training program, I thought I had been listening until I discovered the teachings of Otto Scharmer.

Dr. Otto Scharmer is an economist and the creator of *Theory U*.[15] *Theory U* is a change and innovation framework that focuses not only on solving problems and finding solutions, but also on helping individuals, teams, and organizations experience conscious transformation. Scharmer posits that fundamental transformation requires an open heart—seeing the world through others' realities; an open mind—approaching with curiosity rather than judgment; and an open will—releasing the grip on what feels safe and familiar. An open heart, mind, and will require a different level of engagement, which Scharmer calls generative listening and questioning.

Scharmer teaches four levels of listening:

### Level 1: Downloading

Downloading is listening from well-formed habits, through our lens of the world and all of its biases, to confirm what we already believe. Downloading leads to asking questions that fit with what I already know. No new learning happens at this level.

> *"Can you use the same approach as you did last time this problem occurred?"*

### Level 2: Factual

Factual listening is paying attention to anything that may challenge our current assumptions. We listen for disagreement and notice anything new or unique. We are open to surprising facts.

> *"What other approaches have you considered?"*

### Level 3: Empathic

Empathic listening is about understanding another person's perspective and the emotions and feelings associated with it. By seeing the world through their eyes, we want to build trust and a relational connection.

> *"How is this problem impacting you?"*

### *Level 4: Generative*

Generative listening is full-bodied presence—listening with profound curiosity and openness to what is trying to emerge. It's a co-creative space where both listener and speaker step into shared uncertainty, holding the moment with wonder and suspended judgment.

>*"What is this problem here to teach us?"*

Generative listening and questioning are the essential skills for breakthrough—the path to new insights, solutions, beliefs, and possibilities. They are foundational to "partnering with clients in a thought-provoking and creative process that inspires them to maximize their personal and professional potential."

It is this breaking open of the new that fuels my love for coaching. Coaching is a sacred space where we can access new levels of realities and learning that are readily available. The process is chilling and mysterious when we can suspend all that we know and be open to what we cannot yet see.

## Question like a coach.

Questions are the currency in coaching. The quality of our questions mirrors the depth of our listening. Shallow listening yields surface-level questions. But when we listen with the depth, presence, and curiosity of generative listening, we unlock questions that illuminate, inspire, and transform.

Coaches don't just ask questions. They ask generative questions that evoke awareness and help coachees gain insight, explore possibilities, and deepen self-awareness.

Generative questions rarely begin with What, Who, or Why. Questions that generate transformational insight and lead to new discoveries and possibilities typically begin with How or What.

- *How are you thinking about moving forward?*
- *What are you noticing right now?*
- *How have you handled similar situations in the past?*
- *What would be most beneficial to your future self?*
- *What opportunities have you not yet explored?*

---

## NAVIGATE TO RESOURCE
50 Generative Coaching Questions: PDF

---

## Delegate intelligently.

A wise mentor told me, "Sherry, you can have control or you can have growth. But, you can't have both in equal proportion at the same time."

Let's discuss delegation. Delegation is the number one way to develop others, scale your capacity, and experience the full benefits of the Interaction Strategy.

Many leaders I support hesitate to delegate. The reasons range from not wanting to burden others to fear that people will think the leader is incompetent. I often hear from clients, "It's just faster if I do it myself," and "If I want something done right, I do it myself."

Just because you CAN do something doesn't mean you SHOULD.

When you fail to delegate, you fail to serve the people who look to you for leadership and growth. Whether intentional or not, you signal that you don't trust them or believe they're capable. You prioritize your need to control over their development. The result? You won't grow, and neither will your team or organization. Every time you say *no* to delegation, you also say *no* to your high-impact leadership responsibilities, such as strategic thinking and planning.

When we delegate, we multiply our impact and empower our team. When we don't, we waste our time and withhold growth from those who need it most.

The key to delegation is to provide what the brain needs: clarity, autonomy, and accountability. Below are five criteria for delegating that ensure we meet those needs and set the delegation up for success.

### Clarity

Successful delegations require absolute clarity. Clearly state what winning looks like with this delegation, why it is important, and why this delegate was selected.

*Example:*

*Please book a meeting room large enough to accommodate 12 people at the Hilton on Main for August 5 from 8:00 a.m. to 12:00 p.m. We are hosting a strategy session for the marketing team. I chose you for this delegation because you expressed interest in assuming additional event planning responsibilities.*

### Level

Michael Hyatt recommends assigning a level to the delegation based on the task and the expertise and reliability of the delegate.[16] Assigning a level ensures that you and the delegate are clear on autonomy and follow-up.

Level 1: Do exactly as I say. Applies to inexperienced delegates and high-compliance tasks.

Level 2: Gather information and report findings. Do not make recommendations or decide. Best when exploring options.

Level 3: Investigate and recommend, but do not decide. Useful when we want to involve others in the process while retaining final decision-making authority.

Level 4: Decide, execute, and inform. Helpful for growing trust and giving autonomy.

Level 5: Decide and execute without the need to follow up. Reserved for highly trusted, capable delegates or low-stakes tasks.

*Example:*

*This is a Level 3 delegation. Please provide your recommendation, but do not confirm the reservation until we have had a chance to discuss it.*

## Expectations

Communicate clearly any expectations or non-negotiables you have, such as budget, time, size, shape, etc.

*Example:*

*We can't exceed $2K. My non-negotiables include a room at least 300 sq ft with a window and movable chairs and tables. We will not need A/V equipment.*

## Accountability

Clearly define when and how to report progress to eliminate the uncertainty of "Is it getting done?"

Set clear expectations for deadlines, timelines, and reporting.

*Example:*

*Please send me an email by the end of this week with an update on your progress. We need to book the room by next Wednesday, January 22.*

### Repeat, Review, and Revise

Repeat: Have the delegate repeat what they heard you asking them to do. Remember: what you say is not always what they hear.

Review: After the delegation is completed, ask the delegate what went well and what can be "even better" next time. Feedback is excellent learning.

Revise: Make the necessary adjustments and continue to improve at delegation.

Delegation is the number one way to develop others and free up your capacity to focus on tasks that belong to you as a leader.

> ### NAVIGATE TO RESOURCE
> The Ultimate Checklist for Effective Delegation:
> Course and PDF

## Schedule regular conversations.

*Conversation* breaks down as follows:

- *con* means "with"
- *verse* means "turn"
- *ation* means "the act of"

*Conversation*, then, means "the act of turning with." If we are going to involve, empower, give people a choice and a voice, we must engage with others in meaningful ongoing conversations (turnings with).

We encourage a practice called CHECK-ins. These are meaningful, recurring conversations held privately with each team member. CHECK-ins allow for an exchange of thoughts and ideas rather than a status update.

A CHECK-in conversation is:

- Positive and forward-focused to improve individual and collective work performance.
- Centered on the team members' ideas, needs, and concerns.
- A safe place to communicate.

To lead a CHECK-in:

### Connect

Lower threat and increase trust by beginning with a personal connection.

**NAVIGATE TO RESOURCE**

CHECK-in: Template

*Hi Jill. How did your daughter's soccer game go last weekend?*

### Hear

Use generative listening and questioning to hear what is important right now for the team member.

*What accomplishments are you celebrating?*

*Who has been particularly helpful?*

*What challenges are you encountering?*

*What can I do today (or this week) to help you move forward?*

*Empower*

Resist the urge to solve and tell. Stay in coaching mode and involve the team member in finding solutions.

*You mentioned tight deadlines as a challenge.*

- *What recommendations do you have?*
- *What would be helpful?*
- *What has worked well in the past?*
- *How do you suggest we communicate these changes to the team?*

**Commit**

Recap the conversation and ensure you and the team member are clear on the next steps.

*To clarify, I will discuss login requirements with IT. I can do that today. You will add the security alert to our agenda in next week's team meeting. Did I get that right? I look forward to our next CHECK-in on DATE.*

**Keep**

Follow through and follow up on all commitments. Prioritize CHECK-ins on your calendar.

# FINAL THOUGHTS ON THE INTERACTION STRATEGY

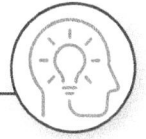

Brain-antagonistic leaders would rather be right than rich. High-performance leaders would rather be rich than right. They release control to reap growth.

The Interaction Strategy fosters cultures where leaders lead with curiosity, stay open to new possibilities, and measure their success by how others thrive. These are empowered cultures where the teams take initiative, collaborate to solve problems creatively, and assume ownership of their work. Leaders grow themselves, their teams, and the organization by giving people both a voice and a choice, by involving rather than telling. As a result, they don't settle for compliance and ignite genuine, lasting commitment.

# WHAT MAKES A LEADER WORTH FOLLOWING?

*We asked real people. We got real responses.*

Here are just a few. Would anyone say the same about you?

- ✔ *A true leader doesn't seek credit but instead celebrates the team's accomplishments, ensuring that every member receives the recognition they deserve.*

- ✔ *Their willingness to not only take charge of a situation but understand when to take a step back and support others from behind. A good leader is both a servant and a guide*

- ✔ *One who is understanding, will lead from the front, will protect the team from politics, has answers or willing to get them, willing to do even the most basic and mundane task.*

✔ *Grit, conviction and someone you know has your back, but also isn't afraid to share their feedback and pushes you to grow.*

✔ *Someone that makes me feel appreciated and valued. A great communicator. Someone that I can trust and I know they have my back even when I make a mistake. Someone that makes me feel like they truly care about me.*

# THINK. DISCUSS. APPLY.

*Make it matter*

1. What are the moments in your life that have had a significant impact on your development? What do they all have in common?
2. What is your default leadership style? And, which leadership style(s) are least comfortable for you?
3. What is a leadership challenge you are currently experiencing? Considering the desired result, the stakeholders, and the culture, which leadership style(s) would be most beneficial? Which leadership style(s) would be least beneficial?
4. Where can you release control to grow and develop others?
5. To what extent do you agree with each of the coaching beliefs in this chapter? How do these belief influence how you lead?

# GIVE CHOICE AND VOICE. LET GO.

**C** What does 'done' look like?

**L** What is the level of delegation?

**E** What are the non-negotiables?

**A** What is the cadence of accountability?

**R** Repeat and reflect

## AWE
### (And What Else?)

Just because you CAN do it yourself doesn't mean you SHOULD.

The greater the interaction and accountability, the greater the likelihood of behavior change

Learning is not a spectator sport.

## Coaching Beliefs - Believe Like a Coach

Belief #1: Better solutions result when we come to a conversation in a state of not knowing.

Belief #2: People respond to their view of reality, not to reality itself.

Belief #3: The more choices we generate, the more control and ownership we feel.

Belief #4: People are whole, resourceful, capable beings.

Belief #5: People are more motivated by a compelling vision.

Belief #6: The presenting problem is usually not the real problem.

Belief #7: There is a reward for all choices, behaviors, and actions.

Belief #8: Tell them, they comply. Involve them, they commit.

Belief #9: There is no failure, only feedback.

Belief #10: The meaning of communication is the response you get.

The brain pushes back when told what to do.

✓ CHECK in

Connect • Help • Empower • Commit • Keep

## CONVERSATION

con – with
verse – turn
ation – the act of

*leadership styles:*
» visionary  » democratic
» coaching  » pacesetting
» affiliative  » commanding

Be more interest**ED** than interest**ING**.

### 4 LEVELS OF LISTENING
(OTTO SCHARMER)

Level 1: Downloading
Level 2: Factual
Level 3: Empathic
Level 4: Generative

# CHAPTER 6

# The Using Emotion Strategy

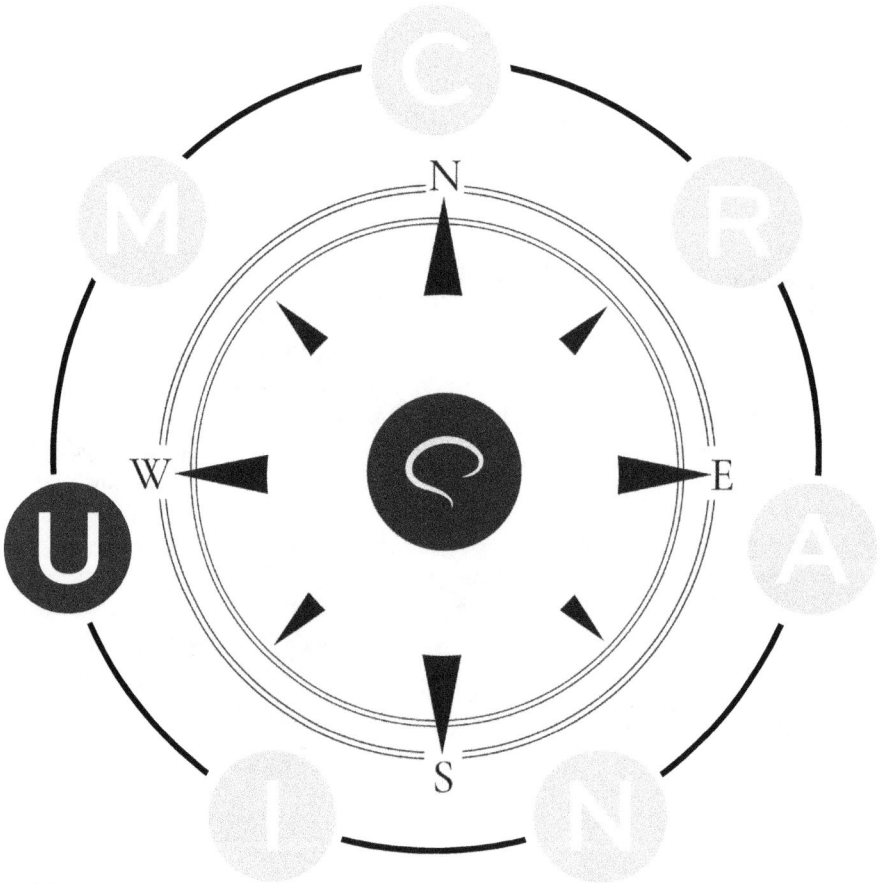

**ENGAGE EMOTIONS.
PRIORITIZE PEOPLE.**

# BIG IDEA

We are all in the relationship business, and the currency of success is connection. Leaders worth following embrace emotional intelligence, recognizing that relationships drive results.

## BREAKTHROUGH BELIEFS

We aren't thinking individuals who happen to have emotions; we are emotional individuals who happen to think.

The question isn't, "How smart are you?" The question is, "How are you, smart?"

Where a problem exists, the solution exists.

# REAL LEADERS. REAL LIFE.

*Emotions run the show.*

It's midweek at an online service company known for innovation and outstanding customer service. On the first floor, Trainer Mark is launching a leadership program for high-potential employees. Today's session focuses on leading with vision and values. Mark invites participants to reflect on leaders they've known personally and identify the traits that made them great. Flipcharts soon fill with words like "trust," "empathy," and "inspiration."

Just down the hall, Cathy, the longtime VP of Sales, notices that one of her managers, recently back from maternity leave, looks weary. Cathy gently invites her in and says, "We can work out a flexible schedule for a while if that would help." The manager smiles through grateful tears.

Upstairs in the call center, Raul, the newest team member, is helping a field technician resolve a login issue. While waiting for the system to connect, they share a few laughs about last night's basketball game. As Raul wraps up the call, his supervisor walks by, gives him a high five, and says, "Nice job—we're glad you're here."

At the service entrance, Sandra backs her truck up to the cafeteria. A former factory worker turned bakery owner, Sandra followed her dream five years ago and poured her savings into opening a shop. Business was slow until she landed her first big contract with this very company. Now, she delivers warm muffins and fresh-baked joy every morning.

Down the hall, Peter, the company's founder and a community legend, meets with a high school student aspiring to attend his alma mater, a prestigious military academy. Though Peter is no longer involved in daily operations, he keeps an open door, welcomes new hires, and mentors future leaders.

As Peter's door closes, Bob walks by and chats with Andrew, who asks for help on a new product design. Bob agrees and offers to share resources, even suggesting that they involve Sonia, a brilliant new hire. "Let's get her in on this," he says.

On the third floor, Lisa opens her team meeting by celebrating everyone's effort in meeting a tight deadline. She gives a heartfelt thanks to two employees who worked over the weekend. Cheers erupt. "It's an honor to lead this team," Lisa says before handing the agenda over to Carlos.

# YOU'RE WIRED FOR EMOTION

*Why your brain thrives on the Using Emotion Strategy*

The Using Emotion Strategy increases returns, loyalty, and profits while decreasing problems, drama, and costs. People are an organization's most valuable, expensive, and challenging asset. It would be easy if leaders only had to plan for what people do, including their schedules, yearly goals, daily tasks, and key deliverables. But we all know we are not humans DOING. We are humans BEING. That's what complicates leading.

Since people and relationships drive results, we are all in the business of people and relationships. It's not enough that we understand the brain's role in what humans DO. We need to know the brain's role in what humans BE. This information on what motivates and influences human behavior is crucial for us to understand, both for ourselves and for those we lead.

# 3 Big Deals and the Big Deal about Emotion

**NAVIGATE TO RESOURCE**

3 Big Deals: Video and PDF

Let's return to the 3 Big Deals every-one should know about the brain.

For simplicity, think about your brain in 3 layers. This visual, though outra-geously oversimplified, is an easy way to explore the Using Emotion Strategy.

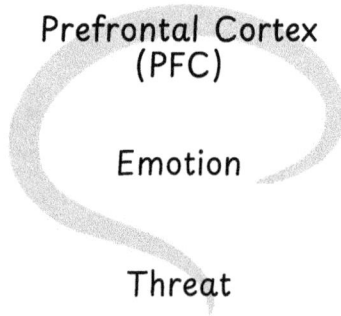

Prefrontal Cortex
(PFC)

Emotion

Threat

## *Big Deal #1: Your Prefrontal Cortex is Priceless*

The PFC is the executive part of the brain that enables us to exhibit various types of self-control, including emotional self-control, demonstrate empathy, consider different perspec-tives, gain greater self-awareness, think strategically, plan, and innovate. Activity in this part of the brain is essential in a world where most of us deliver value through our thoughts and ideas.

## *Big Deal #2: Threat to the Brain is Threat to the Brain*

Your brain doesn't care if the threat is real or perceived, physical or psychological, past, present, or future. It simply responds to threat. So, when we perceive we are in danger, we fight (get defensive and overly committed to being right), we freeze or flee (shut down, check out, or run away), or we flock.

Flocking is a fascinating reaction to threat. It is driven by our need to feel safe and included. If you recall, social rejection is the number one threat in the workplace. The brain has an intense need to belong.

Flocking is when we look to others for validation, support, and connection. You may have experienced this flocking phenomenon in meetings when the leader announces an unpopular change, and people start making eye contact with others who share similar views or are trusted. You may have experienced it when no one speaks up in the actual meeting, but freely shares their opinions in the unofficial meeting after the meeting. You may have experienced it when someone comes to you to talk disparagingly about a person but isn't willing to speak to the person directly.

Our need for support and community drives flocking, but it often results in a lack of accountability and costly, unnecessary drama.

### Big Deal #3: Emotions Run the Show

Ever had a no-matter-what (NMW) moment?

NMW moments are those moments where we harness super-human focus and determination to accomplish a goal. Moments when we were unstoppable. For example, no matter what, you were getting out of debt, finishing your book, getting healthy, running the marathon, landing that promotion, or starting your business. These are moments of almost delirious determination and passion.

You can thank emotion for no-matter-what moments. Emotion fuels the prefrontal cortex and activates what Steven Kotler calls the "flow state cocktail." This is the synergistic blend of dopamine, norepinephrine, endorphins, anandamide, and sometimes serotonin that fuels deep focus, creativity, and peak performance.

You feel unstoppable because you are. The more you flow, the more you grow. The flow state can boost learning by 500% and lead to creative breakthroughs by promoting lateral thinking and silencing the inner critic, all while enhancing neuroplasticity.[1]

Ever had a freak-out moment?

Those, too, can be life-changing moments, but not necessarily for the better. Freak-out moments go viral daily and sometimes end up featured on the evening news. These are moments when we lose our shit. A freak-out moment can include screaming at your spouse, getting ejected from a game, pushing to the front of the line, fighting over toilet paper in the grocery store, or raging on the road.

Thank emotion for those freak-out moments, too. Emotion can fuel the threat response just as it can the PFC. Like a NMW moment, you are equally dialed in, focused, and potentially unstoppable in a freak-out moment. It's also a flow state, albeit a potentially destructive one.

Emotion is an accelerating ingredient. It can reveal the best and worst of who we are. The key is for us to recognize the role of emotion and learn ways to manage it for ourselves and for others. You can work with how the brain works best and achieve better results with less effort, or you can work against how the brain works best and create a costly mess that can sometimes take generations to clean up.

The emotional brain is involved in everything we do. However, its critical role was largely ignored in brain research for a long time. Many believed that information and events were processed first through the thinking brain, the logical prefrontal cortex. From there, information was disseminated throughout the brain, somewhat like how an organization might run. We thought the executive team made decisions and then cascaded them to different departments.

The idea that we are logical beings who happen to have emotions has influenced today's educational models and cultural beliefs. If you want someone to change behavior, give them logical reasons why they should change. If your goal is to influence and persuade others, present data.

The problem is we were wrong.

The brain is not primarily a logical piece of equipment for rational thought. It is mainly an emotional piece of equipment for feeling, making sense of the world, giving meaning to events, looking for patterns, and making predictions. Sometimes, we get it right. Most of the time, we get it wrong, making it harder to connect with people, get them to change, or influence their behavior.

The brain will default to what "feels" true and what action "feels" right. But just because it "feels" true or "feels" right doesn't make it so.

Scientists like Joseph LeDoux have helped us shift our beliefs about how the brain receives and processes information.[2] This shift in thinking is as significant as learning the sun doesn't revolve around the Earth. His work, along with that of many others, has helped us understand the role of emotions better through improved brain imaging. We now know that information and events are processed in the brain's emotional center, involving a complex area called the limbic system. Consider emotion fuel. It can fuel the prefrontal cortex, making high-performance easier, or it can fuel threat, making high-performance less likely.

If the brain ain't buyin', the brain ain't changin'. Emotion is essential for learning, memory, and behavior change.

As we discussed with the Novelty Strategy, the brain constantly makes predictions and looks for patterns. It pays attention to and remembers things outside the predicted pattern. When the brain expects one thing and gets another, it pays attention. It wakes up, and the stage is set for accelerated learning and memory.

We can capture the brain's attention and trigger emotions through strategies such as doing the unexpected, connecting with what is important to that person (WII-FM – What's In It For Me), storytelling, and giving a powerful reason. We must engage emotion to create a memorable experience, influence behavior, or lead change.

Our understanding of emotion is especially critical when it comes to conflict. The ability to effectively navigate conflict is crucial for high-performing leaders and cultures.

Conflict is a crossroads that can lead to growth or collapse. What makes the difference isn't the issue itself, but how we understand and manage emotion. Conflict can catalyze connection, clarity, and progress when leaders navigate emotions effectively. When they don't, it breeds blame, division, and drama.

Conflict surfaces when emotion is involved, something of value is at stake (even if it's only the ego), and opinions differ. In those moments, we have a choice. We can work against how the brain works best and create more conflict. Or, we can work with how the brain works best and increase the likelihood of a greater connection.

Let's apply the 3 Big Deals to effectively addressing conflict.

*Scenario: Your teenager comes home and announces he is attending a party this weekend. Silently, your first reaction is, "Over my dead body."*

The approach parents often take is one that "feels" right: reason, relate, and regulate.

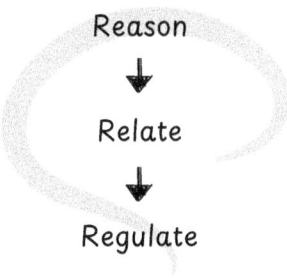

Reason

↓

Relate

↓

Regulate

Reason: Explain the dangers of adolescent drinking.

Relate: Expect them to agree with your concerns.

Regulate: Assume they do not go to the party.

Taking this approach is like going the wrong way down a one-way street. Expect a collision of wills.

And yet, we take this approach all of the time.

- *Leading a change? Show the team data and charts, and expect them to get on board.*
- *Have an employee crying in your office? Offer a tissue, keep talking, and expect the employee to agree.*
- *Having layoffs? Give employees a timeline and a packet of resources and expect them to return to work as usual until their layoff date.*
- *Your child experimented with drugs? Tell them drugs are bad for them and expect them to just say no to drugs.*

There is a better way; a way that works *with* rather than *against* how the brain works best. When conflict starts brewing, we can slow down and go with traffic, remembering we are emotional individuals who happen to think.

Reason

↑

Relate

↑

Regulate

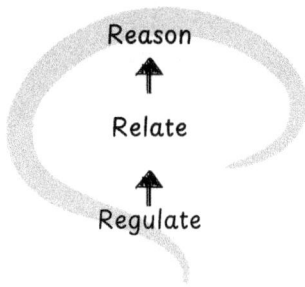

NAVIGATE TO
RESOURCE
Regulate, Relate,
and Reason: Video

Regulate: Take a minute to get yourself in the right state of mind by taking deep breaths or going for a walk.

Relate: Lean in and elevate your curiosity. Use your coaching skills. Listen FOR as much as you listen TO. Engage in generative listening and ask generative questions. Genuinely seek to understand the other person's perspective. (Reread the Interaction Strategy for a refresher.)

Reason: Only by regulating and relating do you have a shot at reasoning.

Next time, follow the path of neurosequencing.

- *Leading a change? Allow the team time to process and ask questions.*
- *Have an employee crying in your office? Ask if they need a few minutes alone before you move forward with the conversation.*
- *Having layoffs? Give employees a timeline and a packet of resources and allow employees time to ask questions or work with a coach.*
- *Your child experimented with drugs? Breathe, sit down with them, and genuinely ask them to share more about what is going on.*

Emotions are involved in everything we do, from learning and remembering to behavioral change and decision-making. Emotions are neither good nor bad. They are all useful indicators that can help us direct or redirect our thoughts and actions. By doing so, we stand a greater chance of strengthening relationships, inspiring high-performing teams, and being leaders worth following.

# THE USING EMOTION STRATEGY IN PRACTICE

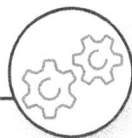

*What a Using Emotion culture looks like*

The Using Emotion Strategy acknowledges and honors the fact that emotions, rather than logic, drive decisions and influence outcomes. If we want to work *with* rather than *against* how the brain works best, we must recognize the powerful role emotions play in our lives and those we seek to lead and influence.

Indeed, we aren't thinking individuals who happen to feel. We aren't driven and motivated by facts and figures, at least not by facts and figures alone. The truth is quite the opposite: emotion rather than logic drives people to move from the possible to the impossible, from where they are to where they want to be.

The human brain makes emotional decisions and then justifies them with logical reasons. I have a Volvo. I justified that purchase because I was in a terrible car accident and wanted the safest car on the road. But if I were being honest, the sound system stole my heart.

We are emotional individuals who happen to think. This human element makes things messy and complex, and a truth we can't ignore. Business is easy until people get involved. If we could remove the human element, most of our problems would not exist. However, if we were to remove the human element, we would never produce anything in the first place. The key is learning how to work *with* the human element.

We've all experienced the inherent challenges of emotion. We can identify a solution or strategy that sounds flawless in theory and looks perfectly simple on paper. But in implementation, all hell breaks loose.

Take the story of the "Miracle on the Hudson," the extraordinary emergency landing by US Airways pilot Chesley "Sully" Sullenberger.[3] After a flock of Canadian geese disabled both engines, Sully made the split-second decision to land the aircraft on the Hudson River, saving all 155 people on board. Despite this heroic act, the National Transportation Safety Board (NTSB) questioned his judgment, suggesting he could have safely returned to LaGuardia. On paper, in simulations, maybe. But real life doesn't happen on paper, and Sully was flying in real time, with real lives on the line.

To test their hypothesis, the NTSB used a flight simulator. As the birds simulate striking the engines, the simulator pilots calmly look at one another. They state that birds are in the engine. Turn left. In the simulation, the plane could have safely landed at the airport. What the simulator doesn't account for is emotion and threat. In real life, the brain must process a complicated wave of emotions and details in milliseconds. What the heck just happened? What options do we have? What are my beliefs and experiences telling me? How can I be sure I'm making the right decision and not one that may cost 155 lives? Unlike in the simulator, making an immediate decision under duress requires time, logic, and the most unpredictable variable of all, emotion.

Great leaders and organizations do not resist the emotions that fuel the human element; they embrace them. They don't work against emotion but rather work with emotion. As Dan and Chip Heath state in their book, *Switch: How to Change Things When Change is Hard*, if we want people to change, we must put feeling first.[4] This fact goes far beyond wanting people to change.

We must put feeling first if we want people to buy into change, learn, remember, self-manage, elevate their thinking, collaborate, build relationships, and be good humans. Emotions run the show; that's the heart of the Using Emotion Strategy.

In cultures where leaders ignore the Using Emotion Strategy, a few observable signs are:

- The environment is toxic and dysfunctional.
- Employees work "for" the leader rather than "with" the leader.
- Vulnerability is perceived as a sign of weakness.
- Self-centered, ego-driven leaders are tolerated and sometimes rewarded.
- Learned helplessness becomes the norm.
- The workforce experiences higher rates of illness and depression.
- Information is hoarded out of fear that sharing will reduce job security.
- Organizational behaviors are misaligned with the vision and values.
- Threat is high and trust is low.
- Team members operate as individuals rather than as a united team.
- Mistakes are covered up instead of owned and addressed.
- Status quo rules.
- Initiative to innovate or take risk is discouraged.
- Coaching is used only as a form of punishment rather than development.
- The workforce focuses on criticism and blame rather than accountability.
- Unacceptable and unprofessional behavior is tolerated.
- High drama adds hidden costs and drains performance.

These cultures suffer unnecessary costs. By not honoring the human element, they create excessive people problems. People problems and the ensuing drama are invisible line items on the budget, destroying productivity and profits. You cannot outwork a toxic culture.

Cultures that recognize the power of emotion experience a different reality.

In cultures where leaders embrace the Using Emotion Strategy, a few observable signs are:

- The environment supports growth, development, and well-being.
- Leaders and teams are willing to be vulnerable without fear of retribution.
- Team members feel they work "with" the leader and not "for" the leader.
- Leaders who invest in personal and team growth are rewarded.
- Accountability and ownership are cultural norms.
- Employee engagement and retention is high.
- Collaboration is embedded in the culture.
- Recognition is timely, and credit is given freely.
- Trust anchors relationships among teammates and with customers.
- All are encouraged to challenge the status quo.
- The right people are placed in the right jobs.
- Risk-taking and innovation are embraced rather than feared.
- Coaching is ongoing and focused on development.
- The workforce is quick to hold themselves and others accountable.
- Expectations are clearly communicated.
- Unprofessional behavior is not tolerated.

There is power and profit in the Using Emotion Strategy. Leaders and organizations that align with how the brain works best are those that survive financial crises and pandemics, attract the top talent, and lead in their industry. They honor emotions and realize that individuals are driven by passion, purpose, and feeling. They intentionally build on strengths and are equally concerned with the health of their people as they are with a healthy bottom line. They have significantly fewer people problems.

| WITHOUT THE USING EMOTION STRATEGY | WITH THE USING EMOTION STRATEGY |
| --- | --- |
| • High threat | • High trust |
| • Work "for" the leader | • Work "with" the leader |
| • No vulnerability | • Vulnerability |
| • Self-centered and ego-driven | • Selfless and others-focused |
| • Learned helplessness | • Self-directed |
| • Increased sickness and depression | • High satisfaction and retention |
| • Silos and information hoarding | • Collaborative |
| • Cover ups | • Give credit where credit is due |
| • Maintain status quo | • See failure as learning opportunities |
| • Punitive coaching | • See development as a right and feedback as a gift |
| • Low engagement and loyalty | • Challenge the status quo |
| • Blame and complain | • Developmental coaching |
| • Tolerate unacceptable, unprofessional behavior | • Meaningful conversations |
| • High drama | • Low drama |

# BE A LEADER
# WORTH FOLLOWING
*How to live out the Using Emotion Strategy*

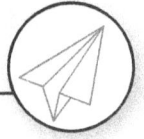

The Using Emotion Strategy is most powerfully applied through the lens of two foundational theories: multiple intelligences and emotional intelligence.

Howard Gardner's work on multiple intelligence theory is an epic example of how a shift in belief can open new worlds of possibilities.[5] Through a blend of interdisciplinary studies, he challenged the conventional view of intelligence as a single, quantifiable measure that an IQ test could assess. His theory proposed that the brain processes information and solves problems in many ways. Gardner challenged us to stop asking "How smart are you?" and to start asking, "How are you, smart?"

So, how are *you*, smart?

- Are you word smart (linguistic intelligence, think Maya Angelou)?
- Are you number smart (logical-mathematical intelligence, think Albert Einstein)?
- Are you picture and proportion smart (spatial intelligence, think Gutzon and Lincoln Borglum, Mount Rushmore sculptors)?
- Are you body smart (bodily-kinesthetic intelligence, think Serena Williams)?
- Are you music smart (musical intelligence, think Rodgers and Hammerstein)?
- Are you pattern and nature smart (naturalist intelligence, think Jane Goodall)?
- Are you big questions smart (existential intelligence, think Friedrich Nietzsche)?

Gardner redefined intelligence from a test score to the ability to create products or solve problems that are important to the culture or the situation. So, the need for clean drinking water may require a different intelligence than the need for a poem.

In the theory of multiple intelligences, "smart" is defined by the culture, not the test takers. This is great news for those of us who struggle with test-taking.

Let's apply this belief to leadership. What is "smart" when the culture is leadership? What intelligence counts when meeting the culture's needs involves leading change, creating resonance within teams, resolving conflict, collaborating, and influencing stakeholders?

The answer lies within the work of multiple intelligence theory (MI) and emotional intelligence theory (EQ). Both emphasize that when people and relationships are involved, the intelligences that matter most are intrapersonal intelligence, the ability to know and manage oneself, and interpersonal intelligence, the ability to connect with and influence others.

**Emotional intelligence is the fusion of intrapersonal and interpersonal intelligences, and it's one of the most powerful predictors of success.** When we strengthen emotional intelligence, results aren't just slightly better, they're exponentially better. Research consistently shows that boosting emotional intelligence delivers a substantial return in performance, leadership, and relationships.

EQ significantly outweighs IQ as a predictor of success in virtually every success marker, from creativity and innovation to pay, job satisfaction, marital happiness, team loyalty, and organizational influence. Teams prioritizing EQ have increased retention and engagement scores, higher-quality ideas and solutions, better conflict resolution skills, a deep sense of curiosity, an inclusive environment, and fewer drama costs.

- Leaders perceived as having empathy perform over 40% higher in employee engagement, decision-making, and coaching.
- Emotional intelligence has a 58% influence on job performance.
- 90% of top-performing employees have high emotional intelligence.
- 71% of hiring managers value EQ over IQ when looking for employees.
- Leaders higher in EQ saw enhanced team cohesion, improved decision-making, increased trust, and enhanced creativity.
- 75% of workplace conflicts are attributed to a lack of emotional intelligence.
- The average employee spends 2.5 hours a day engaged in workplace drama.[6]

**Leaders worth following are deeply committed to growing emotional intelligence—in themselves and in those they lead.** They intentionally cultivate both intrapersonal and interpersonal awareness and skills, recognizing that self and social mastery are essential to achieving a lasting impact. Thanks to discoveries in neuroplasticity, we now know emotional intelligence isn't fixed—it can be strengthened at any age. As long as we're alive and willing, growth is always possible. There is no final exam. No graduation day.

## Intrapersonal Intelligence: Knowing and Managing Your Self

A Hindu proverb says the three greatest mysteries of life are air to the birds, water to the fish, and man to himself.

Psychologist Daniel Goleman, known for his groundbreaking work, describes an emotionally intelligent person as someone who can:

- Stay self-motivated
- Control impulse
- Delay immediate gratification
- Regulate and manage one's moods
- Demonstrate compassion
- Maintain optimism and hope
- Extend empathy

An emotionally intelligent person can do all of this not only under ideal circumstances, when there is plenty of praise, energy, time, and money, but also in times of frustration, when facing high levels of stress, uncertainty, resistance, and risk.[7]

The literature on EQ is vast, resulting in an endless number of valuable resources, including graduate programs, assessments, podcasts, books, and more. My goal is not to delve deeply into the theory, but to highlight key behaviors and practical applications that we can use to live out the Using Emotion Strategy.

### Self-Awareness

Rate how frequently you exhibit the following:

|  | Almost Always | | | | Almost Never |
|---|---|---|---|---|---|
| I know when I experience mood shifts. | 1 | 2 | 3 | 4 | 5 |
| I know when I become defensive. | 1 | 2 | 3 | 4 | 5 |
| I know the impact my behavior has on others. | 1 | 2 | 3 | 4 | 5 |

Self-aware leaders and teams are fully present, mindful, and connected to what their bodies and minds are telling them. They easily identify what they are experiencing and choose what they want to do with it before the emotions have power over their behavior. They know how to adjust to the feelings in the room and the situation. They can dial up and dial down both empowering and disempowering emotions. They know when they become defensive and territorial, how their behavior impacts others, and they can keep situations in perspective. They respond rather than react.

Self-awareness is the most critical capability a leader can develop, but it's also one of the most elusive. Research by organizational psychologist Tasha Eurich found that while 95% of people believe they're self-aware, only 10–15% are.[8] The gap between perception and reality is wide, and closing it takes intentional reflection, feedback, and humility.

### ACTIONS

- Rigorously seek feedback. Proactively ask others how they see you limiting yourself, one or two areas where you can improve, and what you are doing well. When you receive praise, ask, "Even better if?"

- Realize there are no good or bad emotions. They are simply signals we should pay attention to. Your brain and body are constantly communicating with each other. Recognize what they say and decide what you want to do with that valuable information.
- Tasha Eurich includes helpful strategies in her book Insight: *The Surprising Truth About How Others See Us, How We See Ourselves, and Why the Answers Matter More Than We Think*. One strategy is to ask "what" questions rather than "why." Let's say you were passed over for a promotion. Rather than asking, "Why was I passed over for that promotion?" ask instead, "What can I learn from this event in my life?"

### Self-Confidence

Rate how frequently you exhibit the following:

|  | Almost Always | | | | Almost Never |
|---|---|---|---|---|---|
| I welcome constructive feedback. | 1 | 2 | 3 | 4 | 5 |
| I ask for help. | 1 | 2 | 3 | 4 | 5 |
| I am confident in my strengths and weaknesses. | 1 | 2 | 3 | 4 | 5 |

Leaders and teams who are self-confident are more open and vulnerable with each other. They are as confident in discussing and admitting their weaknesses as they are in discussing and acknowledging their strengths. They aren't attached to protecting their ego; they don't have to be right or the most intelligent person in the room. They hold themselves accountable and responsible. They will admit mistakes and avoid criticizing, condemning, or blaming others, including themselves. When mistakes are made, they lean in to see what they can learn from them and move forward. They give credit where credit is due.

---

### ACTIONS

- When you feel yourself blaming or criticizing, ask different questions, such as:
  - How did I create (or contribute to) this outcome?
  - What is and what isn't mine to own?
  - What problem needs to be solved?
  - What actions can I take?
  - What support do I need to take the appropriate actions?
- Ask for help and delegate.
- Accept feedback as a gift. Some gifts are kept forever, and some are tossed in the trash. When you receive constructive feedback, evaluate the message and choose what to keep and what to toss.

---

### *Self-Control*

Rate how frequently you exhibit the following:

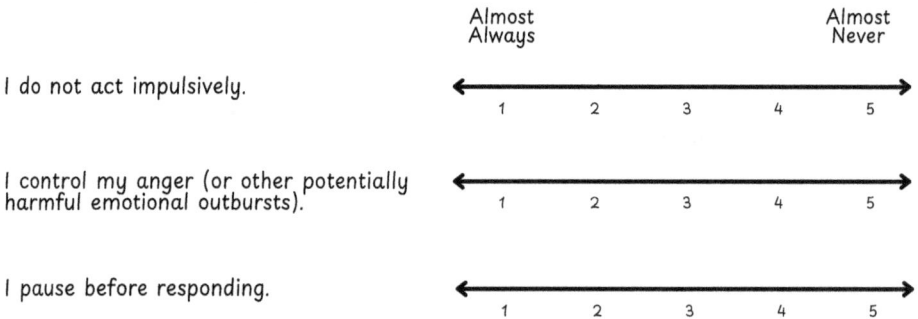

| | Almost Always | | | | Almost Never |
|---|---|---|---|---|---|
| I do not act impulsively. | 1 | 2 | 3 | 4 | 5 |
| I control my anger (or other potentially harmful emotional outbursts). | 1 | 2 | 3 | 4 | 5 |
| I pause before responding. | 1 | 2 | 3 | 4 | 5 |

Leaders and teams who exercise self-control know their point of no return. They know how far they can push themselves and others. They know their triggers, manage their disempowering emotions appropriately, and proactively manage stress and pressures. They are mindful and intentional.

- Know your "yellow lights" and slow down. A yellow light at an intersection means to slow down and pay attention. Most drivers speed up, which can result in deadly collisions. When your life's "yellow lights" appear, such as irritation, health issues, or lack of concentration, slow down and use caution to avoid costly consequences.
- Challenge the stories in your head. Just because something "feels" true doesn't make it true. When a situation triggers you, ask yourself a few generative questions:
  - What meaning am I giving the situation?
  - What meaning do I want to give to the situation?
  - What else might be true?
  - What might I be missing?
  - How do I want to respond in a way that aligns with how I want others to experience me?
- Stop, drop, and roll. This is a proven strategy when someone is on fire. It's equally helpful when our emotions are on fire.
  - Stop: Recognize what you are feeling and what you need.
  - Drop: Move, take deep breaths, go for a walk, ask a few generative questions.
  - Roll: Choose the response that will move you toward the desired outcome.

## Adaptability

Rate how frequently you exhibit the following:

|  | Almost Always | | | | Almost Never |
|---|---|---|---|---|---|
| I deal effectively with change and uncertainty. | 1 | 2 | 3 | 4 | 5 |
| I pursue better ways of doing things. | 1 | 2 | 3 | 4 | 5 |
| I seek different perspectives. | 1 | 2 | 3 | 4 | 5 |

Leaders and teams who are adaptable realize that becoming defensive and overly committed to one way increases threat and decreases activity in the prefrontal cortex. They recognize that a lack of adaptability is often a result of a lack of clarity. Therefore, they seek answers and solutions in times of change. They own only what is theirs to own and stay focused on what they can control. They respect the decisions of others even if they do not wholly agree with them. They search for the good in changes.

### ACTIONS

- The either/or continuum. When you find yourself saying either/or (either I do this or I do this), write "either" on one end of a continuum and "or" on the other. Then, generate as many different options as you can. This helps your brain move out of the tunnel into a space of possibilities.
- Ask, "And what else?" Oftentimes, a stuck mind simply needs more options, so keep asking "And what else?", "And what else?", "And what else?"
- Make a list with three columns: Positives, Uncertainties, Solutions

- In the Positives column, list the positives of the change. Use generative questions like:
  - What do we have here that's good?
  - What becomes possible that wasn't before?
  - What is this showing up to teach me?
  - How might this be happening FOR me rather than TO me?
- In the Uncertainties column, list the worries, concerns, and confusion associated with the change.
- In the Solutions column, brainstorm solutions to the list in the Uncertainties column. Identify where you need greater clarity and where to find it.

### Initiative

Rate how frequently you exhibit the following:

| | Almost Always | | | | Almost Never |
|---|---|---|---|---|---|
| I openly admit mistakes. | 1 | 2 | 3 | 4 | 5 |
| I stay the course when a decision is right despite opposition. | 1 | 2 | 3 | 4 | 5 |
| I proactively address ineffective behaviors. | 1 | 2 | 3 | 4 | 5 |

Leaders and teams who take initiative see themselves as owners. They have an entrepreneurial spirit and mindset. They work *on* their business and *in* their business. They quickly address and stop ineffective behaviors, holding themselves and others accountable. They are both candid and respectful. They create opportunities rather than waiting for them. They move to solutions once problems are identified and involve others as appropriate. They meet expectations without being told or reminded.

## ACTIONS

- Life isn't The Price is Right. Growing up, I watched end-less episodes of this gameshow with my grandmother. It's a show where audience members patiently wait for the host to call their name, followed by the famous line "come on down," so they can come to the front and play the game.

  In life, don't wait to be "called on down." Use generative questions to clarify what you want or need, and then make it happen.
    - What is it that you *really, really* want?
    - What makes this important to you right now?
    - How will you know when you get there?
    - Who can help you?
    - What resources do you have?
    - What are your next steps?

- Study your calendar. Do you have time on your calendar for planning and thinking strategically? Identify how to carve out time in your "green zone," the time of day when you have the most cognitive energy.

- Who in your life shows initiative without coming across as off-putting to others? Who in your life is direct but respectful, forceful but not aggressive, and confident but not arrogant? Study them. Ask them to mentor you in this area.

## Optimism

Rate how frequently you exhibit the following:

|  | Almost Always | | | | Almost Never |
|---|---|---|---|---|---|
| I maintain a positive outlook. | 1 | 2 | 3 | 4 | 5 |
| I deal constructively with mistakes and setbacks. | 1 | 2 | 3 | 4 | 5 |
| I believe where a problem exists, the solution exists. | 1 | 2 | 3 | 4 | 5 |

Optimistic leaders and teams leverage the power of positivity, giving their brains a happiness advantage, as Shawn Achor explains in his TED talk.[9] When setbacks or disappointments occur, optimists approach them constructively while maintaining a positive outlook. They create an uplifting environment for those around them. They move through life enthusiastically and passionately, seeing the bigger purpose in their actions and helping others do the same.

### ACTIONS

- Gratitude journal. Each morning, write 3 things you are grateful for. When you get to a hundred, start over.
- Express your appreciation. Each day, commit to sending at least one text or email to someone expressing thanks or appreciation for their contributions.
- Helper's high. Engage in volunteer work or find a meaningful way to help someone around you. Studies show that volunteering can elevate dopamine, improve your health, and potentially extend your life. Even better if? You bring your team with you.

# Interpersonal Intelligence: Influencing and Developing Others

The most important topic you'll ever study is yourself. The second most important topic is how to connect more meaningfully with others. How others experience you determines your legacy. Connection is essential in being a leader worth following.

As Brene Brown says, "Connection is why we're here; it is what gives purpose and meaning to our lives."[10]

### Empathy

Rate how frequently you exhibit the following:

|  | Almost Always | | | | Almost Never |
|---|---|---|---|---|---|
| I am present and listen to others fully. | 1 | 2 | 3 | 4 | 5 |
| I easily recognize what others are feeling. | 1 | 2 | 3 | 4 | 5 |
| I stay out of judgment. | 1 | 2 | 3 | 4 | 5 |

It is fitting to begin this section on influencing and developing others with empathy. Unless we first manage ourselves, we cannot recognize opportunities to demonstrate empathy, let alone live it out.

Leaders and teams who embrace empathy are highly self-managing. They have the awareness and the resources available when others need help. They genuinely care about others as human beings and are committed to slowing down, staying curious, and listening to better understand rather than rushing in and offering solutions. They truly consider others' perspectives, avoid judgment, and hold unconditional positive regard.

I visualize empathy as sitting in a chair across from someone, facing them and observing them, but seeing the world from my viewpoint. True empathy occurs when I pick up my chair and place it beside the other person. I'm no longer looking *at* them; I'm looking *with* them. Side-by-side, I begin to see the world from their viewpoint. That's empathy. No hugging required.

## ACTIONS

- Notice and listen. We don't need to agree, disagree, change, or judge. Just pay attention.
- Be there. We don't need to validate, silver line, or solve. We don't need to rush or force any answers.
- Show gratitude. Empathy is a divine moment when someone trusts us enough to share something. Thank them for trusting you.

Empathy may be the laziest, yet most powerful behavior a leader can demonstrate.

When I think of a leader worth following, I recall a time when my son was just two months old. I was struggling, but I was putting on a brave face at work. My leader, Kathy Price, called me into her office. We sat for a moment in silence, and she said, "You know, Sherry, we can design a flexible work schedule if you're interested."

Today, my son is 26. It's a moment I'll never forget. Empathy is truly one of the deepest connections we can have with another human being.

## *Service*

Rate how frequently you exhibit the following:

| | Almost Always | | | | Almost Never |
|---|---|---|---|---|---|
| I serve those around me, even if it is uncomfortable or inconvenient. | 1 | 2 | 3 | 4 | 5 |
| I actively build trust with others. | 1 | 2 | 3 | 4 | 5 |
| I give feedback. | 1 | 2 | 3 | 4 | 5 |

Leaders and teams who demonstrate service go the extra mile, expecting nothing in return. They are willing to put others ahead of themselves, even if it is hard, uncomfortable, or unpopular. They have the courage to give the feedback people really need to hear. They evaluate the impact of their decisions and commitments on the people who depend on them. They not only meet the spoken need but also detect the underlying, unspoken needs of others. No task is too menial.

### ACTIONS

- Share feedback. Feedback is one of the highest forms of service. Recently, I debriefed a 360 assessment that contained feedback that I knew would be difficult to receive. I wasn't surprised when she started crying. I was surprised, however, when she explained she wasn't crying because of the feedback. She was crying because no one cared enough about her to share this feedback earlier. She had worked with some of the raters for over 10 years. I'm guessing they did care, but that's not how it landed with her.

- "Even better if?" When we offer help or someone asks for help, add "Even better if?" to see if there is one more way you can serve them.
- Open doors. One of the most effective ways to serve others, especially as an established leader, is to make connections for them. You have resources and relationships that others may not. Opening a door for them simply by making an introduction to someone in your circle can change that person's life.

## Inspiration

Rate how frequently you exhibit the following:

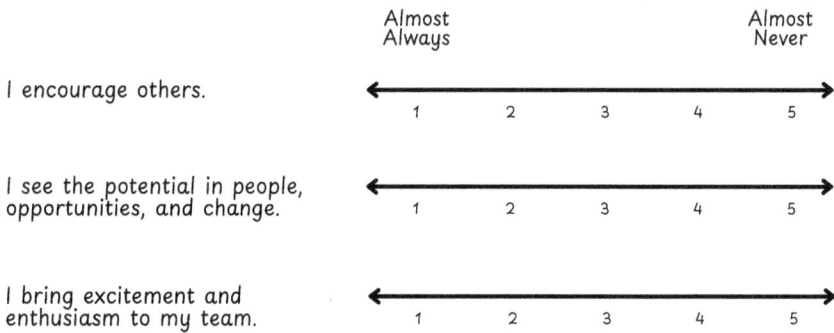

| | Almost Always | | | | Almost Never |
|---|---|---|---|---|---|
| I encourage others. | 1 | 2 | 3 | 4 | 5 |
| I see the potential in people, opportunities, and change. | 1 | 2 | 3 | 4 | 5 |
| I bring excitement and enthusiasm to my team. | 1 | 2 | 3 | 4 | 5 |

Emotions are contagious. Have you made anyone sick, lately?

To *inspire* means "to breathe into" or "give life." Are you breathing fresh air into others? Or blowing second-hand smoke?

Leaders and teams who inspire give life. They are encouragers and energizers. They realize emotions are contagious and seek to spread enthusiasm and passion. They continuously see the potential in people, in new opportunities, and in times of change. Others frequently seek them out because of their contagious, uplifting spirit.

## ACTIONS

- Commit to your morning routine. What must you do each morning to show up to life as your best self? What do you need to do each day before you open the door to the office or turn on your computer screen to inspire others?
- Manage self-talk. People who inspire are not insulated from reality. Some days are hard, and some situations suck. People who inspire choose to believe:
  - They are 100% successful in making it through hard days.
  - Life is happening *for* them, not *to* them.
  - Everything happens in divine timing, and it serves them.
  - Where a problem exists, the solution exists.
- Regulate, relate, reason. When the team needs inspiration, leverage the role of emotions and how the brain works best.
  - Regulate: Listen with empathy and meet people where they are without judgment.
  - Relate: Stay curious and ask generative questions.
  - Reason: Connect to the bigger why (the vision, the values, and the mission) and the greater good.

## Conflict management

Rate how frequently you exhibit the following:

| | Almost Always | | | | Almost Never |
|---|---|---|---|---|---|
| I stay curious and see conflict as a place of possibilities. | 1 | 2 | 3 | 4 | 5 |
| I encourage debate and open discussions. | 1 | 2 | 3 | 4 | 5 |
| I speak my truth with candor and respect. | 1 | 2 | 3 | 4 | 5 |

Leaders and teams that effectively manage conflict confront situations and initiate conversations collaboratively and promptly. They handle difficult situations and conversations, as well as challenging personalities, with diplomacy and tact. They focus on the goal and the real issue, not on personalities and opinions. They listen fully and ask questions to see the situation from others' perspectives. They avoid mind-reading, making assumptions, and jumping to conclusions. They strive to keep the solution as close to the problem as possible and avoid involving others unnecessarily.

### ACTIONS

- Sooner is smaller; later is larger. The "wait and see approach" typically results in waiting and seeing that the conflict and its consequences escalate, and the hard conversation becomes even harder.
- Keep the solution closest to the problem. As a guiding principle, address conflicts directly with the person involved, rather than through others. The more people we involve, the more confusion we create, and the less control we have over the outcome.

- Assume good intent. Our brains are exceptional story-tellers, and left to default, they tell a story of sabotage and conspiracy. Discipline yourself to assume good intent when approaching a conflict conversation.
- GROW. GROW is a collaborative framework for addressing conflict. Below is an overview of GROW and the science behind it.

### Step One: Goal

Clearly state a goal for this conversation that is compelling to everyone involved.

> Why? If we start with reality, we trigger the brain to get defensive and listen for disagreement. If we start with a compelling goal, we tap into the brain's WII-FM (What's In It For Me?) and trigger the brain to listen for agreement.

*Can we discuss ways to build greater trust on our team?*

### Step Two: Reality

Clearly share what you are experiencing and invite the other person to share their own experiences.

> Why? The purpose is to regulate and relate. You don't have to agree with each other's reality to move forward. You simply need to establish a gap between where you are and where you want to be.

*I want to share some things I'm experiencing, and I want to hear what you are experiencing.*

### Step Three: Options

Generate options to move from reality to the goal. Share ideas you have, invite the other person to share ideas they have, and generate other ideas together.

> Why? The more options *we* generate, the more control and ownership *we* feel. Keep asking, "and what else?" and "even better if?"

*I had some ideas for the team, and I want to hear your ideas.*

### Step Four: Way Forward

Recap next steps, timelines, and responsibilities, and schedule a follow-up GROW conversation.

> Why? What we say is not always what people hear. Schedule the follow-up meeting. As a reminder from the Action Strategy, there is only a 16% follow-through rate if we hear an idea and like it. However, the likelihood of implementation increases to 90-95% if we like and adopt the idea, create a plan, and then report to someone on whether or not we did it.

*Let's reconnect next Monday at 10am to check in our progress.*

The GROW framework gives courage and structure to those who *avoid* conflict and encourages collaboration for those who *like* conflict a little too much.

If you find you are not closer to the goal at the follow-up meeting, have another GROW conversation. Restate the goal, review reality, and generate and act on different options. A high-performance belief is that if we create a result that isn't serving us, we can create a different result that will.

> **Goal**: *Hi Patty, can we talk about how to ensure we get our bonuses this year?*
>
> **Reality**: *I'd like to share a few obstacles I'm seeing, but I want to hear what you are experiencing.*
>
> **Options**: *I've had a few ideas on how to close the gap I'd like to share. I'm sure you have ideas also.*
>
> **Way Forward**: *So, I'll take the lead on the process changes, and you'll take the lead on talking with IT. When can we regroup to see if we are getting better results?*

### *Influence*

Rate how frequently you exhibit the following:

|  | Almost Always | | | | Almost Never |
|---|---|---|---|---|---|
| I model the behavior I want to see in others. | 1 | 2 | 3 | 4 | 5 |
| I listen for and care about what is important to others. | 1 | 2 | 3 | 4 | 5 |
| People seek out my opinion and expertise. | 1 | 2 | 3 | 4 | 5 |

Influential leaders and teams model the behavior they want to see from others. They communicate directly, providing a realistic and straightforward view of reality, and do not distort the truth to make it more appealing. They are committed to integrity and helping others move in a positive direction. They recognize that *influence* and *influenza* come from the same root word; they can either lift others up or make them sick.

---

### ACTIONS

- **Flow through.** In the word *influence, flu* means "flow" and *in* means "through." Thus, *influence* means "to flow through." Just like flowing water, influence is extremely powerful to change behavior for the positive or the negative.
- **Regulate, relate, and reason.** To influence, we must regulate by self-managing, modeling credibility, and setting aside our agenda. We relate to others by listening to what is important to them, building trust and rapport. Then, we move to reasoning.
- **3 words.** Identify 3 words you want people to think of when they think of you. What are 3 words you would like for your legacy to be? (honest, steady, trustworthy, fun, kind, etc.). Have those 3 words visible every day. Be mindful to respond to every situation in alignment with who you aspire to be and how you want to be known.
- **Commit to integrity.** Are you the same even when no one is looking? Are you the same with team members as you are with clients? Consistency of character builds trust, and a trustworthy person is foundational to high-performance leadership and being a leader worth following.

## Teamwork

Rate how frequently you exhibit the following:

|  | Almost Always | | | | Almost Never |
|---|---|---|---|---|---|
| I create a sense of belonging with those on my team. | 1 | 2 | 3 | 4 | 5 |
| I protect and promote my team's reputation with outsiders. | 1 | 2 | 3 | 4 | 5 |
| I advocate for my team. | 1 | 2 | 3 | 4 | 5 |

Leaders and teams that work together recognize the sophisticated skills required to be an effective team member. They value unity. They are loyal to each other and their word. They honor the absent and refrain from speaking negatively of someone if they are not present. They actively seek ways to demonstrate appreciation for one another, and they reward and recognize their achievements. They hold each other accountable for living out the team's vision and values. They promote a welcoming, friendly, and cooperative environment. They protect and promote the team's reputation with outsiders. They know their leader always has their back and the courage to advocate on their behalf when necessary.

### ACTIONS

- Give clarity, meaning, and purpose. The brain craves clarity, meaning, and purpose. Without it, it moves to confusion and threat. One of your roles as a team leader is to provide clarity and a compelling why behind every decision.
- Establish non-negotiables. What are your team's non-negotiables? If those have not been clearly defined,

each person operates from their standards. Spend time as a team identifying the team's non-negotiables and keep them visible.

- Ongoing development. No team wins the World Cup by accident. And even when they win, they never stop practicing. Professional sports teams constantly train. They continuously reinforce the fundamentals and work with a coach, if not a team of coaches. Why should your team be any different? Invest in your team's development. It is one of the highest-return investments you can make.

## NAVIGATE TO RESOURCE

Team Non-Negotiables: PDF

# FINAL THOUGHTS ON THE USING EMOTION STRATEGY

Not surprisingly, companies with healthy, emotionally intelligent cultures achieve better business results, including greater talent attraction, retention, innovation, productivity, and a healthier bottom line. They truly are a "best place to work," not just one that received the award for social media purposes.

If culture drives results, what drives culture?

The number one influence on culture can be traced back to the actions of one person: the immediate leader.[11]

Leaders who drive healthy cultures recognize the power of the Using Emotion Strategy for themselves and for those they seek to influence, lead, and develop. They embrace the human element. They realize that regardless of the industry, they are in the relationship business, and all eyes are on them.

# WHAT MAKES A LEADER WORTH FOLLOWING?

*We asked real people. We got real responses.*

Here are just a few. Would anyone say the same about you?

✔ *The leader must walk the talk with empathy, fairness and respect for others.*

✔ *They are trustworthy, grateful, empathetic, and compassionate. They have effective communication skills and inspire and empower others.*

✔ *Authentic connection; common principles.*

✔ *Character first. Credibility second (due to their relational investment, their personal capability or their track record). Positional authority last (a person isn't worth following simply because they've been given the authority by the powers that be).*

✔ *Empathy's another big one; they get what drives people and don't treat them like just another rung of the ladder. They're not pushovers. They're also usually good at letting people shine, rather than hogging the spotlight.*

# THINK. DISCUSS. APPLY.

*Make it matter*

1. If a respected colleague described you as a leader, what might they say?
2. If a direct report described you as a leader, what might they say?
3. Describe a time in which you were successful in managing yourself. What were the benefits?
4. Describe a time in which you were not successful in managing yourself. What were the costs?
5. How frequently do you display the intrapersonal behaviors discussed in this chapter?
6. How frequently do you display the interpersonal behaviors discussed in this chapter?
7. As you consider the behaviors discussed in this chapter, which one could you intentionally increase to better handle a current challenge or improve your effectiveness moving forward?"

## NAVIGATE TO RESOURCE

Go here to schedule a complimentary call to discuss how EQ assessments can inform your leadership.

Reason

↑

Relate

↑

Regulate

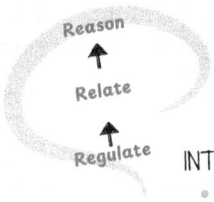

## ENGAGE EMOTIONS. PRIORITIZE PEOPLE.

### INTRAPERSONAL INTELLIGENCE

- Self-Awareness
- Self-Confidence
- Self-Control
- Adaptability
- Initiative
- Optimism

### INTERPERSONAL INTELLIGENCE

- Empathy
- Service
- Inspiration
- Conflict Management
- Influence
- Teamwork

*Culture drives results.*
*Leaders drive culture.*

> Abilities such as being able to motivate oneself and persist
> in the face of frustrations; to control impulse and delay
> gratification; to regulate one's moods and keep distress from
> swamping the ability to think; to empathize and to hope.
>
> (Goleman, Emotional Intelligence, 1998)

## WHERE A PROBLEM EXISTS, THE <u>SOLUTION</u> EXISTS.

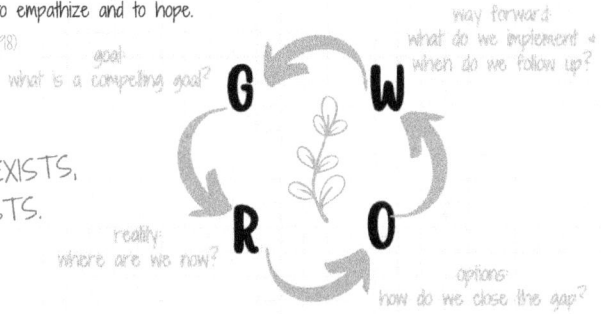

goal:
what is a compelling goal?

way forward:
what do we implement &
when do we follow up?

G    W

R    O

reality:
where are we now?

options:
how do we close the gap?

The question isn't
'how smart are you?'
The question is 'how
are you smart?'

We aren't thinking individuals who happen
to have emotions; **we are emotional
individuals who happen to think.**

EQ is four times a better
predictor of success than

IQ in virtually every
success marker,

# CHAPTER 7

# The Mosaic Strategy

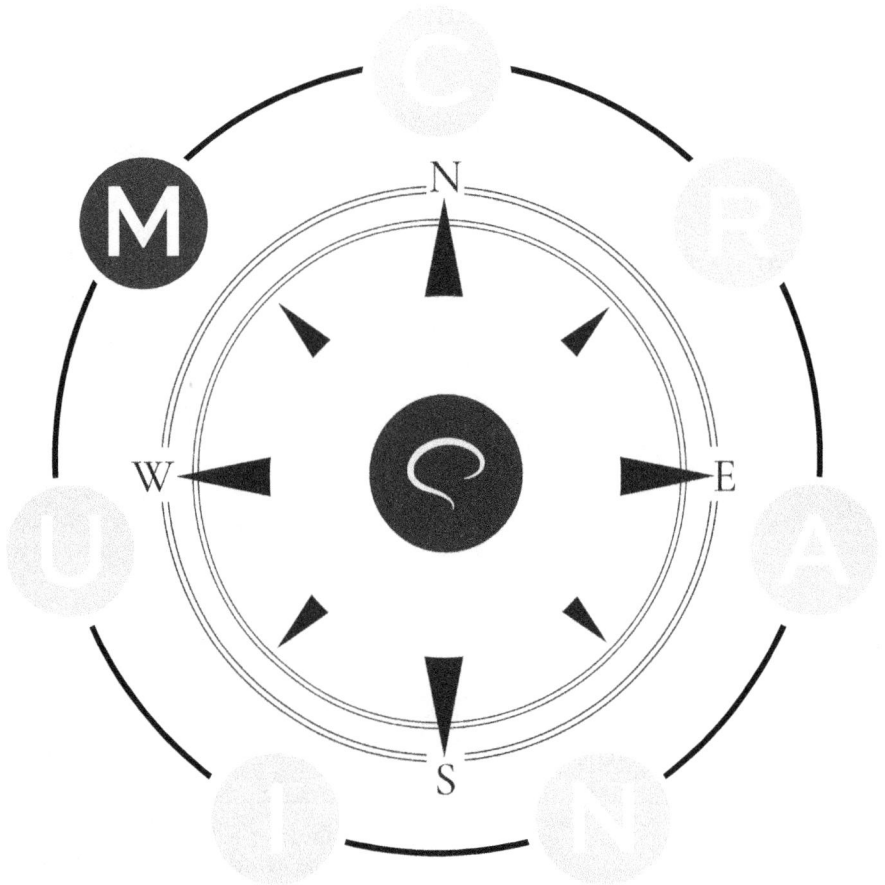

**VALUE DIFFERENCES.
CREATE BELONGING.**

## BIG IDEA

Belonging is not a nicety; it's a neurological necessity. Inclusion transforms unique parts into a resilient, lasting force.

## BREAKTHROUGH BELIEFS

Great minds don't think alike.

Social rejection and physical pain are virtually identical in the brain.

You have a message and a style of delivering that message that hasn't been given to anyone else. Honor and protect that gift. No. Matter. What.

# REAL LEADERS. REAL LIFE.

*More than a chair.*

Ruth sat in deep reflection at her first executive team meeting, one month after her hiring. When she initially walked in, there wasn't a chair for her at the table. Though everyone was friendly and introduced themselves as the team gathered, she noticed one seat was missing: hers. So, she rolled over a chair from the room next door. The CEO gave her a warm introduction as the hospital system's Chief Culture Officer, a newly appointed position. But when he asked if anyone had questions about Ruth or her role, the team was silent. Thirty minutes into the meeting, she realized it was dominated by three members. Each had a business background from the same university, had a long tenure with the company, and approached every situation from similar perspectives. Ruth noticed that a couple of team members had attempted to challenge their recommended solution but were quickly shot down. When a vote was taken to move to the next agenda item, the room was silent.

Ruth knew why this group needed a Chief Culture Officer, but she was questioning whether they were truly committed to the changes that were necessary. As the meeting progressed, she began to reflect on her first 30 days since taking the position.

She was drawn to the hospital system because it served a diverse community. It provided health services in several neighborhoods with extreme economic differences; the population served ranged from young families to those in assisted living. Several large, global companies had recently relocated their headquarters to this city, bringing employees and their cultures from all over the world.

At her interview, Ruth received a tour of one of the group's busiest hospitals. She immediately took notice of the different ages, economic backgrounds, and nationalities sitting in the waiting room. And yet, the diversity of the staff did not reflect the people they served. That day, Ruth saw a Spanish-speaking mother with a sick child who asked a staff member for directions to the lab. The employee did not speak Spanish, nor did he offer to find a translator. She also observed an Indian family grieving in a nearby room. Meanwhile, just outside of the hospital, an older woman, looking very confused, was pushing her husband in a wheelchair.

Ruth sat in on a physicians' leadership meeting later in the day. The physicians were making decisions without considering the staff's input or the impact these decisions would have on staff scheduling. She had multiple private conversations where staff voiced concerns of working in silos, a lack of collaboration with other departments, feeling their opinions were not valued, and that going along with the status quo was easier than trying to make a change.

Next, she visited with HR leaders who voiced concern over the competition for qualified healthcare workers in the city and discussed the need to attract, hire, and keep good staff. A local university had been their main source for recruitment for years; however, their compensation plan simply could not compete with another healthcare system in the area. Ruth's organization had a retention problem as well; many of the most promising recruits left within the first year, seeking growth and development opportunities at other places.

In her first month, Ruth had become aware of organizational culture. The hospital system, established more than 100 years ago, had rich traditions in its ways of thinking and acting. Those who attempted to challenge those traditions, change procedures, introduce new ideas, or share best practices from other hospitals or industries were immediately met with resistance.

Snapping back to the present moment as the executive team meeting concluded, Ruth was confident her seat at the table would make all the difference for this organization.

# YOU'RE WIRED FOR MOSAIC

*Why your brain thrives on the Mosaic Strategy*

Like the art of mosaics, the Mosaic Strategy embraces the endless complexities of the brain. Each brain is as unique as its owner's fingerprints and constantly changing. The brain is a network of billions of individual parts, neurons, working efficiently to form neural networks. Your brain's neural networks result from innumerable variables, including genetics, life experiences, perspectives, strengths, struggles, talents, etc. The optimal environment is one of inclusion, where all individual differences and similarities are more than tolerated; they are valued. Like a mosaic, the ordinary combine to create the extraordinary. The whole is far greater than the sum of its parts.

An inclusive culture isn't just a moral imperative—it's a strategic advantage. Seeking out and leveraging differences is essential for business results because it is essential to the equipment that drives business results – the brain.

The Mosaic Strategy matters to high-performance leadership because it

- lowers threat,
- values life experiences,
- embraces bias,
- celebrates our brains' differences,
- fuels innovation,

- honors the need for belonging, and
- enhances each of the CRANIUM Strategies.

## Lowers threat

Negative threat is the #1 killer of empowering learning environments, living environments, working environments, and human potential. The most impactful action parents, teachers, spouses, co-workers, and leaders can take is to replace high-threat cultures and interactions with high-trust cultures and interactions.

We choose to create trust or threat with every word we say, action we take, and belief we adopt. When the brain perceives something as negative threat, cortisol increases, learning and memory are compromised, emotion is triggered, activity in the prefrontal cortex is limited, and our ability to view options, think creatively, and see from other people's perspectives is narrowed.

As mentioned in previous chapters, the top threats I have encountered in working with thousands of leaders for nearly 30 years include change, perceived favoritism, unrealistic or unclear expectations, risk of loss, humiliation, micromanagement, lack of meaningful work, lack of resources, lack of trust, and social rejection. All of these situations share common characteristics: some level of risk and confusion, the fear of adverse consequences, and a lack of choice and voice.

We can minimize each of these threats by creating an inclusive culture. In an inclusive, or Mosaic culture, members welcome differences and value perspectives resulting from diverse life experiences.

## Values life experiences

All of our life experiences, the life experiences of those who came before us, and even the life experiences of those around us shape who we are.

For example:

- *Did you grow up in poverty, wealth, or somewhere in between?*
- *Were you physically safe?*
- *Did you play video games inside or play creatively outside?*
- *Did you go to private, public, or home school?*
- *Did you have a strong family unit?*
- *Did you have people who encouraged, invested, and believed in you?*
- *Did you play individual or team sports? Did you play sports at all?*
- *Did you travel often?*
- *Have you lived in different cities or countries?*
- *Did your parents read to you?*
- *Did you have access to a variety of experiences?*
- *Was your home multicultural?*
- *Did you have access to healthy foods?*
- *Were you exposed to trauma?*
- *Did you receive healthcare?*
- *Did you have siblings and extended family?*
- *Did you live in an urban, suburban, or rural area?*
- *Were you brought up with specific spiritual values?*
- *Were you a first-generation college student?*
- *Were your parents or your grandparents immigrants?*

These experiences, whether encountered, observed, or inherited, influence how we develop, who we are today, and who we will be tomorrow. They shape our beliefs about ourselves and our world, our values, our actions, and our results. The better we can understand each other's life experiences, the better we can appreciate how those experiences influence today's actions, perspectives, and results.

## Embraces bias

If you're human, you have bias. The human brain constantly distorts, deletes, and generalizes everything it encounters.

The Mosaic Strategy isn't about ignoring or even necessarily suppressing biases. It's about recognizing them, acknowledging them, and then deciding what we want to do with them. It's about bringing our biases to the surface, not to judge or criticize, but to stay curious. Where is that bias from? What purpose is it serving? How does it influence our decisions and results? And most importantly, do we want to keep it?

It's comforting to think our brain chooses a logical response to the events in our lives, that we consciously create the outcome we want. This gives us a sense of security and control. The reality, however, is that our brain's response is filtered through all our biases.

$$E + R = O$$

(events)    (response)    (outcome)

For example,

**Event**: I see someone with tussled hair wearing baggy pants, flip-flops, and a T-shirt walking across the street with a menacing look, carrying a large black trash bag tossed over his shoulder.

**Response**: My response is neutral; he's just another pedestrian. I let him cross the street.

**Outcome**: I drive to my class and continue with my day, not giving it a second thought.

But that's not what happens at all.

Our brains are predicting, meaning-making machines. Hopefully, the predictions and stories they create will keep us on the planet for longer. Every second of the day, our brains work to make sense of the world by assigning meaning to events.

Our brains give meaning to every event, whether we are conscious of it or not. We give meaning to every email, text, conversation, news story, pedestrian crossing the road, etc. The meaning comes from all the direct and indirect experiences and beliefs we've adopted throughout our lives.

In milliseconds, our brain creates a story between an event and the response.

So, the process actually looks like this:

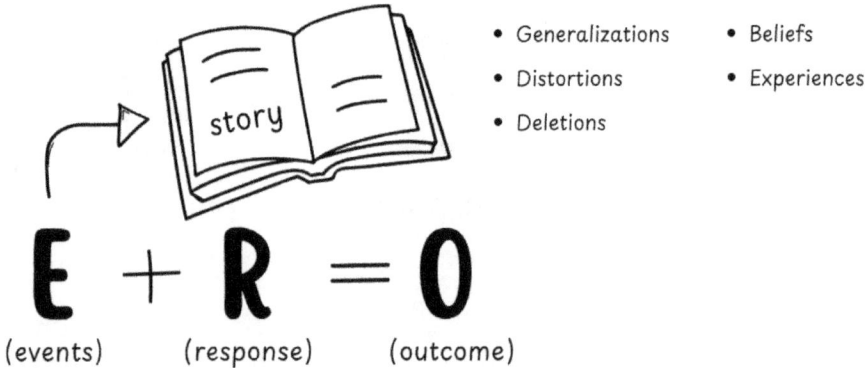

- Generalizations
- Distortions
- Deletions
- Beliefs
- Experiences

$$E + R = O$$

(events)  (response)  (outcome)

**Event**: I see someone with tussled hair wearing baggy pants, flip-flops, and a T-shirt walking across the street with a menacing look, carrying a large black trash bag tossed over his shoulder.

**Story**: This man is homeless. Our country has such a serious problem with homelessness. What will we ever do? What is the solution for this terrible situation that will soon overtake our neighborhoods?

**Meaning**: He's a dangerous nuisance. He's not even paying attention to oncoming traffic. He must be on drugs or mentally ill. He is likely dangerous.

**Response**: I let him cross the street feeling concerned, sad, and fearful.

**Outcome**: I go to my class and complain to participants about the growing homeless problem in our city, imposing my fear and worry onto them.

Our brains constantly distort, delete, and generalize information. Some scientists predict that we have anywhere from 2 to 4 million bits of information hitting our brains every second, and our brains can only process about 126 bits.[1] Therefore, our brains constantly try to be as efficient as possible through distorting, deleting, and generalizing.

The problem is we often get it wrong. We don't always focus on the right 126 bits of information. We constantly misread people, situations, and opportunities, which can come at a significant cost.

The real story?

I led a class at NASA Goddard Space Flight Center, a critical hub for NASA's space science research, technology development, and satellite operations. It is also home to some of the most advanced solar research in the world.

When I arrived at the building where I was to teach my class, I shared my concern of the "homeless" guy with one of the participants. He responded with, "Oh, Jim? Yeah, I know him. Nice guy."

It turns out that the man I saw crossing the street that morning was not homeless or dangerous; he was an award-winning scientist.

**A few facts to remember about bias:**

- We all have bias.
- Ninety-nine percent of bias is unconscious.
- Bias operates at lightning speed.
- Bias is deeply ingrained and difficult to unlearn.
- Bias is often wrong and limits our ability to perform at our best and to assume the best of others.

## Celebrates differences

The Mosaic Strategy is about better understanding our differences and similarities, appreciating them, and leveraging them to accomplish great things.

The list of how our brains differ is endless, but the point is that even if you have a handful of things in common with one group, you most likely have twice as many differences. Even identical twins have been found to have multiple anomalies, because no two brains are alike.

Beyond our vastly different life experiences, we all bring to work different styles and preferences in how we communicate, resolve conflict, learn, behave, etc. The assessment market is roughly around $3 billion annually. In our practice, we use EQ assessments, 360 assessments, DiSC, Thomas-Kilman Conflict

Mode Instrument, Hogan, CliftonStrengths, Enneagram, and many more. We can tell you your color, letter, profile, number, and percentile. We can run individual reports, comparison reports, and team reports. Why? Because assessments provide valuable data points to help leaders and their teams better understand each other, mainly their differences. This leads to stronger relationships and results, and an informed leader who can place people in roles where they thrive.

## Fuels innovation

As the Novelty Strategy highlights, innovation requires diverse perspectives collaborating in a safe atmosphere where people feel free to challenge one another and take risks. This makes it easier for ideas to emerge and to "sell" them to stakeholders. As a reminder, a great idea doesn't sell itself. To gain buy-in and support, we must understand and address all stakeholders' perspectives, communication styles, concerns, and needs.

## Honors the need for belonging

The #1 threat to the brain is social rejection, which may be the most debilitating of all. When people feel shunned or rejected, the pain circuitry in their brains is activated. Brain scans of physical pain and brain scans of social rejection are virtually identical. As with threat, the brain perceives pain, regardless of whether the pain is physical or emotional, real or perceived. In many ways, pain to the brain is pain to the brain in the same way threat to the brain is threat to the brain.

The Gallup Q12 are the twelve questions we discussed in the Challenge Strategy. According to Gallup, these questions assess the key drivers of engagement. All twelve questions have a common denominator: people have an innate need to be seen, to be heard, to be valued, and to belong.

## Amplifies CRANIUM

The Mosaic Strategy is not just the 7$^{th}$ strategy. It is the culmination and amplifier of all the CRANIUM strategies.

It lowers threat and increases trust, creating a stimulating, challenging environment (The Challenge Strategy). It values individual strengths and allows each to see how they contribute to the bigger vision (The Relevance Strategy). It honors that each brain is unique, and all brains have limitations (The Action Strategy). It ignites the collaboration critical to innovation (The Novelty Strategy). It provides an environment for people to show up and speak up fully (The Interaction Strategy). Finally, it evokes positive emotions and promotes long-term resilience (The Using Emotion Strategy).

# THE MOSAIC STRATEGY IN PRACTICE

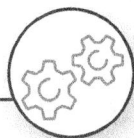

*What a Mosaic culture looks like*

Mosaic means "of the Muses" and refers to the nine daughters of Zeus who granted inspiration to those seeking something sacred, expressive, and greater than themselves. Mosaic artists create with reverence, intentionally shaping meaning from fragments. Similarly, leaders see the divine in human differences. They recognize that diversity isn't a disruption to manage, but an asset to honor and that variety is essential to innovation, resilience, and survival.

A mosaic unites individual fragments to form a lasting masterpiece. Similarly, the Mosaic Strategy illustrates that the full potential of any system, whether a brain, a team, or an organization, is realized only when individual elements are purposefully aligned to a greater vision.

The Mosaic Strategy recognizes that every interaction with another human being is a sophisticated, highly complex encounter of thoughts, experiences, beliefs, strengths, and weaknesses. It is about honoring, valuing, and welcoming everyone to the table, regardless of title. That requires an inclusive culture.

Cultures that exclude:

- Discourage authentic two-way communication
- Avoid rich conversations and debate
- Discourage disagreement
- Limit constructive feedback
- Hire and promote those who look, think, and act in similar ways
- Form cliques
- Have leaders who mentor and develop people only like themselves
- Address new problems with the same methods used to address old problems
- Limit possibilities for the future
- Create environments where people lack an overall sense of belonging
- Reprimand people who speak up and challenge the status quo
- Miss out on the contributions of highly talented people
- Handicap their future as they lack adaptability and flexibility
- See vulnerability as a weakness
- Risk being left behind

Cultures that include:

- Expect healthy tension and see continuous agreement as a disadvantage
- Value different ways of looking, thinking, acting, and learning
- Encourage two-way communication
- Freely give constructive feedback
- Have leaders who mentor and develop people different from themselves
- Address new problems with new methods to find new solutions
- Inspire unlimited possibilities for the future
- Create environments where people feel a sense of belonging and worth
- Capitalize on the contributions of highly talented people
- Embrace a changing marketplace and position themselves for current and future business opportunities
- See vulnerability as a core competency
- View conflict as an opportunity to grow themselves, their relationships, and their businesses
- Will lead the way

| WITHOUT<br>THE MOSAIC STRATEGY | WITH<br>THE MOSAIC STRATEGY |
|---|---|
| • Surface agreement | • Healthy debate |
| • One-way communication | • Free exchange of information |
| • Sidestep conflict | • Embrace conflict as possibilities |
| • Avoid constructive feedback | • Constructive feedback |
| • Closed-minded | • Open-minded |
| • Cliques | • Freedom of personal expression |
| • Mentor a similar mentee | • Mentor diverse mentees |
| • Tired, dated methods | • Cutting-edge solutions |
| • Social rejection | • Deep sense of belonging |
| • Conventional talent | • Unconventional talent |
| • Resist exploring new markets, new products and services, or new clients | • Explore new markets, new products and services, and new clients |
| • Risk-averse | • Risk-tolerant |
| • Temporary: will be left behind | • Resilient: will lead the way |

# BE A LEADER WORTH FOLLOWING

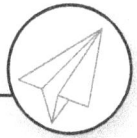

*How to live out the Mosaic Strategy*

The mosaic is more than a metaphor; it's a guide for becoming a leader worth following. Both mosaics and inclusive cultures require a deep commitment to vision, thoughtful strategy, discernment in placement, courageous decision-making, and the patience to bring it all together over time.

## Vision and values

A mosaic is a masterpiece of intention. Like a Mosaic culture, these intricate works do not emerge by accident. They begin with a compelling vision. The artist sees the whole before it exists and then purposefully places each fragment to tell a story. Across centuries and civilizations, these tiny pieces were meticulously arranged to contribute to a greater truth and capture the struggles, heroics, and values of the culture.

In the 2nd century BCE, Sosus of Pergamon, a master mosaicist, set a new standard with his renowned *The Unswept Floor*.[2] Composed of over one million tesserae, the mosaic depicts the scattered remains of a lavish banquet, including bones, shells, fruit peels, nuts, and even a mouse nibbling at crumbs. The precisely detailed image mirrors the Hellenistic values: elite indulgence, wealth on display, and the fleeting nature of pleasure and life.

More than two thousand years later, a mosaic of a very different kind was created by multiple artists for the Hiroshima Peace Memorial Hall.[3] The panoramic artwork encircles a water basin at the heart of the memorial and depicts the devastated cityscape from the hypocenter shortly after the bombing that occurred on August 6, 1945, at 8:15 am. The 140,000 tiles that compose the mosaic represent the lives lost by the end of that year. This mosaic tells a different story, one of grief, loss, and collective longing for peace. Unlike Sosus' telling of excess, this mosaic is an expression of mourning and hope.

**If you created a mosaic to reflect your organization's culture, what story would you tell?**

Hildreth Meière was a 20th-century American mosaicist who created a stunning mosaic that adorns the ceiling of the Rockefeller Chapel at the University of Chicago.[4] It represents

St. Francis of Assisi's Canticle of the Creatures and celebrates nature's elements, the sun, moon, water, fire, and the sacredness of life. Her work reflects her personal values as an artist: harmony, reverence, and the belief that beauty elevates the human experience.

**If you created a mosaic to reflect your leadership values, what story would you tell?**

## Discernment

Once the vision is clear, the mosaicist takes inventory, examining the tesserae available, selecting those that align, and setting aside those that do not. Some fragments may need refining through careful chipping or polishing. So, too, must inclusive leaders evaluate the people, strengths, and gaps within their teams. Both work with what is available, not with what is perfect. Neither seek perfection but possibilities.

Inclusive leaders see what is and what could be. They recognize the potential in unconventional talent, nurture growth and development, and match people with opportunities that bring their best to life. Like a skilled mosaicist, they balance creativity with clarity, trusting that something greater will emerge when each piece is honored and purposefully placed.

## Courageous decision-making

Vision requires courage. Not every tesserae will fit the mosaic. Similarly, leaders with a vision must sometimes make hard choices and unpopular decisions. They risk resistance, rejection, and discomfort. Since the brain strives for belonging, inclusive leadership often requires courage, grit, and determination to stand alone and be wildly unpopular.

Like a mosaicist, an inclusive leader works with flaws and not against them. But even then, discernment means knowing when a piece doesn't fit. To summarize Steve Jobs, A players don't want to work with C players who get equal opportunity. Inclusion is not blind tolerance. It requires setting boundaries, maintaining accountability, and sometimes separating from individuals who are not a fit with the mission.

## Patience

Mosaic art demands time and patience. The *Unswept Floor* likely took years to complete. Every painstaking detail, including selecting, shaping, and placing sub-centimeter fragments, was deliberate. Mosaics, like inclusive cultures, are slow masterpieces.

As an added challenge, cultures are living mosaics, constantly evolving and never truly "done." The creative process is messy; things get complicated before they get meaningful. The work of culture is not about speed but rather depth. The Action Strategy emphasizes that some things, like inclusive cultures, can't be rushed. They must be nurtured through time, presence, and persistence. The artist and the leader holding the vision must have faith in the process.

## From metaphor to action

Building a mosaic culture isn't just poetic; it is profoundly practical. The artistry of inclusive leadership requires more than a belief and a vision; it requires deliberate action. Like the mosaicist placing each tessera with care, inclusive leaders shape culture one choice, one conversation, and one connection at a time.

The following actions offer concrete ways to bring the vision of an inclusive culture to life:

- Lower threat.
- Build trust.
- Acknowledge bias.
- Honor differences.
- Create belonging.
- Champion inclusion.

## Lower threat, build trust

Inclusive cultures minimize negative threat by actively building trust. When people feel safe, their brains move from fight or flight to connection, from flocking to collaboration. Below are actions to create environments where threat decreases and trust increases.

### ACTIONS

### Love It or List It

Inspired by the HGTV show, invite your team to identify what they "love" about the culture and what they want to "list" or change. Use this feedback to design a workplace people want to stay in.

### Build Trust

Don't wait for trust to happen; build it proactively. Share stories, keep commitments, and show consistency in action.

### NAVIGATE TO RESOURCE
25 Simple Trust-Building Actions: PDF

### Create a Manifesto

Craft a public declaration of your leadership or team values. This becomes your cultural North Star to articulate what matters most clearly.

**NAVIGATE TO RESOURCE**

Yellin Group Manifesto: PDF

### Go Beneath the Surface

Use the iceberg visual to explore identity, bias, and belonging. We only see 10% of who a person is (race, gender, physical attributes, etc.). The other 90% is below the surface (experiences, motivations, values, etc.). The 90% is where real understanding and connection begin.

**NAVIGATE TO RESOURCE**

Iceberg: PDF

### Connection Questions

Start meetings with low-stakes, emotionally safe questions like, "Where was your first job?" "What is the last book you read?" or "What did you want to be when you grew up?"

**NAVIGATE TO RESOURCE**

Connection Questions: PDF

### Tell Your Story

Model vulnerability. Share moments that shaped you. Invite others to do the same.

### Discuss the Beliefs Model

Explore how beliefs are shaped and reinforced by life experiences. Ask generative questions like, "What life experiences have shaped your beliefs about conflict?" Or, "What beliefs have changed in you recently?"

> ## NAVIGATE TO RESOURCE
> Beliefs Model: Video

## Embrace bias

Bias is human; we all have it. The advantages of inclusion begin when we acknowledge it and actively work to manage it.

### ACTIONS

### This or That?

Use light, neutral preferences to spark bias conversations. Ask fun, preference questions like:

- Aisle or center seat?
- Coffee or tea?
- Mustard or ketchup?
- Cats or dogs?

### What's Your Bias of Choice?

Introduce common types of bias (i.e., confirmation bias, negativity bias, positivity bias) and encourage reflection. How might these be shaping decisions, interactions, or personal and professional results?

> **NAVIGATE TO RESOURCE**
>
> Common Biases: PDF

### Social Circle Inventory

List the names of 10-15 people you trust the most and enjoy spending time with. Then place a check beside those names that are different from you in terms of:

- Political views
- Religious beliefs
- Race
- Gender
- Sexual preference
- Country of origin
- Language
- Physical ability
- Education level

Notice what you notice. What might this exercise reveal about your exposure to differences?

## Honor the brains' differences

Understanding how people think, communicate, and respond is essential to inclusion. Assessments are one way to fast-track a better understanding and connection with others. Below are a few of my favorites.

### 360 Feedback

Although most people claim to be self-aware, few truly are. A 360-degree assessment enables us to compare how we see ourselves with how we are experienced by others. Requesting feedback across various roles helps surface blind spots and gain valuable insights. The Science of High-Performance Leadership 360 measures how frequently others observe you demonstrating the CRANIUM strategies.

> ## NAVIGATE TO RESOURCE
> HPL CRANIUM 360 Assessment

### DiSC Communication Styles

Use DiSC to explore how team members interact. This easy-to-understand tool builds self-awareness and appreciation for differences. DiSC can save teams years in trial and error and unnecessary misunderstandings.

### CliftonStrengths

This assessment uncovers strengths, talent, and potential. Choose the full 34-theme report to maximize insight for development and placement.[5]

> ## NAVIGATE TO RESOURCE
> Tips for Selecting Assessments: PDF

### Enneagram

The Enneagram is a robust personality framework that reveals distinct motivations, fears, and behavior patterns. Understanding the "why" behind our thinking and acting accelerates self-awareness and understanding of others.[6]

## Fuel innovation

Innovation flourishes where diversity is valued and risk feels safe.

ACTIONS

### Who's at the Table?

Audit your team or project group. Whose perspectives are present? Whose are missing? Why?

### Tiny Experiments

Reframe innovation as a series of micro-tests. A "laboratory" mentality reduces fear of failure, fosters playful curiosity, and increases momentum.

### Cross-Pollinate

Learn from other industries. Attend new conferences, listen to different podcasts, and explore solutions outside your field and comfort zone.

### Create Belonging

Belonging is the ultimate expression of inclusion. It's what happens when people feel fully seen and accepted and do not have to hide any part of who they are.

### Meeting Greeter

Arrive early to meetings with the sole purpose of welcoming people. Keep a sharp eye out for those who are new, quiet, or seem out of place.

### Design for Fun

Somewhere along the way of metrics, goals, and budgets, we forget to play and have fun. Fun accelerates focus and trust. Create time for joy. A team at NASA Goddard had a "Fun Czar" whose role was to keep laughter, play, and connection a team priority.

### Say Thank You

Simple, specific gratitude builds connection. Start your day with a note, text, or shoutout to someone in your circle to whom you can express thanks or appreciation.

## Champion inclusion

In 2016, Deloitte published a seminal study on inclusive leadership, revealing "four global mega-trends" reshaping business: the need for diverse markets, diverse customers, diverse ideas, and diverse talent.[7] The study highlighted six leadership characteristics essential to meeting the inherent challenges in these trends:

- **Commitment**: an authentic commitment to inclusion that aligns with the leader's values, not because it is mandated.
- **Courage**: the courage to speak up and challenge the status quo, even if it is uncomfortable or unpopular.

- **Cognizance of bias:** developing self-awareness of biases and how they impact preferences and decision-making.
- **Curiosity**: keeping an open mind and a desire to understand different perspectives and experiences.
- **Cultural Intelligence:** investing effort in better understanding other cultures and how to interact with them respectfully.
- **Collaboration:** empowering others, building trust, and fostering collaboration across boundaries.

The pandemic and the years following have magnified these trends. Now more than ever, there is a demand for leaders who champion inclusion through these six characteristics of inclusive leadership. They are critical to creating a Mosaic culture where people feel appreciated and heard. When people feel included, the culture enjoys less drama, high-functioning teamwork, and co-created solutions that inspire ownership and new possibilities. When people feel excluded or "overpowered," they feel undervalued and ignored, leading to silence and apathy. They leave, or even worse, they stay—unhappily.

## CRANIUM Accelerator

The Mosaic Strategy speaks directly to creating an inclusive culture where our shared humanity and unique differences are fully recognized. However, each CRANIUM strategy is vital in bringing inclusion to life. All 7 brain-based strategies equip leaders with the mindset, tools, and behaviors needed to make inclusion actionable and lasting.

## CHALLENGE

The Challenge Strategy minimizes threat and increases trust, two essentials in an inclusive environment. When people feel safe, they are more open to taking risks, questioning assumptions, and challenging outdated norms. But they can only do so when they feel supported. In a high-trust culture, individuals don't need all the answers or the "right" answer. They feel safe exploring the unknown, owning their growth, and learning about cultures and viewpoints different from their own. Inclusive leaders create this high-trust, low-threat environment, giving people the courage to be curious, vulnerable, and bold.

## RELEVANCE

The Relevance Strategy ensures inclusion is not a side initiative but central to the vision and values of the organization. Inclusive leaders clarify where the organization is headed and communicate why it matters. They help individuals connect their personal purpose and strengths to the bigger picture, reinforcing meaning and building on strengths at every level. This alignment deepens commitment, inspires collaboration, and ensures that diversity is fully engaged. When people can see how their voice and their strengths fit into the mission, inclusion becomes personal, not just professional.

## ACTION

The Action Strategy acknowledges the brain's limitations as much as its potential. Inclusive leaders understand that people operate differently. Rather than force-fitting everyone in the same cookie-cutter mold, they design flexible processes that support healthy integration of work and life. They lead with presence and empathy, knowing that inclusion lives in the day-to-day adjustments that allow people to thrive.

### NOVELTY

The Novelty Strategy teaches us that innovation, diverse thinking, and creativity is a natural outcome of creating inclusive cultures. Inclusive leaders foster this by encouraging experimentation, welcoming unconventional thinking, and valuing contribution over credit. They set aside ego in favor of exploration, knowing innovation requires humility and intense curiosity. They know new possibilities surface when people feel free to collaborate, make mistakes, challenge, and co-create without fear of being dismissed.

### INTERACTION

The Interaction Strategy is where inclusion becomes visible. Inclusive leaders engage others by inviting participation, ownership, and voice. They operate from a stance of "power with" versus "power over," asking more than telling and listening more than talking. They intentionally draw out perspectives different from theirs and prioritize commitment over compliance. Through inclusive interaction, they model humility, equality, and the belief that everyone deserves a seat and a say at the table.

### USING EMOTION

The Using Emotion Strategy is the entry point to human connection. Inclusive leaders know that people are not just thinkers who feel; they are feelers who think. Leading inclusively means recognizing that change, learning, and belonging are profound emotional experiences. Every inclusive leadership trait, including commitment, courage, cognizance of bias, curiosity, cultural intelligence, and collaboration, requires emotional presence. Inclusive leaders lead people first, regardless of the initiative, role, or strategy. They never forget that the human brain runs on emotion.

# FINAL THOUGHTS ON
# THE MOSAIC STRATEGY

Each tile in a mosaic has limited potential on its own. But when placed with vision and intention, it becomes part of something enduring. In ancient times, mosaics weren't just decorative; they were structural. Embedded into the floors, walls, and vaulted ceilings of buildings, they added not only beauty but also strength, resilience, and cohesion. Many have survived earthquakes, floods, centuries of wear, and even burial for over 2,000 years. What endures isn't just the art; it's the meaning woven into every deliberate piece.

Inclusive leadership is no different. When we place people, values, and stories into our organizations with the same care, we don't just build culture. We build a **legacy** that outlasts us, withstands pressure, and tells a story worth remembering.

And never forget that **you have a message—and a way of delivering that message—that hasn't been given to anyone else. Honor and protect that gift. No. Matter. What.** You are one of the pieces. Your voice is a treasured part of the design. Stand up and be heard.

In a rapidly changing world, one of the most valuable business strategies an organization can have is to create an inclusive environment that leverages the endless returns of the Mosaic Strategy.

Differences make us all the same; our differences are our similarities. When we shift from erasing differences to embracing them, we open a whole new world of possibilities for leadership, business results, human performance, and a better, happier life.

# WHAT MAKES A LEADER WORTH FOLLOWING?

*We asked real people. We got real responses.*

Here are just a few. Would anyone say the same about you?

✔ *They are willing to consider other perspectives.*

✔ *A leader worth following is someone who will actively listen to the needs of others, who shows respect regardless of title or status, who genuinely cares about their people, who values the efforts that others put in day in and day out, who looks for ways to help others succeed, and who regularly looks for ways to get better every day.*

✔ *A leader is worth following when they inspire me to believe in their cause. When a leader connects with me by demonstrating that my skills and talents have a meaningful role within the team and contribute to a greater purpose, I am more inclined to follow them. It is this ability to align individual strengths with a shared vision that makes a leader truly worth following.*

✔ *Value everyone's contributions.*

✔ *Treats those around them with the respect that they hope to be shown.*

# THINK. DISCUSS. APPLY.

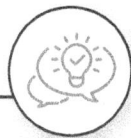

*Make it matter*

1. Describe when you felt your suggestion or input was not valued. What impact did that have on you? How did it impact relationships in your life?
2. Make a list of the people on your team. What are 10 similarities and what are 10 differences among them?
3. Think about the people you work with. Who would you say is the most different from you? How often do you engage with them and listen to their perspective? How might you learn something about them one level deeper than you know today?
4. Describe a time when a different perspective led to a better solution. What was that experience like? What did you contribute to the breakthrough?
5. Look around the table (or screen) at your next meeting. What similarities do you notice? What differences do you notice?
6. Be a curious observer in your next meeting. Who speaks and how often?
7. What has your experience working with a mentor (formally or informally) been like?
8. Who are you mentoring now (formally or informally)?
9. Rate the degree to which you agree with the statements on the following page:

| | Strongly Disagree | | | | Strongly Agree |
|---|---|---|---|---|---|
| I seek out perspectives different from my own. | 1 | 2 | 3 | 4 | 5 |
| I can be vulnerable with others at work. | 1 | 2 | 3 | 4 | 5 |
| I value those who disrupt conventional ways. | 1 | 2 | 3 | 4 | 5 |
| I feel like I belong in my organization. | 1 | 2 | 3 | 4 | 5 |
| I learn about new cultures. | 1 | 2 | 3 | 4 | 5 |
| I go out of my way to make sure others feel included. | 1 | 2 | 3 | 4 | 5 |
| My first response to a different idea is to become curious. | 1 | 2 | 3 | 4 | 5 |
| I do not become defensive when someone disagrees with me. | 1 | 2 | 3 | 4 | 5 |
| I treat each person as a whole, resourceful creative human being. | 1 | 2 | 3 | 4 | 5 |
| I am aware of my biases. | 1 | 2 | 3 | 4 | 5 |
| I seek ways to lead change. | 1 | 2 | 3 | 4 | 5 |
| I adapt easily to other cultures. | 1 | 2 | 3 | 4 | 5 |
| I consider multiple perspectives before making a decision. | 1 | 2 | 3 | 4 | 5 |
| I speak up when I feel others are not being included. | 1 | 2 | 3 | 4 | 5 |
| I hold people accountable for inappropriate behavior. | 1 | 2 | 3 | 4 | 5 |

# VALUE DIFFERENCES. CREATE BELONGING.

## A MOSAIC CULTURE REQUIRES:

- lowering threat
- building trust
- acknowledging bias
- honoring differences
- creating belonging
- championing inclusion

> You have a message and a style of delivering that message that hasn't been given to anyone else.
>
> **Honor and protect that gift.**
>
> No. Matter. What.

99% of all processing is unconscious.

Our brains are always distorting through bias

inclusive cultures amplify

**every CRANIUM strategy.**

## Signature Traits of Inclusive Leaders

Commitment
Courage
Cognizance
Curiosity
Culturally Intelligent
Collaborative

**Bias:** the lens through which we see the world and make decisions

story

- Generalizations
- Distortions
- Deletions
- Beliefs
- Experiences

# E + R = O

(events)    (response)    (outcome)

## PAIN TO THE BRAIN IS PAIN TO THE BRAIN

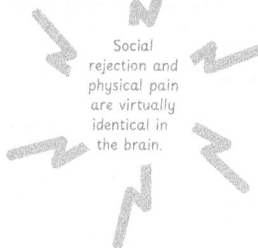

Social rejection and physical pain are virtually identical in the brain.

## Great minds don't think alike.

# Final Thoughts

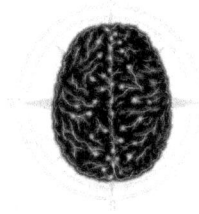

If we aspire to be a leader worth following and achieve the results of high-performing leaders, we must continually learn about the three-pound miracle in our heads. Our brains are the most marvelous, complex, and awe-inspiring technology in history, and we are still in the beginning stages of understanding their capabilities. Your brain is your most significant advantage, the source creating those "no-matter-what" moments and the life of your dreams. Your brain is also your most significant constraint, the source fueling those "freak-out" moments and limiting your ability to see beyond your current reality.

When we apply what we know about the brain, we make things easier. We can accomplish more, make smarter decisions, live out the better version of ourselves, develop those around us, and care for things that matter. We become leaders worth following.

We make things harder when we do not apply our knowledge of the brain's abilities. We add unnecessary stress, live in conflict, hold ourselves and others back from reaching full potential, and ignore or harm the things that truly matter. Ultimately, the choice is ours: we can harness what we know to create positive, lasting legacies or disregard it and leave behind unintended consequences.

I am proud to live in a small community with a history rich in farming. Listen to farmers talk, and you will quickly appreciate the importance of respecting universal laws. Farmers simply have no control over weather patterns, rainfall, drought, or the invasion of unwanted pests. In addition, farmers have no control over specific universal laws. For example, if a farmer wants to grow corn, that farmer must plant corn. If a farmer wants to harvest during one season, that farmer must plant in the appropriate season for that crop to be harvested. Farmers can either battle, argue, and work *against* the variables and universal laws, or they can opt to work *with* the variables and universal laws. The latter typically yields better results and a longer, happier life for the farmer.

As leaders seeking to develop ourselves and those around us, we can learn a few lessons from farmers. We, too, can focus on the variables, such as the unpredictability of human behavior and the economy, and we can stay in a reactive mode when faced with the increasing complexities of a rapidly changing, competitive world. Or, we can focus on the universal truths, the unchanging, guiding principles of how the brain works best. When we focus on the 7 CRANIUM Strategies, we create the optimal environment for the best results, regardless of the change, the subject, or the situation.

First, we must honor the **Challenge Strategy**. If we wish to operate at our best and influence others we care about to do the same, we must build trust and minimize threat. This is perhaps the most important of the CRANIUM Strategies. The health of our brain is everything, and it is dramatically impacted by threat and high-threat environments. So, if we want to gain unforgettable results like collaboration, cooperation, innovation, creativity, and self-control, we will intentionally and purposefully seek ways to challenge ourselves and others in a high-trust environment.

We can continue leading through threat-producing tactics like humiliation, micromanagement, favoritism, and posturing. But if we make that choice, we forfeit the right to blame, complain, criticize, or point fingers when we don't see results or when no one chooses to follow us.

The **Relevance Strategy** explains why the human brain performs best when it is motivated by purpose and passion. I often ask people attending my workshops to think of a time when they were successful in achieving a personal or professional goal. I've heard, "I lost 40 pounds last year," "I traveled to Europe," and "I took my family to five different national parks over the summer."

When asked why they thought they were successful in achieving those goals, as opposed to others they had set in their lives but had not accomplished, I often hear an inspiring purpose. I lost the weight because... "I was on the verge of becoming a diabetic." I went on the trip because... "It was my 50th birthday, and I have wanted to travel to another country my entire life." I booked the trip to the national parks because... "My kids are growing up so fast; I wanted to experience that with them before they graduated."

What I never hear is - "Because my boss told me to."

Of all the questions we ask, the most important may be, "What matters to you?" If we fail to honor Relevance, we may gain compliance, but we will never achieve commitment.

The **Action Strategy** calls us to learn and embrace the brain's limitations. Though the brain is marvelously complex and efficient, its limitations must be respected, or there will be natural consequences. If we constantly multitask, there are natural consequences—tasks get done, but not correctly. If we don't ensure enough sleep, push harder in times of stress, work longer at the expense of healthy eating and exercise, or fail to repair the brain when it is not working properly, there are natural conse-quences, such as illness. Of all the strategies, Action highlights the importance of working with, rather than against, how the brain works best.

The **Novelty Strategy** fuels innovation and creativity, prized commodities in a rapidly changing world where competition is fierce. However, often, we give more attention to the result we seek than to the conditions needed to promote that result. Novelty requires a safe environment to pursue innovation and creativity, and yet most of our organizations operate under threat and low trust, where mistakes aren't tolerated.

Novelty, like Relevance, requires leveraging strengths, and yet most of our organizations still try to close gaps rather than build on strengths. Novelty craves change, yet most organizations do not effectively manage the change process. Novelty depends on collaboration, and yet most of our organizations still oper-ate in silos. Organizations that give the appropriate attention to the required cultural conditions for novelty will thrive. They will leave the competition far behind and change the world.

Tell them; they comply. Involve them; they commit. When we violate this belief, we ignore the **Interaction Strategy.** If we want to foster engagement, ownership, and accountability, we must *involve* rather than *tell*. If we want the people around us to truly develop, generate the best solutions, and become mature problem-solvers, we must first facilitate discovery. If we want to create cultures where everyone speaks up—respectfully and boldly—regardless of hierarchy, to strengthen relationships and raise performance together, we must move away from "boss" and move toward "coach." We must venture away from solving problems, giving orders, and sharing advice to meeting people where they are in a way that promotes discovery, increased awareness, and new learning.

The **Using Emotion Strategy** calls on us to engage emotion intentionally to lead change, enhance learning, and motivate. Our emotions are contagious; they can propel us forward and build commitment and engagement or make us sick, both figuratively and literally. We cannot ignore emotion, the human element, as we seek to accomplish tasks and achieve results. Doing so only makes progress slower and creates greater stress and conflict.

Finally, the **Mosaic Strategy** represents how an extraordinary masterpiece begins with valuing each piece. Every brain wants to feel welcomed and included. Every brain has value to add. Every brain has limitations, biases, and blind spots. And every brain is wildly unique. An inclusive environment quickly moves beyond the old notions of diversity as gender, race, and age. It embraces the idea that different ways of being in the world, resulting from unlimited experiences and influences, produce better results. Great minds don't think alike. The whole is greater than the sum of the parts. An inclusive leader values and strives to create an environment where all our differences and all our similarities merge to create an extraordinary masterpiece.

Before we close, love is the only thing we bring into this world and the only thing we take with us when we leave.

So, love your life, including the 90,000 or more hours you spend at work.

Lead with intention and make those hours meaningful for yourself and others.

Leave a legacy that lasts.

Being a leader worth following isn't rocket science—it's brain science.

The science of learning shows us the way. The CRANIUM strategies light the path.

Trust the process. Activate the potential. Enjoy the results.

Simple? Yes. Easy? No. Worth it? Every time.

You now hold the blueprint.

**Lead like it matters. Because it does.**

# Notes

## Introduction Chapter Sources

1. Gamble, M. (2024, April 22). *85% of workers suffer from burnout, study shows. The Times.* https://www.thetimes.co.uk/article/85-percent-workforce-burnout-mental-health-reed-pvcqwt3l3.
2. Society for Human Resource Management. (2024, January). *Anxiety is now the top mental health issue in the workplace.* SHRM. https://www.shrm.org/topics-tools/news/benefits-compensation/anxiety-top-mental-health-issue-workplace-compsychshrm.org+4shrm.org+4shrm.org+4.
3. The HR Digest. (2024, January 11). *Employee engagement in the U.S. hit a 10-year low in 2024.* https://www.thehrdigest.com/employee-engagement-in-the-u-s-hit-a-10-year-low-in-2024.
4. Fit Small Business. (2024). *40+ leadership statistics: Trends and insights for 2024.* https://fitsmallbusiness.com/leadership-statistics.
5. American Psychological Association. (2024). *Work in America: 2024 work and well-being survey.* https://www.apa.org/pubs/reports/work-in-america/2024/2024-work-in-america-report.pdf.
6. Gallup. (2024). *Gallup's 2024 workplace report: The alarming state of employee engagement and why this has to change.*
7. Goleman, D., Boyatzis, R., & McKee, A. (2002). *Primal leadership: Realizing the power of emotional intelligence.* Harvard Business School Press.

## The Challenge Strategy Chapter Sources

1. Csikszentmihalyi, M. (1990). *Flow: The psychology of optimal experience.* Harper & Row.
2. Medina, J. (2008). *Brain rules: 12 principles for surviving and thriving at work, home, and school.* Pear Press.
3. Howard, R. (Director). (1995). *Apollo 13* [Film]. Universal Pictures.

4. Jensen, E. (2022). *Teaching with poverty and equity in mind: Succeed with the students who need you most.* ASCD.
5. Fukuyama, F. (1995). *Trust: The social virtues and the creation of prosperity.* Free Press.
6. Kross, E., Berman, M. G., Mischel, W., Smith, E. E., & Wager, T. D. (2011). Social rejection shares somatosensory representations with physical pain. *Proceedings of the National Academy of Sciences, 108*(15), 6270-6275. https://doi.org/10.1073/pnas.1102693108.
7. Gallup. (n.d.). *Q12: The 12 Elements of Great Managing.* https://www.gallup.com/workplace/356063/gallup-q12-survey.aspx.
8. Buckingham, M., & Coffman, C. (1999). *First, break all the rules: What the world's greatest managers do differently.* Simon & Schuster.
9. Centers for Disease Control and Prevention. (2021). *Mental health, substance use, and suicidal ideation during the COVID-19 pandemic—United States, June 24–30, 2020. Morbidity and Mortality Weekly Report, 69*(32), 1049–1057. https://www.cdc.gov/mmwr/volumes/69/wr/mm6932a1.htm.
10. World Health Organization. (2022, March 2). *COVID-19 pandemic triggers 25% increase in prevalence of anxiety and depression worldwide.* https://www.who.int/news/item/02-03-2022-covid-19-pandemic-triggers-25-increase-in-prevalence-of-anxiety-and-depression-worldwide.

## The Relevance Strategy Chapter Sources

1. Hebb, D. O. (1949). *The organization of behavior: A neuropsychological theory.* Wiley.
2. Beilock, S. (2010). *Choke: What the secrets of the brain reveal about getting it right when you have to.* Free Press.
3. Jensen, E. (2022). *Teaching with poverty and equity in mind.* ASCD.
4. Merzenich, M. (2013). *Soft-wired: How the new science of brain plasticity can change your life.* Parnassus Publishing.
5. Gallup. (2016). *How millennials want to work and live.* Gallup.
6. Spring Health. (2025, January 27). *Engagement isn't just an HR problem: The $8.9 trillion reason why.* https://www.springhealth.com/blog/engagement-isnt-just-an-hr-problem.
7. Gallup. (2024). *State of the global workplace.* Gallup.

8. Clifton, D. O., & Buckingham, M. (2001). *Now, discover your strengths*. Free Press.
9. Rath, T. (2007). *StrengthsFinder 2.0*. Gallup Press.
10. Sullivan, D., & Hardy, B. (2021). *The gap and the gain: The high achievers' guide to happiness, confidence, and success*. Hay House.
11. Howard, R. (Director). (1995). *Apollo 13* [Film]. Universal Pictures.
12. Dweck, C. S. (2006). *Mindset: The new psychology of success*. Random House.

## The Action Strategy Chapter Sources

1. Amen, D. G. (2015). *Change your brain, change your life: The breakthrough program for conquering anxiety, depression, obsessiveness, lack of focus, anger, and memory problems* (Revised ed.). Harmony Books.
2. American Psychological Association. (2006). *Multitasking: Switching costs*. https://www.apa.org/research/action/multitask.
3. Chis, M. A. (2023). *Investigating the cognitive load-productivity tradeoff in multitasking* (Master's thesis, University of Pittsburgh). D-Scholarship@Pitt.
4. Mark, G. (2022). *Multitasking in the digital age*. MIT Press.
5. Foerde, K., Knowlton, B. J., & Poldrack, R. A. (2006). Modulation of competing memory systems by distraction. *Proceedings of the National Academy of Sciences, 103*(31), 11778–11783.
6. Hirshkowitz, M., Whiton, K., Albert, S. M., Alessi, C., Bruni, O., DonCarlos, L., et al. (2015). "National Sleep Foundation's sleep time duration recommendations: methodology and results summary." *Sleep Health, 1*(1), 40–43.
7. National Highway Traffic Safety Administration. (2023). *Drowsy driving: A serious problem*. U.S. Department of Transportation. https://www.nhtsa.gov/risky-driving/drowsy-driving.
8. National Public Radio. (2016, April). *Why sleep matters: The cost of sleep deprivation*. https://media.npr.org/assets/news/2016/04/sleep.pdf.
9. Centers for Disease Control and Prevention. (n.d.). *Stress: The health epidemic of the 21st century*. https://www.cdc.gov/

10. American Institute of Stress. (n.d.). *Workplace stress.* https:// www.stress.org/workplace-stress

11. Lyra Health. (2024). *2024 State of workforce mental health.* https://www.lyrahealth.com/state-of-workforce-mental-health -2024/.

12. Centers for Disease Control and Prevention. (2023). *Overweight and obesity statistics.* https://www.cdc.gov/obesity/data/adult .html.

13. Holmes, T. H., & Rahe, R. H. (1967). The Social Readjustment Rating Scale. *Journal of Psychosomatic Research, 11*(2), 213–218.

14. Swenson, R. A. (2004). *Margin: Restoring emotional, physical, financial, and time reserves to overloaded lives.* NavPress.

15. Medina, J. (2008). *Brain rules: 12 principles for surviving and thriving at work, home, and school.* Pear Press.

16. Shekerjian, D. (1991). *Uncommon genius: How great ideas are born.* Viking Penguin.

17. Burchard, B. (2017). *High performance habits: How extraordinary people become that way.* Hay House.

18. Pink, D. H. (2018). *When: The scientific secrets of perfect timing.* Riverhead Books.

19. Amen, D. G. (2013, November). *The most important lesson from 83,000 brain scans* [Video]. TEDx Talks. https://www.ted.com/ talks/daniel_amen_the_most_important_lesson_from_83_000_ brain_scans.

## The Novelty Strategy Chapter Sources

1. Heath, C., & Heath, D. (2017). *The power of moments: Why certain experiences have extraordinary impact.* Simon & Schuster.

2. Volkswagen. (2009). *The Fun Theory* [Advertising campaign]. DDB Stockholm. https://www.dandad.org/awards/ professional/2010/digital-advertising/18245/the-fun-theory/.

3. Achor, S. (2011, May). *The happy secret to better work* [Video]. TEDxBloomington. https://www.ted.com/talks/ shawn_achor_the_happy_secret_to_better_work.

4. Centers for Disease Control and Prevention. (2021, January 29). *Prevalence of overweight, obesity, and severe obesity among adults aged 20 and over: United States, 1960–1962 through 2017–2018* (NCHS Health E-Stats). U.S. Department of Health

and Human Services. https://www.cdc.gov/nchs/data/hestat/obesity-adult-17-18/obesity-adult.htm.

5. Sorbet. (2024, July 24). *New survey reveals one-third of U.S. employees' vacation days go unused; 68M Americans losing out on PTO value.* PR Newswire. https://www.prnewswire.com/news-releases/new-survey-reveals-one-third-of-us-employees-vacation-days-go-unused-68m-americans-losing-out-on-pto-value-302204102.html.

6. Gallup. (2025). *Indicator: Life Evaluation Index.* https://www.gallup.com/394505/indicator-life-evaluation-index.aspx.

7. Murphy, M. (2016, September 18). *The way you check email is making you less productive.* Forbes. https://www.forbes.com/sites/markmurphy/2016/09/18/the-way-you-check-email-is-making-you-less-productive/.

8. Centers for Disease Control and Prevention. (2023, July 18). *Adults: Sleep facts and stats.* U.S. Department of Health and Human Services. https://www.cdc.gov/sleep/data-research/facts-stats/adults-sleep-facts-and-stats.html.

9. Amen Clinics. (2023, May 30). *If you're struggling with mental health issues, welcome to normal.* https://www.amenclinics.com/blog/if-youre-struggling-with-mental-health-issues-welcome-to-normal/.

10. Morris, D. Z. (2018, November 27). *Elon Musk thinks everyone should work 80–100 hours per week.* Fortune. https://fortune.com/2018/11/27/elon-musk-100-hours-work-week/.

11. Pencavel, J. (2014, April). *The productivity of working hours* (IZA Discussion Paper No. 8129). Institute of Labor Economics (IZA). https://docs.iza.org/dp8129.pdf.

12. PricewaterhouseCoopers. (2023, March 12). *Trust in U.S. business survey: The current state of trust in business.* https://www.pwc.com/us/en/library/trust-in-business-survey.html.

13. Gallup. (2024, May 14). *Only 23% of U.S. employees strongly agree they trust their leadership.* https://www.gallup.com/workplace/612228/employees-don-trust-leaders.aspx.

14. Knight, R. (2018, August 9). *How to make time for deep work.* Harvard Business Review. https://hbr.org/2018/08/how-to-make-time-for-deep-work.

15. Rogelberg, S. G. (2019). *The surprising science of meetings: How you can lead your team to peak performance.* Oxford University Press.

16. Rath, T., & Conchie, B. (2008). *Strengths-based leadership: Great leaders, teams, and why people follow*. Gallup Press.
17. Lovell, J., & Kluger, J. (2006). *Apollo 13*. Houghton Mifflin Harcourt.
18. NASA. (2010, April 1). *Tank paint removal helped reduce weight on shuttle*. https://www.nasa.gov/mission_pages/shuttle/behindscenes/paint_tank.html.
19. Weihenmayer, E. (2002). *Touch the top of the world: A blind man's journey to climb farther than the eye can see*. Dutton Books.
20. Murray, C., & Cox, C. B. (1989). *Apollo: The race to the moon*. New York, NY: Simon & Schuster.
21. Rogers, E. M. (2003). *Diffusion of innovations* (5th ed.). Free Press.
22. Duhigg, C. (2012). *The power of habit: Why we do what we do in life and business*. Random House.
23. Freeman, R. E. (1984). *Strategic management: A stakeholder approach*. Pitman.
    Kaushik, A. (2007). *Web analytics: An hour a day*. Wiley.
24. Mendelow, A. L. (1991). *Environmental scanning: The impact of the stakeholder concept*. In Proceedings of the International Conference on Information Systems (pp. 407–418). Cambridge, MA: ICIS.
25. Kaushik, A. (2007). *Web analytics: An hour a day*. Indianapolis, IN: Wiley Publishing.

# The Interaction Strategy Chapter Sources

1. Freifeld, L. (2023, November 14). *2023 Training Industry Report*. Training. Retrieved from https://trainingmag.com/2023-training-industry-report/.
2. Dale, E. (1969). *Audio-visual methods in teaching* (3rd ed.). Holt, Rinehart and Winston.
3. Bloom, B. S. (1956). *Taxonomy of educational objectives: The classification of educational goals*. Longmans, Green.
4. Jensen, E. (2005). *Teaching with the brain in mind* (2nd ed.). ASCD.
5. Johnston, C. A., Rost, S., Miller-Kovach, K., Moreno, J. P., & Foreyt, J. P. (2013). A randomized controlled trial of a community-based behavioral counseling program. *The American Journal of*

*Medicine, 126*(12), 1143.e19–1143.e24. https://www
.amjmed.com/article/S0002-9343(13)00672-4/.

6. Eyre, L., & Eyre, R. M. (1994). *Teaching your children responsibility.* Simon & Schuster.
7. Lombardo, M. M., & Eichinger, R. W. (1996). *The career architect development planner* (3rd ed.). Lominger Limited.
8. Beheshti, N. (2019, January 23). Improve workplace culture with a strong mentoring program. *Forbes.* https://www.forbes.com/sites/nazbeheshti/2019/01/23/improve-workplace-culture-with-a-strong-mentoring-program/.
9. International Coach Federation. (2009). *ICF Global Coaching Client Study.* PricewaterhouseCoopers. https://coachingfederation.org/research/global-coaching-client-study.
10. Merzenich, M. (2013). *Soft-wired: How the new science of brain plasticity can change your life.* Parnassus Publishing.
11. Seligman, M. E. P., & Maier, S. F. (1967). Failure to escape traumatic shock. *Journal of Experimental Psychology, 74*(1), 1–9.
12. Goleman, D., Boyatzis, R., & McKee, A. (2002). *Primal leadership: Unleashing the power of emotional intelligence.* Harvard Business Review Press.
13. International Coaching Federation. (n.d.). *Why ICF?* https://coachingfederation.org/why-icf.
14. TEDx Talks. (2019, November). *Michael Bungay Stanier: How to tame your advice monster* [Video]. https://www.ted.com/talks/michael_bungay_stanier_how_to_tame_your_advice_monster_feb_2025.
15. Scharmer, O. (2009). *Theory U: Leading from the future as it emerges.* Berrett-Koehler Publishers.
16. Hyatt, M. (2019). *Free to focus: A total productivity system to achieve more by doing less.* Baker Books.

## The Using Emotion Strategy Chapter Sources

1. Kotler, S. (2014). *The rise of Superman: Decoding the science of ultimate human performance.* New Harvest.
2. LeDoux, J. (n.d.). *Joseph LeDoux: Neuroscientist, author, musician.* https://www.joseph-ledoux.com.
3. Eastwood, C. (Director). (2016). *Sully* [Film]. Warner Bros. Pictures.

4. Heath, C., & Heath, D. (2010). *Switch: How to change things when change is hard*. Broadway Books.
5. Gardner, H. (1983). *Frames of mind: The theory of multiple intelligences*. Basic Books.
6. Soocial. (2023). *Emotional intelligence statistics*. https://www.soocial.com/emotional-intelligence-statistics/.
7. Goleman, D. (1995). *Emotional intelligence: Why it can matter more than IQ*. Bantam Books.
8. Eurich, T. (2017). *Insight: The surprising truth about how others see us, how we see ourselves, and why the answers matter more than we think*. Currency.
9. Achor, S. (2010). *The happy secret to better work* [Video]. TED Conferences. https://www.ted.com/talks/shawn_achor_the_happy_secret_to_better_work/transcript?subtitle=en.
10. Brown, B. (2010, June). *The power of vulnerability* [Video]. TEDxHouston. https://www.ted.com/talks/brene_brown_the_power_of_vulnerability.
11. Goleman, D., Boyatzis, R., & McKee, A. (2002). *Primal leadership: Unleashing the power of emotional intelligence*. Harvard Business School Press.

## The Mosaic Strategy Chapter Sources

1. Csikszentmihalyi, M. (1990). *Flow: The psychology of optimal experience*. Harper & Row.
2. Sosus of Pergamon. (2nd century BCE). *The unswept floor* [Mosaic]. Pergamon, Ancient Greece.
3. Hiroshima Peace Memorial Museum. (n.d.). *Hall of Remembrance mosaic* [Memorial mosaic installation]. Hiroshima Peace Memorial Hall, Japan. https://www.hiro-tsuitokinenkan.go.jp/en/.
4. International Hildreth Meière Association. (n.d.). *Rockefeller Chapel ceiling mosaic*. https://www.hildrethmeiere.org/commissions/university-of-chicago-rockefeller-chapel.
5. Gallup. (n.d.). *CliftonStrengths*. https://www.gallup.com.
6. Integrative Enneagram Solutions. (n.d.). *iEQ9 Enneagram profile*. https://www.integrative9.com.
7. Deloitte. (2016). *The six signature traits of inclusive leadership*. Deloitte Insights. https://www2.deloitte.com/us/en/insights/topics/talent/six-signature-traits-of-inclusive-leadership.html.

# About the Author

**Dr. Sherry Yellin**
*Leadership Strategist | Author | Founder, The Yellin Group*

Dr. Sherry Yellin is an author, executive coach, and founder of The Yellin Group, where the science of learning meets the art of leadership. With a Ph.D. in cognitive learning and certifications from the International Coaching Federation and Center for Credentialing Education, she helps leaders get extraordinary results with less effort by aligning how they lead with how the brain works best. Sherry equips multi-industry leaders to build cultures that bring out the best in people.

Her bold mission:
**To equip a world of leaders worth following.**

**To learn more about her work,**
**visit** www.yellingroup.com

https://www.youtube.com/@YellinGroup

**To join one of her complimentary monthly LEADing**
**Lab sessions, visit https://yellingroup.com/events**

www.ingramcontent.com/pod-product-compliance
Lightning Source LLC
Chambersburg PA
CBHW030452210326
41597CB00013B/632